Towards a New Sociology of Social Work

ROGER SIBEON
Department of Sociology, Social Policy
  & Social Work Studies
University of Liverpool

Avebury

Aldershot · Brookfield USA · Hong Kong · Singapore · Sydney

Published by
Avebury
Gower Publishing Company Limited
Gower House
Croft Road
Aldershot
Hants GU11 3HR
England

Gower Publishing Company
Old Post Road
Brookfield
Vermont 05036
USA

ISBN 1 85628 028 4

Printed and Bound in Great Britain by
Athenaeum Press Ltd., Newcastle upon Tyne.

Contents

1 Introduction

Howe (1988) observes that sociological analysis of social work '... is still ... surprisingly underdeveloped ...' (ibid., p.65). There have been some recent attempts to incorporate contemporary sociology into this field of study (Davies, 1991; Sibeon. 1989a and 1991) but these have barely scratched the surface in identifying the future direction and scale of work that remains to be done in constructing a modern sociology of social work. At the beginning of the 1970's Heraud had suggested 'There is no reason why a sociology of social work should not develop in Britain ...' (Heraud, 1970, p.12). That this development failed to materialise is partly a function of sociologists' general lack of interest in social work. This is not to say that no work has been undertaken in this field. Some social scientists involved in social work education have made significant sociological contributions to the analysis of social work; examples include the work of Webb (1981a, 1981b, 1985), Webb and Evans (1976), Hardiker (1977, 1981), Hardiker and Webb (1979), Hardiker and Barker (1981), Rojek (1989) and Rojek et al. (1988, 1989). Also, a number of academics associated either with social work writing per se or with other academic disciplines (such as social policy or philosophy) have employed social science constructs in ways that have contributed to an analytic understanding of social work issues; this is true of, for example, the widely differing analyses provided by Stevenson (1981), Jones (1983), Timms (1983) Timms and Timms (1977), Howe (1987), Harris (1983, 1985, 1988), Harris et al. (1985) and Harris and Webb (1987). In general, however, the sociology of social work is characterized by a remarkably low level of empirical, theoretical, and methodological development (Sibeon, 1991. p.18).

Sociology of social work is an exercise in intellectual understanding, its primary purpose being to sociologically analyse social work as an organized social activity in society; it is not directed towards the goal of providing sociological knowledge of a kind intended for 'practical' application. The objective in sociology of social work is to add to the sum of knowledge about social work. This objective rests upon intellectual values which specify that knowledge is worth having for its own sake. In contrast, a sociology in or for social work may be defined as the attempt to furnish 'relevant' sociological knowledge in the form of theoretical insights and empirical data intended for practical application by social work policy-makers and practitioners. This distinction between sociology 'of' and sociology 'in' or 'for' social work is analytically important for the reason that it relates closely to questions of purpose. However in reality the distinction often becomes blurred. In the social sciences, as in the physical sciences, 'pure' research far removed from practical concerns may turn out to have unanticipated applied connotations. Also, many substantive areas of inquiry are intrinsically difficult to assign to one or the other of the two categories just referred to. An example is sociological analysis of social work organizational structures: this topic is integral to a sociology of social work (Smith, 1979) but analysis in this area is also capable of generating a range of insights and data with potentially practical value for social work practitioners and for policy-makers (Barker, 1981).

It could be argued that a sociology of social work which succeeds in clarifying social work issues and in contributing to an understanding of them (particularly when the issues in question are ambiguously formulated within social work discourses) is of itself a practical movement towards a sociology 'in' or 'for' social work. This view, though not entirely without merit to the extent that it recognizes sociological understanding may inform policy and practice in various ways, does, however, raise some problems. These problems partly stem from internal disagreements and ambiguities within and amongst those social work discourses which specify the structure and forms of social work knowledge (see chapter four), and from long-standing complications surrounding the relation of academic knowledge to social work practice (see chapter two) and also to social work education and training (see chapter seven). Other problems are to do with controversies that revolve around value-conflicts in the politics of social work (see chapters two and five) and controversies surrounding professionalizing goals and organizational and service-delivery issues (see chapters two and six). More generally, much of the controversial history of the relation between sociology and social work (Webb and Evans, 1976) centres upon the question of whether the sociologist should be confined to providing data for the achievement of professionally defined goals, or also be involved in analytic critique of the nature of the goals themselves and of the social work organizational frameworks and practice methods used for achieving them (Gouldner, 1965). The question posed by Gouldner is not restricted to social work. Academic research problems of various kinds (not to mention moral-political problems) arise if it is argued that social investigators should simply 'accept' professional actors' accounts at their face value and that, say, the 'proper' role of policing in society should be defined entirely by police officers, or that doctors should have exclusive defining rights in specifying how medical service-delivery systems should be organized (Lee, 1978, p.19).

An uncritical 'servicing' role in a sociology for social work is in any case problematic for a pragmatic reason implicit in the preceding paragraph. To ask 'is sociology relevant to social work?' is to pose a facile question. It would be necessary to ask the questioner which 'social work' she or he has in mind and to which academic sociology

2

might be unproblematically harnessed. Within social work's own 'internal' literature there are widely differing theories and perspectives concerning definitions of what social work is, concerning how to 'do' social work, and concerning the types of knowledge deemed to be 'relevant' to social work practice (Timms and Timms, 1977. p.17; Sibeon, 1989b, p.34). There is evidence that social work educators, who have responsibility for teaching social work students and assessing their competence prior to the award of the professional qualification, do not have any clearly formulated, shared view of what constitutes 'appropriate' social work knowledge nor even what constitutes 'appropriate' professional practice (Brandon and Davies, 1979, p.345). As will become evident in the following chapters, there is no single, unambiguous or consensually agreed version of social work to which academic knowledge (such as sociology) might be 'made relevant'. Therefore the question of the relevance or otherwise of academic social science disciplines to social work only begins to make sense if the question if rephrased in a form which asks - relevant to which definition of 'Social Work'?

The following chapters will provide numerous illustrations of the analytic motif and methodological procedures that characterize a sociology of social work that moves far beyond an uncritical 'servicing' role. One such illustration is Armstrong's (1980) observation that analytic problematization is necessary in sociology. Armstrong's (1980) understanding of problematization as an analytic procedure is illustrated with reference to the social work concept 'relevance' (ibid., p.17)

> ... when the issue of "relevance" is raised this provides an opportunity to open up a range of different perspectives and their underlying assumptions ... what does "relevant" mean? What knowledge is "relevant" to social work and why? Why is other knowledge not considered "relevant"? What purpose does "relevant" knowledge serve? In other words, "relevance" can be treated as problematic as a way of understanding the nature of social work or of any other profession.

For theoretical reasons outlined in chapter three, the form of analysis employed in this book avoids any notions that social workers' discourses (regarding the concept 'relevance' or any other social work matters) are surface reflections of so-called 'objective' structural 'needs' or of any putative 'deep' cultural 'logic' embedded in society. In the theoretical terms developed in chapter three, social workers are regarded as actors who employ discourses; but these discourses are contingently produced in particular conditions of action, rather than being 'necessary effects' of the social totality.

To say that discourses (ways of thinking and of acting) are not structurally predetermined in the sense implied by, say, structuralism (Gibson, 1984), structuralist linguistics (Silverman and Torode, 1980, p.329) or structural theories of social work discourse (Philp, 1979), is not to say that the discourses used by actors are necessarily 'free' of self-limiting forms of cognitive closure. Some social work 'materials' (particular ways of thinking, policies, practice styles, organizational conventions, etc.) are widely disseminated through time, and also across social space (i.e. from one social work physical setting to another). Through the institutionalization of the meanings associated with these materials they may become habitualized, routinized and 'taken-for-granted' (Berger and Luckmann, 1972, pp.56-58). Regular occupational immersion in and repeated use of these temporally and spatially circulated materials may lead to an inability to cognitively 'step outside' the routinized occupational views of the world supplied by these internalized materials. When meanings become objectified into consciousness in this way they become part of a 'natural attitude' (Holzner, 1968. p.1) that fails to reflexively grasp the implications that might arise from an understanding that 'We see and hear and otherwise experience very largely as we do because ... our ... (discourses) ... predispose certain choices of interpretation' (Sapir, 1966, p.69). A similar point, though framed in theoretical terms that differ from the ones just mentioned, is made by Rojek et al. (1988). A central theme of their text is that 'received ideas' in both 'traditional' and 'radical' social work discourses involve a form of cognitive closure. Commentaries on social work written in terms confined exclusively to the meanings and forms of thought contained in social work discourses sometimes embody a remarkably narrow, restricted view of the social world and hence of social work's relation to that world (Timms, 1968, p.12). Pearson (1975) in a critical account of 'traditional' social work, suggests professional socialization is a form of cognitive closure and a narrowing of awareness that puts the subject into a '... professional sleep' (ibid., p.127). According to Pearson, most aspects of the social world are oversimplified in professional social work's ways of thinking. This happens to such an extent that the complexities of social life are '... not observable from <u>within</u> professional culture' (ibid.).

To move beyond and 'step outside' the cognitive closure associated with social work's 'received ideas' (Rojek et al.. 1988) does not mean that <u>sociology</u> of social work can legitimately claim any exclusive defining rights. No discourse, sociological or otherwise, is omniscient: any such claims should be viewed with the utmost suspicion. Webb (1981a), in an account of the relation of sociology to social work, notes (ibid., p.121) that a sociological

> ... sense of doubt or systematic scepticism towards the way in which explanations are given rests upon an understanding that knowledge only <u>approaches</u> an ultimate truth, and sociology is pretty certain that what knowledge purports to describe is not the full totality of a phenomenon. Knowledge is partial ...

A sociology of social work (or of anything else) can properly aspire to provide relatively adequate explanations of the phenomenon being investigated. This aspiration refers to empirical explanations that are claimed to be 'relatively adequate' rather than ultimate truths. It is therefore incumbent upon sociologists (and other academics and researchers) to make fully explicit the basic, underlying theoretical assumptions upon which empirical interpretations of social phenomena are constructed. This rarely happens in the 'received ideas' of conventional social work discourses: nor should it, however, be allowed to happen in sociology. It is not enough to make interpretations and draw conclusions; the underlying theoretical concepts and postulates upon which empirical interpretations are based should be explicit and thereby made 'publicly' available for the critical scrutiny of others. It is necessary to state the grounds for selecting particular theoretical assumptions and for rejecting others. Even where this is done there remains a sense in which all social theories are relative and open to challenge. Actors in general attempt to convince others of the adequacy of their accounts; this is also the way sociology has to go about its work (Callon, 1986, p.200).

The fact that a particular interpretation may be sociological is hardly a reason for its automatic acceptance; as well as the points just made, theoretical disagreements exist among sociologists. This means a reflexive sociology of social work has to also be a sociology of sociology: the individual sociologist of social work necessarily has to select from the range of different sociological approaches available, a process of conscious selection which involves providing explicit reasons for rejecting some particular sociological perspective(s) and for selecting others. It is often terminologically convenient to refer to 'the' sociology of social work; this is acceptable provided it is remembered that, in principle, many different sociologies of social work are possible. In more general terms, there are no good reasons for supposing that 'everyone' will accept and endorse any particular social interpretation, whether of a sociological or some other kind: nor are there good reasons for supposing that any theoretically uncontextualized 'supra-content' concepts or any conceptual or methodological devices exist as a referee for conclusively arbitrating between two or more conflicting interpretations in a way that will be acceptable to all the parties concerned. Controversies surrounding the study and interpretation of social life are interminable and sociology cannot legitimately claim epistemological privileges: sociological narratives are no more, but no less valid than others (Callon, 1986, p.200). This being so, and in the light of what was said earlier, the essential point to be made here is that sociological interpretations should be accompanied by a clear, explicit statement of their underlying conceptual assumptions; it is intended to hold to this precept in each of the following chapters.

In the future it may be that an increasing number of sociologists (and also social policy academics) working in other fields will develop interests in social work: it is possible that this development will be stimulated through dissemination of the academic material currently being formulated by the few sociologists actively involved in this field. At the present time, however, it is mainly a relatively small number of sociologists based in social work education (together with an equally small number of sociologically-inclined social work academics) who are involved in the construction of a contemporary sociology of social work. Social work writing per se is almost wholly uninformed by recent developments in sociology and in academic social science generally. This also applies, as Webb (1987) has noted, to some ostensibly 'sociological' writing on social work. As a body of academic knowledge, the sociology of social work has trailed far behind the pace of change that has occurred within sociology as an academic discipline: set against this background, the purpose of this book is to identify empirical and theoretical issues relevant to the construction of a modern sociology of social work.

2 Social work in perspective

The construction of a 'new' sociology of social work builds upon the anti-reductionist conceptualizations discussed in chapter three. The later emphasis upon recent forms of sociology may at first sight appear at odds with an insistence that analysis of modern social work should be grounded in a knowledge of social work history. However it will be demonstrated in this chapter that historical data are an essential analytic resource in the sociology of social work. Many problems and issues in modern social work are contemporary re-activations (or 're-workings') of 'perennial' social work problematics (Lee, 1982). It need hardly be said that the social and political contexts in which these 'perennial' problematics arise, and the ways in which they are socially constructed and responded to by social work (and other) actors, exhibit discontinuities and variation in time and place. But this does not mean no continuities exist: the social work wheel is not wholly 're-invented each time'. The point was made in the last chapter that some social work 'materials' (social work forms of thought, policies, forms of practice, organizational conventions, etc.) are disseminated temporally and spatially across the social work community. For theoretical reasons that will be made more explicit in chapters three and four, an important concern in an anti-reductionist sociology of social work is the investigation of both continuities and discontinuities in the dissemination of social work materials across time and social space. Framed in these terms, the main purpose of the present chapter is to relate historical materials to more recent developments in a way that will also serve to provide a general overview of social work. To this end the chapter will be concerned with three perennial-but-also-contemporary social work problematics. These are analytically separable, although empirical interconnections exist between them: these interconnections will emerge at various points in the chapter and throughout the book as a whole. The first of these problematics is social work knowledge and its relation to social work practice; the second is value-conflict in the politics of social work; the third concerns professional, organizational, and service-delivery issues. These 'core' social work problematics will be re-examined in later chapters when each of them will be separately analysed in closer detail, drawing where appropriate on the theoretical sociological postulates developed in the next chapter.

Social work knowledge and its relation to social work practice: the 'theory-practice' problematic

The 'theory-practice' problematic arises from conflicting opinions within the social work community as to whether formal, academic social science knowledge 'does' or 'should' relate to social work practice; and from ambiguities and confusions as to what form(s) a relationship between theory and practice might take. Throughout the book the term 'theory' will be used as a convenient shorthand expression that encompasses formal academic knowledge in general, including both theoretical and empirical knowledge. On occasion, particularly in chapter four, use of the term will be extended to include 'informal' theory. A 'theoryless practice' is a contradiction in terms: practitioners' use of, for example, cultural commonsense or 'practice-wisdoms' extrapolated from the practical experience of doing social work, does not mean that no 'theory' is being employed. Social work theories may be of the formal or informal variety (or more complexly, some fusion of the two) and on this broad definition, 'theories' are inevitable and unavoidable features of practice. This means that a relevant choice for social work practitioners is not whether but which theories to use (Curnock and Hardiker, 1979, p.10).

The term social work was first used in Britain around the turn of the present century (Seed, 1973, p.3) in connection with the activities of the Charity Organization Society (COS). Philanthropy is the work of amateurs. A key objective of the COS was '... to transform philanthropy from an unskilled "duty" of the rich to an expert and professional activity undertaken only by those who were prepared by social theory and trained in the appropriate methods' (Jones, 1983, p.81). Embryonic social work professionalism allied to a 'use of theory' was expressed in a paper by Loch (1906), the Society's secretary who wrote 'Doctors have to be educated methodically, registered and certified. Charity is the work of the social physician. It is to the interests of the community that it should not be entrusted to novices, or to dilettanti, or to quacks' (ibid., p.xix). The first British programme of social work education was established in 1903 in the COS's School of Sociology at London University. Urwick (1904), the newly appointed Director of the School argued that '... the impulse to do good may, if untrained, lead straight to evil doing ... the good heart unschooled by the good head will probably fall into dangerous paths ...' (ibid., p.180). From the beginning, this association between academic knowledge and social work practice was highly problematical.

Some years before the School of Sociology was established, Loch (1877, quoted in Timms, 1983, p.70) reported that a critic of the Society had said to him 'It is all very well for you to read and study. But, you know, the members of your Committees don't. They plod along with their cases; but you are quite wrong if you think they are troubling themselves about general causes, principles, or any other questions'.

7

The professionalizing ethos of the COS's programme was based on '... a definite attempt to induce people not to shrink from applying theory to practical work' (Bosanquet, 1914, pp.404-5). Prior to the formal inauguration of the COS's School of Sociology in 1903, the Society's leadership had expressed concern about students' and COS trainees' attitudes to intellectual learning in the COS's local training schemes. Bosanquet reported there was 'prejudice against theory' and the COS trainees were criticized by Bosanquet for holding attitudes expressed in the form 'There is too much real work to be done; I have no time for your books and theories' (Bosanquet, 1900, quoted in Smith, 1965, p.87). These early theory-practice tensions were magnified following the establishment of the COS's School of Sociology in 1903 at London University. From the outset, the university had doubts about housing a social work training course. These doubts persisted and in 1912 the university suggested the social work course should be taken over by the COS (Armstrong, 1980, p.6). The London University Executive Committee on Social Work Education (1903) had earlier reported that '... Social Science ... (disciplines) ... rouse but little interest ... and their real meaning is not understood, while the students ... regard them only as ... bookwork' (London University Executive Committee on Social Work Education, 1903, quoted in Smith, 1965, p.40, emphasis added). In the light of this it was perhaps not surprising that the senior university academicians sitting on this committee of 1903 were perplexed as to the purpose of locating basic social work training in the university.

The 'timeless' (perennial) dimension of social work's theory-practice problematic was noted many years later in Satyamurti's (1983) account of a social work student who spoke of wanting to help people and who asked 'so how can reading help?' (ibid., p.36, emphasis added). According to Satyamurti, social work students in the 1980's reject theory 'from the contributory disciplines' (ibid.) and also reject theory of a kind that is '... directly related to social work intervention' (ibid.). Like Bosanquet (1900) more than eighty years previously, Satyamurti (1983) expressed her frustration that 'The students do not ... feel that they will get anything that is important to them from a book' (ibid., p.36). Satyamurti's observations concerning social work students' scepticism about the relevance of intellectual learning and the use of academic social science knowledge, are mirrored in empirical data reported in studies by Cox (1982) and Waterhouse (1987) and numerous other empirical studies referred to in the last section of chapter three and also in chapter seven.

The unwavering persistence with which a large number of empirical studies reveal similar findings spanning the best part of a century (see chapter seven) indicate that the theory-practice problematic in social work education and training is a truly 'perennial' material that cannot be explained as a 'failure' of social work students to grasp the relevance of academic social science knowledge nor as a 'failure' of social work educators to correctly teach academic knowledge in a way that is directly 'applied' to social work practice. The theory-practice problematic in social work has appeared with such regularity in too many places at too many different times for these types of 'explanation' to have any credence: any such 'explanations' would have to presuppose a massive perennial incompetence on the part of both teachers and learners and would have to demonstrate why this assumed incompetence has remained unremedied for as long as social work has existed. For rather more than a century, professional(izing) social work actors (Loch, 1877; BASW 1977) have portrayed social work practice 'as if' it were, or was about to become, or might realistically be expected to become, an activity

8

based on the application of formal academic social science knowledge that 'therefore' requires that social work training 'must' be based in academic institutions of higher education. This 'as if' portrayal of 'professional' social work is not and never has been an accurate reflection of the socially constructed and historically reproduced reality of social work practice and its cognitive foundations (Loch, 1877; Bosanquet, 1900; Eliot, 1924; Karpf, 1931; Kadushin, 1959; Carew, 1979; Pratt and Grimshaw, 1985). In this respect, professional(izing) social work founders on a historically institutionalized and professionally reproduced 'credibility-gap'. Most of the available empirical evidence suggests that social work practice is based almost entirely upon practical 'commonsense' and experientially acquired occupational 'practice-wisdoms' (Carew, 1979) that are learned on-the-job rather than in academic institutions. When each generation of students and practitioners inevitably reject formal academic disciplinary knowledge, this perennial rejection is not because the academic knowledge has been 'incorrectly' taught by academics, nor either is it because of any idiosyncratic or personal 'incompetence' on the part of particular social work students and practitioners: it is because the socially constructed reality of social work practice in general is such that formal academic knowledge (i.e. social science knowledge, there being no other formal academic disciplinary knowledge base that social work might draw upon) is simply not 'required' for social work practice. Whether academic knowledge 'could' or 'should' be employed in social work practice is another matter: the issue being discussed here concerns the socially constructed and historically institutionalized and reproduced reality of social work practice as it actually exists. These issues will be returned to in chapter seven.

A closely related problematic is that there is wide disagreement among social work writers as to what social work's knowledge-base 'does' or 'should' consist of. Hardiker (1981) advocates the use of academic social science knowledge. In contrast, Morris (1975) suggests that reading novels, poetry, and plays, is a crucial way of enabling social work students and practitioners to acquire 'sensitivity and insights which enrichen ... contacts with others ... and ... deepen ... understanding' (ibid., p.7). Valk, (1983) too, advocates reading fiction and poetry and she comments that there are 'elements of ... experience ... (that) ... cannot be communicated through the social and behavioural sciences' (ibid., p.17). Irvine (1975) also argues that 'creative literature' should have a major role in professional social work education, because academic disciplines such as sociology and psychology 'inevitably oversimplify' (ibid., p.5) and while 'the behavioural sciences provide ... knowledge about human beings, social workers also need to have a more intimate knowledge of them' (ibid.). It is possible that Irvine has in mind a distinction between nomothetic and idiographic constructs. Some radical social work writers have advocated that direct 'lived' experience of structurally induced oppression and disadvantage is a crucial source of emancipatory knowledge, and that social workers should therefore be recruited directly from the ranks of unemployed persons, discharged prisoners, recovering alcolics, and various other categories of 'non-expert' (White, 1972; Priestly, 1975). A different dimension of the theory-practice problematic is the view of some writers that it is not any particular 'type' of formal academic or professional knowledge that makes for effective practice, but the personality attributes and attitudes of the casework counsellor or groupworker (Kahan, 1979; Traux and Carkhuff, 1967; Garfield and Bergin, 1978).

Davies (1985) argues that social science has no significantly useful role in social work practice (ibid., p.220). He suggests the four 'essential ingredients' for social work practice are practice-wisdoms or 'practice know-how' (ibid., p.223), a knowledge of law affecting social work (ibid., p.225) and of clients 'welfare rights' entitlements to financial benefits (ibid., p.227), and lastly, a working knowledge of the local community (ibid., pp.239-42). This cognitive checklist implies an agency 'in-service' model of on-the-job occupational training, perhaps supplemented by short training or induction programmes. In terms of this checklist, there would be no point in locating social work training in those academic institutions that teach formal academic disciplinary knowledge such as social policy, sociology, and psychology. Yet Davies (1981c) simultaneously argues that social work training should be based in academic institutions, particularly in universities (ibid., pp.282-83). This contradiction will be discussed in the last section of chapter three, with particular reference to what will be identified in that chapter as a 'technical-professionalist' paradigm of social work. Heraud (1979) suggests the inclusion of social sciences in social work training curricula may serve to '... give a spurious legitimacy and status to the activities of utilizers ... to persuade others that "knowledge" is being put to use, as in the case of professions ...' (ibid., p.22). Heraud's observation has particular relevance to sociological analysis of social work education and its role in the professionalization of social work.

The 'theory-practice' problematic is not simply a conflict between social work educators 'versus' field practitioners. Internal theory-practice tensions within social work education have a long history. It was noted earlier that the COS's School of Sociology established in 1903 had an academically inauspicious start. Largely as part of the university's attempt to inject some academic content into the social work course established by the COS in the School of Sociology, that school was in 1912 re-located within London University to the London School of Economics (LSE). This meant that LSE university academics, who were not social work tutors, became involved in providing lectures for social work students. The COS leadership quickly became alarmed not only at 'socialist' influences entering social work training but also at the LSE lecturers' more academic approach to social work training. The movement towards a relatively more academic, 'university' type of approach to social work training after 1912 lessened the ability of the COS leadership to control the way in which social work's 'theory-practice' problematic was constructed and insulated from the scrutiny of university intellectuals: the COS desired that 'professional' social work tutors as ex-practitioners unhindered by university academic social science should define this problematic in the process of teaching social work students. In the terms just described, the fate of the School of Sociology after 1912 was '.. from the standpoint of the COS something of a tragedy' (Mowat, 1961, p.171) This reflected a much larger problem. On the one hand social work training can not successfully claim to be a 'professional' form of training unless it is located in academic institutions; but on the other, the actual relationship between social work training and academic disciplinary knowledge is tenuous to say the least. This is one reason why, throughout the history of social work, courses of social work training in academic institutions of higher education have in general always intentionally remained self-contained and marginally located, and in most respects have led a relatively 'separate' existence from the academic community (Donnison et al, 1975, pp.256-7).

With regard to the basic question 'what should social workers know?' reference was made earlier to ambiguities and disagreements in social work responses to this question. A related issue is the existence of a pervasive 'oral culture' in social work (Carew, 1979, p.361; Curnock and Hardiker, 1979, pp.10-11). This co-exists alongside a written social work culture comprised of social work texts and journals; nevertheless, as will be shown in chapter four, empirical evidence suggests that an oral culture is very significant both in the construction of social work knowledge and in its 'word-of-mouth' temporal and spatial dissemination across the social work community. In the 'process-versus-content' debate (Harris et al., 1985) advocates of 'process' learning perspectives refer to a fusion of cognitive and emotional processes in the construction of social work 'insights' and 'understandings' (i.e. in the construction of social work knowledge). In social work, the process-versus-content debate is sometimes described as the 'heart versus head' controversy, in the sense that '... whereas "head work" stresses the importance of being able to generalize, theorize, abstract ... "heart work" stresses the idiosyncratic nature of each situation ... (and) ... the importance of personal experience' (Smith, 1971, p.26, emphases added). Most social work courses subscribe in varying degrees to a 'process' learning approach. This is usually thought of as a 'group dynamics' process based on experientialism (Greenwall and Howard, 1986) and where students, and sometimes staff, are encouraged to fuse their emotional aspects of 'self' (Shaw, 1974) with cognitive learning and to share verbally with others their emotional responses to social work constructs. The approach is compatible with radical social work theories of consciousness-raising, though many social work teachers and practitioners who subscribe to 'process' learning employ various psychodynamic and psychotherapeutic ideas, and Paley (1984) captures the essence of the approach in an article which notes it is not necessarily the case that the things most worth knowing can always be written down on paper.

A sociological illustration of 'process' learning is Barbour's (1985) ethnographic empirical study of social work training, where learning is achieved '... especially through the "sharing" of feelings' (ibid., p.504). Approaches of this kind have attracted criticism (Bandura, 1969). North (1972, chapter 3) is highly critical of the ways in which the concept 'emotional insight' is incorporated into social work training and into psychotherapeutically oriented casework. Yelloly (1972) comments '... not only ... is the concept of insight extremely ill-defined, but the process by which it is thought to mediate change is equally inexplicit' (ibid., p.143, original emphases). Simon (1967) suggested social work preoccupations with 'process' often mean that the intellectual 'contents' of academic knowledge are thrown '... out of the window' (ibid., p.10). Pinker (1989) examines factors that might in the future lead academic institutions in the higher education sector to withdraw from basic, qualifying 'professional' social work training (ibid., p.101). One of the factors identified by Pinker (1989) is that social work's continuing emphasis upon experientialism embodies '... a psychodynamic legacy which still determines the orientation of social casework, holding it apart ... (and) ... keeping it separate from the academic community' (ibid., p.91). Whether social work's 'perennial' theory-practice problematic will in the next decade interact with some other contemporary issues in a way that leads to a separation of social work training and higher education, is a currently professionally troubling problem that will be examined in chapter seven.

The politics of social work

There are grounds for regarding 'the politics of social work' as the second major perennial-but-also-contemporary problematic of professional social work. As in the case of the theory-practice problematic, the Charity Organization Society was a significant precursor of later developments. Conflict between the COS's professional casework ideology and the collectivist politics of the late nineteenth century socialist reformers was not the first expression of conflict in the politics of welfare (Seed, 1973, p.8). Prior to the rise to influence of the COS, the philosophy of welfare represented by 'The Society for the Reformation of Manners' contrasted sharply with the objectives of social movements concerned with structural, political issues centred upon factory working conditions, low wages and poverty, housing, sanitation and public health, and extension of the franchise (Owen, 1965; Harrison, 1966). In effect, the professionalizing activities and individual casework orientation of the COS gave renewed and highly conflictual articulation to already existing opposed philosophies of welfare.

Historical conflicts between 'caseworkers' and 'social reformers' are described in Young and Ashton (1956), Woodroofe (1962), and Stedman Jones (1971). The COS's philosophy rested on a 'personal inadequacy' theory of welfare in which casework was deployed as a method to 'remedy defect in citizen character' (Bosanquet, 1909). Theoretical underpinning for this model was provided by the type of sociology (Spencer's (1877) evolutionary theories and 'social Darwinism') included in the COS's training curriculum at its School of Sociology (Leonard, 1966, pp.4-7; Heraud, 1970, p.4). This was more in the nature of a general reference to Spencerian sociology as a legitimation of the COS's political philosophy of practice. There is no evidence that the COS fieldworkers' practice was itself based on academically-grounded 'scientific casework' in the sense claimed by the COS leadership. The COS's actual fieldwork practice, although portrayed by the society's leadership as 'professional' and based on academic knowledge, was, in reality, based on a mixture of moral-political principles and values combined with what might be termed 'practice-wisdoms' developed out of the practical experience of doing fieldwork (Pinker, 1989, p.87). To return to a point noted earlier, the COS is the first empirically recorded example of a persisting tendency on the part of professionalizing actors, including many professional social work educators, to portray social work practice 'as if' it were or else was on the point of becoming an activity based on formal academic knowledge derived from the social sciences.

The COS's political philosophy of welfare was indicated in Octavia Hill's (1884) suggestion that reform of housing policy would not resolve the problem of bad housing, for the reason that '... the tenants' habits and lives are what they are. Transplant them to healthy and commodious houses and they would pollute and destroy them' (ibid., p.10). The Society's journal in 1881 stated 'There can be no doubt that the poverty of the working classes of England is due, not to their circumstances ... but to their improvident habits and thriftlessness. If they are ever to be more prosperous it must be through self-denial, temperance and forethought' (COS Review, Vol.10, 1881, p.50). The COS's political welfare doctrine was strongly opposed by social reformers influenced by the writings of Edwin Chadwick, Charles Booth and the Fabians (Alden, 1905) who argued for structural reform through a more interventionist role on the part of the state (Townsend, 1911). Some acerbic exchanges took place between the social reformers of that time and the COS advocates of casework (Stedman Jones, 1971) and in castigating the social reformers' use of statistical data as a measure of inequality and social deprivation, the COS stated 'We do not share Mr. Booth's natural affection for his table of causes. His mastery of figures is only exceeded by the mastery of figures over his own imagination' (COS Report, 1892).

Social work education has always been a significant institutional arena for the expression of conflict over social work politics. The COS's training course established in 1903 in the School of Sociology was essentially a self-contained social work course; the school, despite its title, was in effect a school of social work in which training was controlled largely by social work tutors. University academics' perceptions that the social work course lacked any academic credibility, and the problems posed for the COS arising from this perception, were referred to earlier. In 1912, on the brink of closure, the COS's School of Sociology was absorbed into the London School of Economics and became a Department of Social Science. This made it more difficult for the COS to insulate its training course from 'intellectuals' and also from politically contaminating teaching that might in some way challenge its welfare training philosophy based on casework method. The approach to teaching at the LSE was both far more 'intellectual' than it had been at the COS's School of Sociology and, in the eyes of the COS leadership, also far too 'socialist'. An antecedent of some modern social work professionals' fears of the dangers of exposing social work students to politically radical ideas, a theme that will be returned to shortly, was the COS's misgivings after 1912 concerning '... the influence ... of socialist theory on the school's teaching and on the attitudes of its students' (Harris, 1989 in Bulmer, et al., p.30). Some years previously, one of the leading lights of the COS had written that socialists, particularly the Fabians were '... frightfully anti-COS ... I could never work with them or with any of them in any practical effort, we should be at daggers drawn in every detail' (Bosanquet, 1890, in Muirhead 1935, pp.73-74). Although the later development of the welfare state continued to be politically controversial (Cootes, 1966) it was the 1970's before specifically social work political daggers were again drawn in an outbreak of major political conflict between 'professional' casework theorists and advocates of structural reform.

In the 1950's and early 1960's the political cultural climate within and outside social work co-incided. Employment was relatively high and this together with the post-war 'Beveridge' expansion of the welfare state engendered a perception that the 'grinding poverty' of the 1930's had been eliminated and that any remaining problems of welfare would require not major structural interventions but a residue of psychological counselling services directed towards individuals and families. Crosland (1956) in his The Future of Socialism stated that future governments would '... increasingly need to focus attention ... on individual persons and families, not on economic causes of distress, but on social and psychological causes ... not ... cash payments, nor even ... material provision ... but ... individual therapy, casework and ... treatment' (ibid., pp.155-56). This political climate suited social work professionalism and also co-incided with the increased influence of psychodynamic ideas in professional casework theory (Meyer and Timms, 1969). However, the post-war political welfare consensus that had enveloped the social work community began to crumble after the mid to late 1960's. The first major post-war political criticisms of professional social work began to appear in the late 1960's, these criticisms being '... jointly associated with challenge to the psychotherapeutic tradition and with the rediscovery of poverty; the recognition that basic social provisions had not achieved what many had hoped for - the ending of poverty and a gradual movement towards social equality' (Sainsbury, 1986, p.3). The intensity of the conflicts that developed around the 'traditional versus radical' social work debate in the 1970's probably reflects the irony that radical condemnations of professionalism inopportunely surfaced when professional social work was optimistically embarking upon what promised to be a period of unprecedented expansion.

The 1970's, particularly the first half of the decade, may aptly be described as the 'golden era' of social work professionalism in Britain (Richards, 1971). The historically long-standing, but still unachieved, goal of social work professionalism was brought closer by the Seebohm Report (1968) which led in 1971 to the creation of the new 'professional' social services departments in local authorities. Other indicators of professional social work expansion in the 1970's included the formation of a national professional association, the British Association of Social Workers established in 1971; the movement towards a professionally unifying 'generic' mode of practice; and the unification of training in the form of a single nationally recognized professional qualification (the Certificate of Qualification in Social Work) regulated by the Central Council for Education and Training in Social Work following the creation of the training council by statutory instrument in 1971. These developments led to the opening of many new departments of social work training in universities and polytechnics, causing one commentator to suggest that '.. the future of professional social work is its growing intellectualism' (Sainsbury, 1977, p.213). Inevitably, this professionalizing aspiration was doomed to failure because the closer relationship that developed between social work and academic institutions in the 1970's merely served to re-activate social work's perennial 'theory-practice' problematic; in the following decade this was to lead to potentially threatening (Carter, 1985) de-professionalizing policies constructed by 'non-professional' social work actors, including social work employers and administrators. In the 1970's, however, it was primarily conflict over social work politics that threatened to divide the social work community. These conflicts centred on social work education in the newly created professional social work 'schools' in universities and polytechnics. The earlier concerns expressed by the COS leadership after 1912 at the 'radicalizing' influence that lecturers at the London School of Economics were having on social work students, were resurrected on a grand scale.

Radical social work critiques in the 1970's took the form of criticisms that professional social work discourse was politically ideological by virtue of its emphasis upon 'traditional' individual casework and groupwork rather than more radical collectivist, community-based forms of local intervention allied to pressure for larger structural change; and professionally self-interested in the sense of seeking to establish a 'professional' 'status' for social work. Radicals also rejected professional discourse on the grounds that it was a theoretically simplistic discourse. As briefly noted in the first chapter, radical social work writers criticized professional socialization as a form of cognitive closure. Pearson's (1975) view was that professional social work operates at a very low level of 'theoretical appreciation' (ibid., p.127) and he argued that (ibid.)

... the professional eye does not recognize itself in its

operations; the modes of thought and action which characterize any particular professional activity are not observable from <u>within</u> professional culture. There is even a sense in which professional vision can be thought to miss the point of its own enquiries altogether, for, as Alfred Schutz (1964, p.95) observes, one of the functions of culture is "to eliminate troublesome enquiries by offering ready-made directions for use, to replace truth hard to obtain by offering comfortable truisms, and to substitute the self-explanatory for the questionable".

North (1972) indicated that psychotherapeutic casework 'mystique' (ibid., p.84) was pervasive in professional social work which instead of attempting to tackle structural inequalities was merely providing clients with unwanted 'psychic handouts' (ibid., p.81). Deacon and Bartley (1975) in their empirical study argued that social work teachers were attempting to 'cool out' students' radical criticisms of professionalism, through the use of psychological socialization devices associated with the quasi-psychodynamic 'process' learning model referred to earlier in the chapter. According to Deacon and Bartley (1975), social work education is a process of professional socialization based on '... the encouragement of students to adhere to a set of social work professional maxims which ... (are) ... very confused ... (and) ... underpinned by a general disavowal of intellectuality, of theoretical thinking ...' (ibid., p.70). Needless to say, these and countless other 1970's style radical social work and radical sociological critiques of social work professionalism produced a spirited defensive response from professional(izing) social work actors.

The Central Council for Education and Training in Social Work observed that 'certain sociological perspectives ... have had a radicalizing effect' (CCETSW, 1972, p.12). The Gould Report (1977) criticized 'marxist penetration' of the higher education sector, and of the professional training of teachers and social workers. Although it was Marxist sociology that was usually singled out for professional social work criticism, it was sociology of a quite different type that Munday (1972) had in mind when he warned that '... the ideas of writers like Matza, Becker, Cicourel are intellectually fascinating and persuasive, but quite ominous for the social worker' (ibid., p.4). Another writer suggested that exposing professional social work students to critical social science disciplines has a professionally disastrous influence and '... the dangers of undermining the professional commitments of novices in the field parallel those of putting a viper in the cradle of an infant' (Wilson, 1974, p.9). Probably the most vigorous and sustained professional social work criticism of radicalism, and in particular of the allegedly politicizing effects of sociology, came from Davies (1981a, 1981b, 1981c, 1982, 1983, 1985) who warned against academic social scientists' left-wing political subversion of professional social work (Davies, 1981a, pp.194-97). Davies (1981b) stated that social science knowledge and sociology in particular has a 'debilitating' effect upon social work students who as a consequence of being exposed to 'critical perspectives' (ibid., p.19) were becoming '... <u>critical</u>, <u>questioning</u>, even sceptical ...' (ibid., emphases added). One of Davies's (1981b) reasons for being sympathetic to the idea of removing sociology from social work training (ibid., p.19) is that unless the subversive, politically radicalizing effects of social science knowledge, and more particularly sociology, can be contained '... it is theoretically possible that sociology might undermine or <u>destroy</u> social work ...' (Davies, 1981a, p.196, emphasis added). The historical

15

parallel between these acute professional anxieties and those voiced by the COS leadership was drawn earlier when note was made of the COS's profound 'misgivings' after 1912 when its social work training course was opened up to the LSE's academic lecturers whom the COS held responsible for 'the influence of socialist theory ... on the attitudes of students' (Harris, 1989 in Bulmer et al., p.30). These perennial professional anxieties about radical subversion wrongly assume that social work students are extraordinarily susceptible and immaturely naive, if not downright gullible; in reality, there is no empirical evidence to justify Davies's (1981a, 1981b, 1981c) denigratory assumption that social work students are so easily 'led astray' by radical intellectual analyses that subvert an otherwise smooth process of socialization into professional social work's cognitive and political mores.

Professional social work leaders need not have been alarmed at the political 'challenge' posed by radical social work. In real terms, radical social work in the 1970's was essentially a theoretical radicalism which contained very few realistically attainable practical prescriptions for changing the system of 'professional' social work training or for changing the post-Seebohm 'bureau-professional' system of organization and service-delivery. At root, radical social work in the 1970's was an academic radicalism, an intellectual critique of professional social work under capitalism. Two features of these radical critiques should be noted. Firstly, when radical professionals criticized the domain assumptions of their own profession, they did so safe in the knowledge that their profession was rapidly expanding. There was no fear that radical theory might bring about the collapse of bureau-professionalism. Radical social work co-incided with a massive expansion of post-Seebohm professional social work in the social services departments (Webb, 1980, p.285). It was not until the late 1970's that professional social work services began to experience the impact of financial expenditure cuts associated with the 'legitimation crisis' of the modern welfare state, a point taken up in chapter five. Secondly, as already noted, radical social work was largely a theoretical critique: it posed no real or 'practical' threat. The development of an 'abstract radicalism' in the 1970's was noted by Morris (1975) whose rejection of traditional professionalism was counterbalanced by his rejection of a purely theoretical radicalism: he wrote 'The rhetoric of revolution is no less futile than the rhetoric of psycho-therapy' (ibid., p.19). Morris (1975) asked 'having satisfied oneself that one's clients are actually part of the working class movement ... what would support for this struggle actually look like?' (ibid., p.19). Timms (1983) in a comment on radical social work as it existed in the 1970's and early 1980's observes '... the feasibility of a "genuinely" Marxist social work is not without problems, and it is not easy to discern its distinctive features ...' (ibid., p.97). Some years before this, Donnison et al. (1975) had argued that marxist welfare theory is utopian and fails to 'formulate concrete priorities and policies ...' (ibid., p.35). Deacon (1981, p.46) in arguing for democratic socialist welfare based on the idea of service democratization and decentralization made the point that

> Socialists who know their Marxist philosophy have always been keen to point out that there can be no blueprint for the socialist society - no a-priori resolution of issues that can then be simply acted upon .... The problem of letting the question rest there is ... to leave socialists with no positive alternative conception of

the welfare state ... and ... leaves the way open for ... dismissing the Marxist critique as unpractical ...

Where prescriptions for radical practice existed, these generally replicated conventional forms of professional organization and practice. In their text Towards Socialist Welfare Work the claim made by Bolger et al. (1981) was that they had developed '... a form of marxist thought and politics which directly informs day-to-day welfare work' (ibid., pp.18-19). This was disputed by Simpkin (1982) who observed that 'few of the tactics proposed in Towards Socialist Welfare Work differ greatly from those proposed by liberal professionals' (ibid., p.94). These and various other critical accounts may be taken as an indication that the hiatus between 'theory' and 'practice' in traditional professional social work is replicated in professional 'radical' social work.

Replication of professional social work's 'theory-practice' problematic in radical social work has led some critics to interpret radical social work theoreticism as an expression of 'radical careerism'. Parry et al. (1979) suggest that, following the Seebohm Report (1968), the new social services departments established in 1971 created expanded career progression opportunities for professional social workers: they refer to 'substantial promotion opportunities ... (in) ... more powerful bureaucracies' (ibid., p.163). Some critics associate social work careerism with casework based professionalism, as in Jones's (1989, pp.208-9) observation that

Although rooted in the post-1945 expansion of state welfare, modern social work's attachment to social democracy was both weak and at times ambiguous. Thus, while social work opportunistically benefited from social democratic reformism which led to the creation of the social services departments and the expansion of social work as a state activity, its prevalent individualistic and psychologistic versions of human welfare rested uncomfortably at times with the more dominant sociological perspectives of social democracy as represented by groups like the Fabian Society. Indeed the Fabian Society published (Townsend, 1970) a telling critique of the 1968 Seebohm Report arguing (as did the new right fifteen years later) that the major beneficiaries of a reorganized and bureaucratized social work service were the social workers themselves rather than clients.

Writing during the height of the 1970's radical social work movement, Moore (1976) described the expansion of professional social work in the post-Seebohm social services departments and made the unexceptional comment that 'in a short space of time social work has become a thriving profession' (ibid., p.10). More controversially, he suggested radical professionals are '... thinking Left and living Right' (ibid.). In Moore's account of radical social work, radical professionals are unwilling to 'surrender' their monopoly of professional power to clients and local communities and he claims the persons who have gained most 'from the rise of the radical professional are the radical professionals themselves' (ibid.). Pinker's (1989) description of radical social work carries a similar sting in the tail: he writes 'The radical approach to social work has ... introduced a spirit of egalitarianism which conflicts with professional "elitism", except in the case of pay levels and terms of employment' (ibid., p.99).

These critical accounts, together with the observations made earlier, suggest that the schism between radical theory and practice may arise for two reasons. Firstly, failure on the part of radical social work theorists to define identifiably 'radical' practices and radical organizational and service-delivery frameworks; and secondly, for reasons to do with what has been called 'radical careerism'. Concerning the first of these factors, Hearn (1982a) suggests the failure of radical social work theorists to specify 'radical' forms of organization and collectivist practice has a demoralizing effect on social work students and practitioners. He comments 'For some, the whole process of radical socialization within educational establishments and political groups may be so "conscientising" as to be immobilizing' (ibid., p.26) and this paradoxically leads erstwhile radicals to retreat to a conservative professional casework 'psychologism' (ibid., p.27). Hearn (1982a) identifies a second barrier against the development of radical social work organization and practice, expressed in his concept of 'radical careerism' which he argues is a key factory in de-radicalization. Radical careerism in social work consists of '... the inevitable conversion of socialist principles to radical careers in radical social work' (ibid., p.26). Hearn (1982a) suggests radical careerism is a phenomenon that exists in many walks of life, including politics and academic social science, and he goes on to say (p.26)

> There is no special reason why radical social workers should remain immune ... employing organizations ... provide their bread and butter, and they also provide the opportunity for career advancement. Radical careerism - the achievement of career advance through association with a radical cause or causes - always becomes a possibility where radicalism can be talked about without necessarily leading to future radical action. It therefore arises principally in professions whose technology is talk or further radical writing. It is a familiar phenomenon in politics, and an emerging one in social work, especially academic social work.

The issues discussed by Hearn and the other writers referred to earlier, refer to contemporary social work's re-activation of 'perennial' problematics that in various forms have centred on 'theory-practice' and 'social work politics' since the time of the Charity Organization Society. There are, however, some other crucial aspects of modern social work politics to which analytical attention should be drawn; these relate to a recent change of emphasis in radical social work.

Radical social work in the 1970's was largely a Marxist or socialist class-based form of analysis. By the late 1980's radical social work had largely abandoned the earlier concern with social class, and switched its attention to gender issues and racism. The extent of this transition in social work politics is clearly reflected in the social work literature. For example, Bailey and Brake's (1975) Radical Social Work was almost entirely class-based: there were no chapters specifically on racism or gender issues, and in those chapters where these topics were mentioned the references to them were scant. In contrast, hardly any class-analysis figures in Langan and Lee's (1989a) edited collection of papers titled Radical Social Work Today. Their book contains no chapter on social class but a number specifically on gender and racism, the latter topics also being addressed in every chapter. Arising from this transition in radical social work, two interrelated aspects of modern social work politics that will recur in later chapters require some denotation here. The first concerns the failure of radical social work (and of structural sociology) to transcend problems of theoretical reductionism and reification. The

18

second is a recent and usually conceptually confused radical social work bifurcation which asks whether theoretical and practical policy primacy should be given to class or gender or 'race', or whether these three categorizations should be, so to speak, 'considered' simultaneously. These issues require a more theoretical focus than has been the case so far in the chapter and broaching them here will also usefully serve to lay some of the ground for the mainly theoretical material that is the focus of attention in the next chapter.

Radical social work theory in the 1970's, together with the varieties of sociological Marxism that were associated with radical social work at that time, were seriously flawed by a theoretical reductionism in which social class was regarded as an analytical prime mover. Problems of theoretical reductionism are examined in detail in the next chapter. Here, it is necessary only to briefly introduce the core postulate of anti-reductionist social analysis. This is that 'explanations' of social life as a 'necessary effect' of the social totality, or of so-called 'objective' structurally 'given' interests presumed to inhere in 'classes' (or in any other taxonomic collectivities such as 'society', 'men', 'women', 'white people', 'black people', etc.) have no empirical explanatory significance nor any useful role in the construction of social policies (Hindess 1986a, pp.116-17, p.123, pp.124-5; Betts, 1986, p.49). In chapter three, attention will be given to problems that are inherent in reductionist uses of the concepts 'interests' and 'false consciousness'. Social collectivities such as 'classes' do not have 'objective' structurally-determined 'interests', nor do any individual human actors. The claim that individual actors possess structurally 'given' ('objective') but unacknowledged interests that exist by virtue of actors' structural location or membership of a taxonomic collectivity is a claim that is irremediably flawed in both a theoretical and an empirical sense.

Recent anti-reductionist sociology rejects the 'micro' reductionism of methodological individualism (the notion that 'individuals make society'), and also rejects the reductionism (methodological collectivism) inherent in those forms of structural sociology which in the 1970's and early 1980's had involved attempts to 'explain' social life through the analytic use of reified, personified images of social structure. One amongst other manifestations of the almost total isolation of social work discourses from wider forms of intellectual inquiry in the social sciences is the fact that radical social work writers have, as yet, shown no awareness that these recent developments exist in contemporary social science. Therefore, radical social work is unable to offer any theoretically formulated anti-reductionist basis for empirically investigating and practically acting upon those forms of social inequality to which radical social work is addressed. Feminist social work writing, for example, is generally theoretically weak and problematic: it contrasts sharply with the more theoretically informed approaches that exist in feminist sociology (for instance, see Walby, 1988, 1989; Frazer, 1988; Acker, 1989; Crompton, 1989; Charles, 1990). Dominelli and McLeod (1989) in their advocacy of feminist social work take on board the criticism that middle-class feminist social workers may 'impose' their theories upon working-class women clients. To avoid the dangers of 'class superiority' (ibid., p.62) intruding upon what ought to be 'egalitarian' relationships (ibid.) with working-class women clients, it is stated that 'the true test ... is not middle-class intentions but working-class women's experience and perception of what is happening' (ibid., emphasis added). Leaving aside the tacitly invoked and unresolved epistemological conundrums raised by statements

of this kind, the 'test' just referred to is rejected a few pages later
when Dominelli and McLeod (1989) consider the position of women who in
their relationships with, say, spouses, children, or elders, provide
various forms of 'care' in the domestic sphere (ibid., pp.80-81).
Dominelli and McLeod (1989) in rejecting the empirical validity (and
presumably the epistemological status) of data suggesting that some
women may be 'happy with ... (their) ... lives' (ibid., p.80), endorse a
reductionist interpretation analogous to the 'false consciousness'
doctrine. The authors refer to 'the misery' of women (ibid., p.81),
their 'plight' (ibid.), their 'servitude' (ibid.), and their mistaken
sense of 'contentment' (ibid.). Women who experience contentment are
wrong to do so: they do not perceive that they have 'real' or
'objective' interests qua their status as women. Dominelli and McLeod
(1989) argue that '... the revelations from feminist work question
whether the contentment of an unknown number of women is being bought at
a morally unacceptable price in terms of reinforcing a set of social
relations that are fundamentally detrimental to women's emotional
welfare' (ibid., p.81, emphasis added). What, it might be asked, are
the hidden, inexplicable mechanisms of thought control that produce this
'failure' of individuals to perceive their 'real' or 'objective'
structurally determined 'interests'? On what basis are these
'interests' imputed to others? There is, too, the question posed by
Betts (1986) in her sociological critique of reductionist analyses
(ibid., p.54)

> How is it that the observer, who is also a member of society,
> buffeted by all the ideological winds and social pressures that
> beset ... (others) ... how is it that she can arrive at an
> "objective" definition of interests, when they themselves cannot do
> this? How can we tell that this observer's diagnosis of the
> situation and her statement of what people's interests ought to be,
> is not itself an attempt to impose an alternative dogma ... ? The
> answer is that we cannot.

In feminist sociology, Ramazanoglu (1989) rejects notions that 'A
feminist viewpoint can ... be built on the suppression of the voices of
persons with experiences unlike our own' (ibid., p.437). Whether there
exist forms of inequality based on asymmetrical distributions of
economic resources and life-chances, and on prejudice and discrimination
of various kinds, is not in dispute: these inequalities plainly exist
(Reid, 1989; Ringer and Lawless, 1989; Saunders, 1990). What is at
issue for social work discourses is the question of how the various
forms of inequality should be theoretically conceptualized, empirically
analysed, and acted upon in social policy and welfare terms: the issue
for a sociology of social work is different, where the task is to engage
in sociological analysis of the theoretical and practical constructions
of these matters in social work discourses.
    The recent transition in radical social work away from class issues
and towards a centralizing of concerns about gender and racism has
prompted some writers to argue against a 'single-issue' approach in
favour of an approach which addresses issues of gender and racism and
social class. For instance, Dominelli and McLeod (1989) reject the idea
of prioritizing any one of these forms of inequality, because '... doing
so would be at someone else's expense' (ibid., p.8). For this reason
'... we arrive at the position that there are an indeterminate number of
forms of oppression. Work to eliminate those of which we are aware must
be undertaken at one and the same time' (ibid., emphasis added). The

question of _how_ in non-reductionist terms these issues might be theorized 'at one and the same time' is wholly ignored in current radical social work discourses. To separately conceptualize class, gender, and 'race' in reductionist terms, and then to attempt to combine these three separate versions of reductionism into some unified and therefore itself reductionist conceptual whole, would be to merely compound and render even more hopelessly inchoate the initial trilogy of reductionisms. As yet, radical social work has no anti-reductionist conceptual framework for conceptualizing these three categorizations either as 'separate' dimensions of social existence or as interconnected dimensions. It is also the case that most social work writers, while specifying that none of these foci should be 'excluded' from the concerns of radical social work, in reality accord far greater emphasis in their work to one or another of these: that is, radical attention has tended to centre either on class-based Marxist social work (Corrigan and Leonard, 1979) or anti-racist social work (Dominelli, 1988) or anti-sexist social work (Dominelli and McLeod, 1989; Hanmer and Statham, 1988). Set against this background, Langan and Lee (1989b) titled their paper 'Whatever happened to radical social work?'. They criticize radical social work's recent tendencies to marginalize class issues, and reject any approach '... that elevates any _particular_ issue of oppression above others' (ibid., p.11). Langan and Lee (1989b) perceive a tendency towards disunity and fragmentation within the radical social work movement, and to correct this they argue for 'an alliance of social forces' (ibid., p.11). They note, however, that 'It is not yet clear how to achieve strategic or tactical alliances that can enable the movement to confront systematically all forms of oppression' (ibid.). For the moment, it is sufficient to make note of radical social work's placing of these issues on social work's agenda for the 1990's, leaving further analysis of them until chapter five where the limitations of reductionism in radical social work will be re-inspected and where some problems and possibilities arising from the social construction of tactical political alliances within and across social movements (of whatever kind) will be analysed in sociological terms that move beyond the cognitive confines of radical social work discourse.

Professional, organizational, and service-delivery issues

The politics of social work, and in particular the 'theory-practice' problematic discussed in the first part of the chapter, are in various ways related to a third major perennial-but-also-contemporary social work problematic: this concerns the professional-organizational structure of social work. The history of British social work since the time of the Charity Organization Society is the history of a professionalizing occupation (Parry and Parry, 1979, pp.25-26). Professional(izing) leaders, in arguing that social work is or should be a 'profession' rather than, say, a vocation, occupation, or social movement, have in every historical period emphasized the 'intellectual task complexity' of professional social work (Loch, 1906; Flexner, 1915; BASW, 1977; Butrym et al., 1981; Doal, 1990). If this claim cannot be sustained, there is no socially recognized 'profession'. However, another crucial element in the achievement of professionalizing objectives, is professional 'unity' (Gross et al., 1982; Germaine, 1983). This has three dimensions. These are, firstly, theoretical and cognitive unity; secondly, philosophical or political value-consensus; and thirdly, organizational unity. These are empirical variables. No profession possesses absolute unity in all of these dimensions. Nevertheless, without a substantial degree of professional homogeneity professionalizing aspirations are severely threatened, and this is one reason why professions, and professionalizing occupations such as social work, strive for occupational or professional 'integration' (Halliday, 1985, pp.436-41).

Cognitive unity in the structure and forms of professional knowledge is necessary in order to sustain claims that the 'profession' in question is not only based upon an academic-professional foundation of knowledge, but also that this knowledge-base is distinctive to that profession sufficient to mark it off from the knowledge held by various 'others' such as other professional groups, 'lay' people, politicians, and administrators. In the light of the material examined earlier in the chapter, it is evident that a problem facing professional(izing) social work is that no internal consensus exists on the question of what social work's knowledge base 'does' or 'should' consist of. This lack of cognitive consensus seriously damages the credibility of any claims that social work is a 'profession' with, firstly, an academic-professional knowledge base that, secondly, has some cognitive 'unity' and professional particularity and distinctiveness unique to social work. As well as these problems of internal theoretical and cognitive disunity, it was observed earlier that political value-integration is also largely absent in social work: at the present time, political value-conflicts and theoretical dissensions exist not only as tensions between 'traditionalists'-versus-'radicals', but also among radicals.

Nor has professional organizational unity been achieved in social work. In the early and mid-nineteenth century the main welfare response to social problems came not from governments (McCord, 1976) but from voluntary charitable activity and philanthropic welfare (Parry and Parry, 1979, p.21). The COS had become influential by the end of the nineteenth century but social welfare in Britain remained in the form of a highly differentiated, segmented social movement (Wilkinson, 1971, p.26) with a minimal degree of professional-organizational unity. Welfare activities took place in a wide variety of state institutions and voluntary organizations including church and university settlements, charitable philanthropic trusts, and local tenants and workers associations: welfare work included, for instance, the roles of hospital almoners, settlement workers, tenant association organizers, the poor law inspectorate, and reformatory-school workers. There was no homogeneous occupational culture of welfare, and social work also '... lacked specific organizational forms with which its adherents could be associated, and automatically by such association, claim to be "social workers"' (Seed, 1973, p.40). Seed notes that even as recently as the late 1940's the Younghusband Report (1947) had listed the following 'forms of social work': almoning, child care, church work, colonial social welfare, community centre and settlement work, probation and other services connected with the penal system, social work in the civil service, personnel management, and youth leadership (Seed, 1973, p.55). Seed further remarks '... to this remarkable list, the Birmingham Social Studies Course added: housing managers, housemasters and housemistresses in Approved Schools, and social survey investigators' (ibid., p.56). Seed's account, though the point cannot be explored here, raises some interesting questions about the immediate post-war reconstruction of the 'theory-practice' problematic in social work and in welfare training programmes (Sibeon, 1983).

The creation of the social services departments (SSD's) in 1971 was an historical landmark in the development of social work professionalism in

Britain. The SSD's, at that time, seemed to offer the prospect of a unified organizational heartland for professional social work and a long-awaited opportunity to organizationally consolidate '... the profession's perennial search for unity' (Gilbert and Specht, 1977, p.223). However, organizational unification has not been secured. It should be noted that, except in Scotland, the new SSD's were social service departments, not departments of social work. In the SSD's, professional social workers are a numerical minority: most employees are 'social services' workers providing a variety of basic, practical services to clients. After the Seebohm (1968) re-organization, professional social workers became something of a psychotherapeutic casework elite who occupied the upper hierarchical echelons of the SSD's, and it was they who as senior social workers and managers also controlled and directed the activities of 'sub-professional' social-service workers employed in the SSD's (Lee, 1982, pp.28-32). After 1975, this hierarchical division-of-labour was reinforced by a binary system of training that awarded a 'professional' qualification (the Certificate of Qualification in Social Work) to professional social workers, and a 'sub-professional' qualification (the Certificate in Social Service) to social services workers. Critics challenged this linkage between hierarchical training and the professional-organizational hierarchy. Parry et al. (1979) noted that 'One current ambition for professional social work is to ... take over, in time, the whole field of social service provision, by steadily training a higher proportion of social workers and devising "sub-professional" qualifications for their assistants. We think this is undesirable and impracticable ...' (ibid., pp.175-6). In chapter seven, it will be observed that in the 1980's there occurred a major escalation of conflict between social-services workers and the professional social work lobby; and related conflicts between, on the one hand, social work educators and professionalizing leaders, and on the other, social work employers who placed more value on practical social-services work than on the 'esoteric' casework associated with professional social work. These conflicts were 'resolved' in the 1980's in ways that had de-professionalizing consequences which partly reversed the expansion of professionalism in the SSD's that had begun in the early 1970's. A related obstacle standing in the way of 'organizational' professional unification arises from the fact that professionally qualified social workers are not only employed by the SSD's. They are employed in the probation service, the local education authority service, hospitals, and in a wide variety of voluntary organizations providing fieldwork, community work, and residential care services of various kinds. In many of these organizations, and indeed, as we have just seen, even within the social services departments, 'professional social work' is not the only nor even the main organizational function (Young, 1979, pp.vii-x).

Despite these problems, the term 'profession' remains as probably the most frequently cited concept in the social work literature. In sociology, and thus in the sociology of social work, dispute exists as to how the concept ('profession') should be defined and used for empirical analytical purposes. In the 1970's, structural Marxist accounts of professions were widespread in sociology, as in the work of Poulantzas (1975), Navarro (1976), Braverman (1974), Carchedi (1975), and Ehrenreich and Ehrenreich (1979). A recurring theme in most of these accounts is that modern capitalism relies on technical managerial and professional expertise, a factor in Esland's (1980) conclusion that 'The professions ... (are) ... agents of control for a powerful state' (ibid., p.214). Professionals were said to be involved in the reproduction of capitalist labour in a 'docile' form, and portrayed as 'agents' engaged in social surveillance and control of the working class 'on behalf of capitalism' (Cockburn, 1977). The point will be made in chapter three that these structural theories are inherently reductionist. An instance is Bolger et al's. (1981) attempt to relate the hierarchical structure of the SSD's to the 'objective' 'interests' or 'needs' of capitalism (ibid., pp.65-66). In fact, there is good empirical evidence that the post-Seebohm construction and reproduction of hierarchic 'bureau-professionalism' (Parry and Parry, 1979, p.43) was proactively achieved by professional(izing) lobby groups (Whittington and Bellaby, 1979) whose activities were in no sense structurally predetermined (Hindess, 1986b, p.117).

Two other and also largely antithetical approaches in the sociology of professions are the 'trait' approach, and the 'process' approach. The first of these, in differentiating professions from vocations or occupations, defines professions in terms of a number of core professional 'attributes' or 'traits'. The traits most frequently cited are task-complexity and skill based upon knowledge acquired during professional training in academic institutions of higher education; altruistic service; rigorous testing of competence prior to registration as a qualified practitioner; and adherence to a professional code of conduct which maintains professional integrity and regulates relationships between professionals and their clients (Saks, 1983, p.2). In the sociology of professions, conventional analyses of professional activity in terms of the 'trait' model were developed by, for example, Parsons (1968), Goode (1957), Cogan (1953), Greenwood (1957), Vollmer and Mills (1966), and Millerson (1964). The 'process' model of 'profession', an analytic approach grounded largely in interactionist sociology, is outlined in the work of Hughes (1958), Bucher and Strauss (1960), Freidson (1970), Elger (1975), Elliot (1973), and Becker (1962). In rejecting the trait or 'core-attribute' model, researchers involved in the 'processual' interactionist perspective criticize (Bucher and Strauss, 1960) a tendency on the part of 'traits' theorists to define professions as being characterized by professional homogeneity (Goode, 1957) and by internal cognitive and political consensus. In particular, the criticism frequently voiced against the traits approach is that sociologists who employ a 'trait' model for engaging in analysis of professions are wielding a predefined checklist of traits that are inaccurately complimentary to professionals and are therefore merely reproducing professionals' own ideological self-descriptions, a criticism that led Freidson (1970) to suggest that the attributes model in most of its usages represents professional ideology rather than reality. Becker (1962), in rejecting the idea that sociologists employing the traits-model have identified a neutral 'scientific' definition of profession, argues that 'there is no "true" profession and no set of characteristics necessarily associated with the title. There are only those work groups commonly regarded as professions and those which are not ...' (ibid., pp.32-33). Becker (1962) argues that it is more empirically productive to engage in study of the actual processes by which professionalizing occupations 'claim' or 'appropriate' the description 'professional' as a way of describing themselves (ibid., p.39)

> ... we find many occupations trying hard to become professions and using the symbol of the profession in an attempt to increase their autonomy and raise their prestige. Optometrists, nurses, librarians, social workers - these are only a few of the many

occupations engaged in this kind of activity.

In his review of theoretical and empirical problems arising from
analytic use of the trait-model, Dingwall (1976) similarly concludes
that sociological analysis of professional activity should proceed by
'... abandoning any claim to legislate a correct use of the term
'profession', but treating it as a concept invoked by members of
particular collectivities and seeking to describe its practical usage'
(ibid., p.331.
Whether it is necessary to abandon a 'traits' model of professions is
a significant question not only in the sociology of professions but also
for future work undertaken in the sociology of social work, particularly
detailed work in the study of professionalization processes. For this
reason the concept of professional 'traits' requires evaluation in
sociology of social work, rather than an automatic assumption that it is
analytically redundant. A number of critics of the concept appear to
have paid insufficient attention to the fact that although 'trait' and
'functionalist' perspectives are often associated with each other, they
need not be synonymous. The former attempts to identify 'core
attributes' as a method of defining professions, the latter approach
carries an implication that these attributes are 'functional' for
society and for client groups. A taxonomic perspective in the sociology
of professions has in practice frequently blurred trait and
functionalist analysis (Saks, 1983, p.2) leading to criticism that
sociologists in analysing professions have become the 'dupes' (Roth,
1974, p.17) of professional ideologists. However, if trait and
functionalist analyses are not allowed to surreptitiously fuse together
there is in principle no reason why a taxonomic approach in the study of
professions need involve uncritical sociological endorsement of
professional ideologies. It is not necessary in the study of
professions to presume that traits such as altruism and paramountcy of
the ethos of client-service are the <u>only</u> or most significant defining
characteristics of a profession. In many existing critical sociological
accounts alternative 'traits' are already used: these include
'professional privilege' (Portwood and Fielding, 1981), professional
'self-interest' (Perrucci, 1976), exaggeration of task complexity
through the creation of professional mystique (North, 1972, p.63), and
occupational closure and monopolization (Berlant, 1975). Viewed in
these terms the relevant question is not 'whether' traits, but <u>which</u>
traits. One attempted solution to problems in the taxonomic approach is
to avoid the problem of definition by focussing analysis upon
<u>professionalization as a process</u>: however as Johnson (1972, p.31) and
Turner and Hodge (1970, p.23) point out, this does not 'resolve' the
problem of taxonomy, because the concept of professionalization implies
movement towards 'something', which remains to be defined. Freidson
(1983) notes that some definition of the phenomenon under investigation
is essential in social research of occupational and professional
structures (ibid., p.21-2) and therefore what is at issue is not the
question of whether to employ a definition of profession but the
adequacy of the particular defining criteria ('traits') employed. As
Freidson (1983) puts it, the 'definitional problem ... is not one ... to
be solved by eschewing definition entirely' (ibid., p.22) as in
exclusively 'process' perspectives which reject the notion that any
definition is necessary (ibid.). Freidson's contention (ibid.) is that

One can avoid the issue of definition only if one adopts the
patently anti-analytical position that all occupations - whether

casual day-labour, assembly-line work, teaching, surgery or systems
analysis - are so much alike that there is no point in making
distinctions of any kind amongst them.

The problem of definition lies in the tendency to employ a 'static',
unhistorical concept of profession which ignores cultural and historical
changes in the meaning of the concept (ibid.). Freidson (1983) notes a
long historical tradition in Britain where the 'learned' (ibid., p.23)
professions of medicine, law, university teaching, and the clergy are
'status professions' historically associated with 'traditional gentry
status' (ibid., p.24) unlike the 'new' middle-class technical-managerial
professions (ibid., p.25). In some societies attendance at particular
elite educational institutions (no matter what particular occupational
speciality this leads to) convey a 'professional' status. In
nineteenth-century Russia and Poland to '... be a graduate of a
gymnasium was what was important, not one's occupation ... In Germany,
what was important was to be a graduate, an akademiker ... In France,
one's fortunes flowed from attending one of the grandes ecoles ...'
(ibid.).
    In Freidson's (1983) perspective, definition of profession is not
wholly abandoned, as in 'process' perspectives, but neither is a static
taxonomy of universal 'traits' adhered to i.e. the concept of profession
is viewed not as a static definition but as a shifting concept which is
variable in time and place. In this perspective the concept of social
work as profession is temporally and spatially variable. Some of the
underlying assumptions in Friedson's analysis are congruent with those
outlined in the later chapters. The concept of social work as a
'profession', and also rejections of the concept, are socially
constructed and negotiated in the relationships that develop among a
variety of social work actors some of whom, in the terms defined in
chapter three, are 'social' (or organizational) actors such as the
British Association of Social Workers and the Association of Directors
of Social Services. In chapter four it will be argued that key
analytical features of an anti-reductionist sociology of social work are
the study of how social work 'materials' (ideas, policies, conventions
etc.) are spatially and temporally disseminated by actors, and
investigation of whether and if so in what ways the material changes its
form as it 'travels'. The concept 'profession' is historically and
socially situated, and therefore variable. When Flexner (1915) asked
'Is Social Work a Profession?' his concept of profession was not that of
the modern 'bureau-professional' in the social services departments.
This is not to say that some aspects of the definition ('profession')
may not become institutionalized and persist for relatively long periods
of time: but it is to say that the existence of space-time continuities
and discontinuities in social work actors' constructions of 'profession'
are matters for contextual empirical assessment, not for theoretical
pre-definition based on an uncontextual listing of 'universal'
professional traits that are presumed to apply in all times and places.
    There is another dimension of the professionalization process that
merits particular attention. The idea that indeterminate knowledge may
be functional for professionals is related to the notion that ability to
control and then work within an 'area of uncertainty' may help to
sustain professional autonomy and maximize professional freedom from
bureaucratic regulation and from 'external' controls and demands exerted
by administrators; organizational managers; politicians; 'the public' at
large; client groups; and perhaps also other professional or
occupational groups who might otherwise encroach upon the professional's

territory. Other things being equal, professional insulation from external controls is likely to be greatest where the outcomes of professional activities are relatively vague and intangible. If 'everyone' (clients, administrators and managers, politicians, the general public, etc.) is able to 'judge by results', professional autonomy may be weakened. This is why McInlay (1973) suggested one mechanism of professional control is '... the removal of certain activities from external observability and evaluation' (ibid., p.77). This may also be a factor in professionals' attachment to psychotherapeutic casework and analogous 'group dynamic' methods such as family therapy, rather than the more practical and cognitively more externally 'visible' and externally 'assessable' collectivist practices associated with community work in local neighbourhoods.

Atkinson (1983) observes that 'The definition of "indeterminate" knowledge and its preservation is part and parcel of the politics of professional knowledge and professional power' (ibid., p.238). If professional knowledge is successfully portrayed as the antithesis of readily communicable cognitions and techniques it is easier for professionals to claim that '... their work is of such complex character, requiring so much judgement, that formal standards or rules are too arbitrary to be applicable' (Freidson, 1973, p.34). To refer to the 'mystifications' of an 'esoteric' social work professionalism is not to deny that the moral-political calculus of human welfare is ambiguous and complex (Timms and Watson, 1975; Clark and Asquith, 1985). The topic under discussion here, however, is the ways in which particular and additional professionally-constructed indeterminations are 'overlaid' upon existing, extant complexities in the moral-political (and also partly 'technical') calculus of human welfare and of welfare systems. Psychotherapeutic casework is an exemplar of cognitive indeterminacy in professional social work. An advocate of this approach, Gammack (1982) objects that social work is '... under great pressures to produce tangible, immediate, practical services ...' (ibid., p.4). Gammack (1982) tries to defend something that he cannot define, nor, according to Gammack, should any such definition be attempted: he argues that '... societal pressures for concreteness and immediate action ... are paralleled in contemporary trends in social work ... towards an increasing focus on the definable elements in ... social work practice' (ibid., p.5, emphasis added). In similar vein, Perlman (1976) argues professional caseworkers are 'overtrained' (ibid., p.204) for giving basic, practical welfare help to clients and instead should be involved in the use of '... complex knowledge of psychodynamics and fine skill in management of the affectfull and verbal interchanges of casework treatment' (ibid.). In a conference speech, Butrym (1973, cited in Wilson, 1973, p.vi) warned against what she termed the 'dangers' of trying to define social casework and in trying to define '... the complexities involved' (ibid.). Butrym argued that defining the 'complex', intangible elements in casework carried the risk of oversimplification and therefore '... clarity can be a problem' (ibid.).

There are, however, limits as to how far an unbridled emphasis upon 'professional' cognitive indeterminacy can be pushed. Professional power is maximized when it operates in a field of activity that is relatively unpredictable and uncertain (Wilensky, 1964) but 'internal' professional knowledge cannot be wholly ambiguous, esoteric, or totally incommunicable to the external world. If professional cognitive indeterminacy is viewed by other relevant and powerful actors (depending upon the circumstances, these may be organizational managers and administrators, politicians, client groups, etc.) as having been pushed 'to excess', de-professionalizing counter-measures might be taken by these actors who, in most cases, want tangibly and visibly effective services. If there is 'not enough' cognitive indeterminacy, professional power and autonomy will never be achieved: but 'too much' cognitive - practico indeterminacy may provoke others into taking steps that result in a drastic curtailment of professionals' power. Jamous and Peloille (1970) observe that professions are '... occupations or activities whose indetermination/technicality ratio ... is generally high ...' (ibid., p.113). Professional(izing) actors have to strike the right balance in their construction of the indetermination/technicality 'ratio'. If there is 'insufficient' cognitive indeterminacy, the activity in question will be socially perceived as a practical vocation or occupation or some other form of activity that is not a cognitively complex 'professional' activity performed (and performable) only by very highly trained professional virtuosos. If, though, the indetermination/technicality ratio is 'exceeded' in the eyes of other relevant, powerful non-professional actors there is a danger of external controls being imposed in the form of, for example, an 'administrative' or 'managerial' takeover of the profession. The strategic importance of politically 'negotiating' the indetermination/technicality ratio is noted by Collins (1975) who observes that '.. the strongest professions occur in the case of ... (those) ... which are of the right degree of effectiveness and ambiguity ...' (ibid., p.342). Professional social work is widely regarded as having overconcentrated on ambiguity at the expense of externally visible effectiveness.

An element of 'technicality', of clear-cut, externally observable, assessable, and demonstrably effective task performance is necessary in societies where norms of instrumental technical-rationality are culturally and politically significant (Habermas, 1979, pp.116-23). The legitimation crisis of the modern welfare state (see chapter five) is an additional contemporary factor in the increased pressures that arose in the 1980's for social work services to be made more efficient, monitored, evaluated, and more responsive to service-users' expressed practical needs. In summarizing research data from a number of empirical studies, Rees and Wallace (1982, p.155) critically observed that

> social workers' valued images and activities ... (embodied) ... goals which sounded worthy yet esoteric ... major social issues affecting people's lives were not addressed. For example, people who are poor or unemployed or homeless generally feel at a loss in the social service market place, trying to find their way in a maze of alleged social service entitlements. In relation to people with such difficulties some social workers acknowledged that their objectives referred to talking about feelings and heightening self-awareness!

Rees and Wallace (1982) also criticized social work educators (ibid., p.143, p.155). Earlier, reference was made to Butrym's (1973) professional ethos in which 'clarity can be a problem', an ethos propounded by Perlman (1976), Gammack (1982), and many other social work professionals. Critics such as North (1972) regard 'the mystique' (ibid., p.63) of casework professionalism as a simplistic cognitive 'mishmash' (ibid., p.87). Pinker's (1989) indictment of professional social work is that '... social work theory is rarely presented in testable form' (ibid., p.86). However, academic criticisms are rarely as threatening to professionals as the practical, concrete actions of critical policy-makers.

A major threat against professionalizing aspirations enshrined in indeterminate knowledge emerged as part of the movement in the 1980's to simultaneously reform 'professional' social work education and redesign the division of labour in the SSD's. Social work employers and senior administrators condemned what they perceived to be an unacceptable excess of professional cognitive-practico indeterminacy that had accumulated throughout the 1970's as part of the post-Seebohm expansion of social work professionalism. Harbert (1985a), Director of Social Services for Avon, condemned what he called 'professional imperialism' associated with professional social work lobby groups' attempts to control other, less 'professional' but more 'practical' social service occupations in the personal social services (ibid., p.16). He argued, in particular, that professional social workers attempted to exaggerate intellectual task-complexity (ibid., p.14). Having indicated that '... since 1970 ... (social work) ... professionalism has been in steady and consistent decline' (ibid.) he stated it was important that '... professionals understand that in the current climate power will continue to slip away from them' (ibid., p.16). Similar criticisms of social work professionalism were made by Warner (1986), Director of Social Services for Kent, who referred in hostile terms to a 'shrinking cadre of professionals' (ibid., p.15). Warner complained critically of the difficulties involved in persuading professional social workers to '... accept that their accountability should be <u>defined</u> and their performance <u>monitored and appraised</u> ... more appraisal and stricter accountability means <u>bringing things out into the open</u> - not something that professionals ... like social workers like to do' (ibid., emphases added). These conflicts reflect tensions of the kind noted by Atkinson and Delamount (1990) who observe '... there is always tension between the indeterminate and the technocratic and ... (therefore) ... always disputes within occupations' (ibid., p.106). This is particularly noticeable in social work. By the mid 1980's professional social work, in the eyes of powerful, 'non-professional' actors, had acquired the characteristics of a highly esoteric professional activity that had 'exceeded' Jamous and Peloille's (1970) indetermination/technicality ratio. The potentially de-professionalizing implications of this development, some of which are examined in chapter seven with reference to shifts in the relationship between social work training and the organizational division of labour in the personal social services, have led to the recent construction of policies that are likely to affect social work in ways which, in Britain at least, will have major implications for the future existence of 'professional' social work.

3 Sociology as a resource for the analysis of social work

The previous chapter indicated the field of study to which a sociology of social work is addressed; the purpose of the present chapter is to introduce the core theoretical postulates upon which, it will be argued, a contemporary non-reductionist sociology of social work should be based. Within sociology itself, the systematic development of anti-reductionist empirical conceptualizations is comparatively recent. The number of theorists and empirical researchers involved is still relatively small, a factor which accounts for the frequent references in this chapter to the work of a quite small group of sociologists, including Hindess (1986a, 1986b, 1987, 1988); Clegg (1989); Callon (1986); Callon et al. (1986); Latour (1986); and Law (1986a, 1986b). The innovative theoretical and empirical work set in train by these and some other writers has by no means permeated the whole of sociology, though it is beginning to have a significant impact and is likely to fundamentally re-shape sociology and social analysis in the 1990's. The sociology of social work has remained almost totally isolated from recent theoretical transitions in sociology and to this extent the purpose of the chapter is to identify theoretical constructs which contribute towards the construction of a 'new' sociology of social work that is capable of analysing both historical and recent social work materials in explicitly <u>non-reductionist</u> sociological terms.

A theoretical outline of some core postulates in anti-reductionist sociology

Reductionist analysis involves attempts to 'explain' one order of phenomena in terms of another, usually through attempts to employ methodological individualism to 'explain' social structure (or 'society') as the aggregated outcome of the decisions and actions of countless human individuals; or else through an analytic use of methodological collectivism which attempts to 'explain' human agency and action as an 'effect' of and in terms of some internal structural properties or 'needs' of social systems. Methodological collectivism is the main form of reductionism discussed in this chapter: this form of reductionism, exemplified in macro-structural theory, has been more widespread in conventional sociology than methodological individualism. It is true that micro-sociology has always '... found difficulty in dealing with more large-scale structures and processes' (Giddens, 1989, p.701). But this is not to say that microsociology has ever been based on methodological individualism (Cooley, 1902). Symbolic interactionist sociology, in particular, is a form of methodological situationalism (Meltzer et al., 1975, p.54) which explicitly rejects atomistic 'individualism' and instead studies intersubjective processes and interactions amongst individuals in settings of interaction (Knorr-Cetina, 1981, pp.8-9 and pp.16-17).

Reductionism, using the term here to refer to methodological collectivism associated with structural theories, goes hand in hand with reified, 'personified' images of social structure. Structural theory presupposes some 'real' objective factual existence of society as something which has modes of operation that are dictated by some structural 'necessities' of one type or another. The empirical world in which actors formulate objectives, make decisions, act in certain ways, etc., is portrayed as a world that is merely a secondary 'surface reflection' of a 'primary' or 'deep' underlying structure (Whitely, 1977, p.170). In these kinds of theories, the supposed structural generators of social action - though macro-structural theorists disagree among themselves as to what these generators consist of - are presumed to be 'hidden' mechanisms ('deep structures') which are directly or indirectly causally determining (Bhaskar, 1978). In the following pages it is intended to demonstrate the explanatory inadequacy of reductionist theories and to show that alternative empirically productive ways of analysing social affairs are possible.

The term 'actor' is a key concept in anti-reductionist sociology. Hindess (1986a) defines an actor as '... a locus of decision and action where the action is in some sense a consequence of the actor's decisions' (ibid., p.115, emphasis added). This definition includes individual human actors, and also social actors such as 'organizations' of various kinds (ibid.). Broadly similar to Hindess's definition of 'social actor' is Harre's (1981) use of the term 'supra-individuals', examples of which are committees (ranging from the government's cabinet to, say, a local authority social services committee) and 'organizations' of various kinds such as central government departments or local public welfare agencies, trade unions and professional associations, organized pressure groups, etc. Supra-individuals, in Harre's (1981) definition, must be continuous in time; occupy a distinctive and continuous region of space or a distinctive and continuous path through space; and have causal powers (ibid., p.141). In Hindess's and Harre's definitions, taxonomic collectivities such as 'society', 'classes', 'men', 'women', etc., are social aggregates that are not actors. That is, social entities that possess causal powers cannot be empirically proven to exist 'above' the middle-range level of social (or 'organizational') actors. There are individual human actors and social actors, but no other actors. Social categories such as 'men' or 'classes', for example, are not actors because '... even a minimal concept of actor requires that the actor possess means of taking decisions and acting on them ... (merely taxonomic) ... collectivities have no identifiable means of taking decisions, let alone of acting on them' (Hindess, 1988, p.105 emphasis added). Only actors have causal powers, and therefore only actors can have causal responsibility for outcomes: it follows, incidentally, that if outcomes (i.e. any existing state of affairs) are judged 'bad', only actors are capable of taking remedial action to alter them.

When reified, personified images of structure are abandoned, there is no legitimate sense in which actors' behaviour can be said to be a direct 'necessary effect' of social structure nor either an indirect necessary effect (the so-called 'subtle', 'mediated', 'refracted' or 'dialectical' effects). Social structures cannot 'do' anything nor 'ask' for anything, nor 'impose' anything, nor have any 'needs'. Actors such as individuals or organizations can both do things and formulate a sense of having particular preferences, needs, interests, intentions, etc., but collectivities such as 'society', 'classes', or 'men' cannot. These collectivities are not actors. In particular, neither 'society' nor any other taxonomic collectivities have 'objective' or 'real' structurally determined 'interests' that determine the forms of thought, decisions, and actions of individual human actors or of social actors. In the case of an individual human actor it follows that an individual's 'membership' of a taxonomic collectivity ('class', 'white people', 'black people', 'men', 'women', etc.) does not determine the forms of thought and actions of that actor nor of any other individual members of that collectivity. Membership of a taxonomic collectivity (not that anyone can be a member of only one!) may at certain times in particular situations predispose particular actors to think and act in particular ways or formulate a sense of having particular interests, but any such predispositions, if and when they occur, are contingently produced and empirically problematic occurrences: they are not structurally predetermined nor an effect of any structural 'necessities'. To summarize: actors' ways of thinking and behaving and actors' formulations of interests, desires, and intentions are not 'necessary effects' of the social totality, nor of the actors' structural location within a social totality, nor of the actors' membership of a taxonomic collectivity of the kinds just referred to.

One of the most significant points made so far is that actors (as defined earlier) do not have 'real' or 'objective' interests that are a necessary consequence of the actors' structural locations in society. That is, no good reasons exist for supposing that any actor has 'real' but unacknowledged interests that are the structurally determined, 'given' or structurally 'fixed' properties of that actor. Actors regularly formulate (a sense of having) particular interests, and sometimes act or attempt to act on the basis of these formulated interests, but this is different from supposing that any particular interests are the structurally determined (structurally 'given') properties of any particular actors. Reductionist social theories impute structurally 'given' or 'objective' interests to actors. Problems associated with the theoretical assignment to actors of structurally 'given' or 'real' interests are long-standing and it was many years ago that Child (1941) asked 'How is one to know which thoughts, feelings, etc., are, in point of fact, the ones rationally suited to a given class's position?' (ibid., p.218). The answer, stated in non-reductionist terms, is that no particular thoughts and feelings are 'necessary' to or 'rationally suited' to a 'class's' structural position: nor, come to that, to 'men's' position or 'women's' position.

If there is no structurally 'necessary' or 'true' consciousness for actors to follow, it is also pointless for observers to impute 'false' consciousness to actors: this will be discussed later.

It is reductionist to suppose that, for example, social work actors are 'agents' of 'the interests of capitalism' or of any other putative structural 'needs' conjured up by theories that refer to the so-called 'objective' ('real') interests of 'classes', of 'men', of 'women', etc. To take up Child's (1941) point, if these interests are not formulated or recognized by the actors in question ... what next? Reductionist interpretations of power, social action, and 'real' interests, regularly invoke the fallacy of teleological explanation. This involves theoretical efforts to 'work backwards' in an attempt to explain a cause in terms of its effects. Betts (1986) notes that teleological explanation '... both locates the powerful and discovers their "interests" by examining outcomes ... this is logically false for we cannot, in the absence of intentional planning, discover causes by examining effects' (ibid., p.51). Certainly intentional planning is one important factor, among others, in the occurrence of outcomes: but planning can only be done by actors and no actors have 'objective' structurally-determined 'interests'. Hindess (1986b) observes that 'The notion of interests that are real or objective (unlike other interests that actors may believe themselves to have) have no explanatory significance with regard to the actions of those whose interests they are thought to be' (ibid., p.128). There is a connection here to the critical observations made earlier regarding structural determination, in the sense that '... there is no possibility of interests (or norms and values) operating as mere transmissions between social structure and actors' decisions. Interests have consequences only in so far as they enter actors' deliberations and contribute towards providing them with reasons for action' (Hindess, 1988, p.110, emphasis added). This non-reductionist conception of 'interests' does not mean that regularized, patterned features of any particular current social context never benefit some actors more than others, but it does not automatically follow that the actors who benefit most created or were able to create the social context, still less that they created it in order to achieve their interests.

Some additional aspects of the point just made are noted in Polsby's (1980, p.208) observation that

> Even if we can show that a given status quo benefits some people disproportionately, as I think we can for any real world status quo, such a demonstration falls short of showing that these beneficiaries created the status quo, act in any meaningful way to maintain it, or could, in the future, act effectively to deter changes in it.

The implications of this statement are far-reaching, as a moment's reflection will show. However, though this does not invalidate what Polsby says, analysis of the social reproduction (or else change) of social situations must take account of the possibility that some of Polsby's 'beneficiaries' may actually be very proactive in trying to maintain the status quo even though it may not have been of their making. Here, it may be observed that fortuity is one of the most neglected concepts in social analysis. Sometimes actors perceive a fortuitous coincidence between some aspects of the current situation(s) that they are involved in, and their own self-formulated interests: in which case they might try to, and sometimes be able to 'retain' the status quo, or at least, those aspects of it which they perceive brings them advantages. This happens quite regularly in occupations, professions, politics, and in the field of social policy: actors, including social actors, are strategic beings who try to achieve their goals in the particular situations that they find themselves in. In accounting analytically for this aspect of the reproduction of social situations through the grasping of advantages that were unplanned by the 'beneficiary', no teleological explanation is required. Nor is any reductionist conception of power involved, because if it is hypothesized that it is the currently most powerful actor(s) in the current situation who are most likely to be able to 'retain' and perhaps institutionalize and further disseminate those outcomes which fortuitously coincide with their (rather than others') self-formulated interests, their power to do so, when defined and analysed in non-reductionist terms, is regarded as a variable, strategically and contingently achieved capacity, not a structurally-predetermined or 'fixed' and unvarying capacity that is 'given' by the actor's location within the social totality. This conception of power as a fluid, variable and contingently produced outcome of interactions will be returned to shortly.

Problems arising from reductionist uses of the concept 'false consciousness' were touched upon earlier and were also discussed briefly in the previous chapter with reference to radical social work and feminist social work writing. These problems relate directly to the theoretical issues highlighted so far in the present chapter. Clegg (1989) in broadly similar vein to Hindess (1988) identifies the problems involved in imputing 'objective' ('real') but unacknowledged interests to actors who are presumed to 'possess' these interests by virtue of their structural location in a social totality or by virtue of their 'membership' of a taxonomic collectivity (e.g. 'women'). Clegg (1989) contrasts, on the one hand, the formulation of 'women's' 'interests' by lesbian feminist separatists, and on the other, the formulation of 'womens' 'interests' provided by 'Women Who Want to be Women', an Australian interest group which specifies that 'women's' real 'interests' are in the home, as wives and mothers (ibid., p.113). Clegg makes the point that 'Many women may not recognize their interests in either articulation - are they deluded?' (ibid.). Ramazanoglu (1989) refers to a different point, concerning 'cross-cutting' memberships of different social collectivities. She comments 'Women of different social classes, and of different social and ethnic groups do not share the same political interests. Women can oppress and exploit other women, and can benefit from the subordination of others' (ibid., p.435). Here, care is needed to ensure that reductionist analysis predicated on a uni-dimensional categorization ('women') is not compounded by constructing a series of sub-categories ('white middle-class women', 'black middle-class women', 'white working-class women', etc.) as a basis for imputing 'objective' or structurally-determined ('real') interests to these sub-categories as taxonomic collectivities: to do this would add a multiplier effect to the original reductionism, or more precisely, would merely replace it with a series of other reductionisms. Nevertheless, the general point may be taken that diversity and heterogeneity within social collectivities, and actors' multiple memberships across collectivities, together with the other previously outlined problems that are inherent in reductionist theories, are good reasons for abandoning simplistic theoretical efforts to 'explain' the empirical complexities of social life as 'necessary effects' of any single unifying structural principle or structural exigency.

Social systems have no systemic 'needs' and to suppose that they do is to apply an illegitimate teleology to them. This problem is magnified when 'real' or 'objective' interests are imputed to taxonomic collectivities and when reductionist attempts are made to link social systems to social action through the supposed 'actions' of taxonomic collectivities (e.g. 'men') that cannot conceivably be regarded as actors. Reductionist theoretical use of the concept 'patriarchy' is a case in point. Crompton's (1989) feminist sociological analysis refers (ibid., p.576) to Hindess's work and she criticizes analytical uses of the concept 'patriarchy'. She writes 'In particular, the use of the concept makes it difficult to avoid ... "categoricalism", that is, the assumption that men as a category are driven to oppress women as a category - a position which is profoundly unsociological' (Crompton, 1989, p.581). Indeed, it is a position that is absurd if a non-reductionist definition of the term 'actor' is accepted. Recourse in Marxism to the concept 'the interests of capitalism' is another classic instance of the problems just referred to: an account of these problems specifically in relation to Marxism is provided elsewhere (Sibeon, 1991). What is at issue here is the contention that social action is not an 'effect' of some structural 'necessity' or of 'objective' interests. Actors formulate interests and reasons for acting, and engage in action. They do so in terms of the means of action, resources, and discourses that are available to them in particular social situations. While the sociologist may want to examine other discourses and a wide range of conditions-of-action that are external to the actor in question, this does not mean that the study of actors' forms of thought, behaviour, and the contexts and outcomes of action, should be undertaken in terms which suppose that actors have 'objective' ('real') structurally determined 'interests' which, because unacknowledged, are 'therefore' an indication of 'false consciousness' on the actors part.

It was observed earlier that only actors, as previously defined, have the capacity ('power') to produce outcomes. What, though, is power and how do actors become powerful? Analysed in non-reductionist terms, power is not a structurally predetermined or structurally 'given' capacity of actors: it is not a fixed-capacity that inheres in any actor by virtue of the actor's structural location within an over-arching social system. Power is emergent, in the sense of being an outcome of social interactions: power, to paraphrase Law's (1986a, p.5) definition, is an effect not a cause of strategic success achieved by actors during their interactions with other actors in particular situations or in a series of situations. Actors may become more powerful, or less powerful: this is because their capacity to shape events or to obtain their objectives is not a structurally bestowed, predetermined or 'fixed' capacity. Actors contingently grow or reduce in size: they have no structurally predetermined 'size' (Callon and Latour, 1981, p.280). Two illuminating empirical case studies of the acquisition and loss of power are provided by Callon and Latour (1981) and Callon (1986). In these studies of strategic interactions between competitive social ('organizational') actors struggling against each other for 'power', the 'expanding' actors later diminished in 'size'. Strategic success in the acquisition of power is always potentially reversible. It is because power is not structurally predetermined that there are usually formidable strategic problems to be overcome if currently 'ascending' or 'powerful' actors are to be able to stabilize their situation for very long periods by means of irreversibly enrolling and 'consigning' (making durable temporally and spatially) a large number of related ideas, policies, practices, and resources (Callon and Latour, 1981, p.293). Some strategically successful actors may be able to achieve and then sustain relatively long-lasting asymmetries in 'size' between themselves and other actors (ibid., p.286) but these temporally stabilized asymmetries, if and where they occur, are contingently and strategically reproduced, not a 'necessary effect' of the social totality.

The existence of contingency in social life is partly a consequence of there being no structurally predetermined 'hierarchy of sites' (Hindess, 1986a, p.122) with those at 'higher' levels always exerting a structurally 'given' total control over other actors or over other sites of action. There are many loci of power: there is no single temporally and spatially enduring Leviathan. Many sites and social actors are, in usually variable and shifting ways, related to each other spatially and temporally 'But the question of whether ... (any particular) ... local scene has some future historic import is a problematic matter for empirical assessment' (Duster, 1981, p.114). The question to which Duster refers is always a matter for empirical assessment, not for theoretical predetermination. Actors have no structurally predetermined 'size', and therefore their capacities to (spatially) shape events in other sites and to (temporally) shape future events, are empirically contingent and problematic. This is illustrated in Callon and Latour's (1981) empirical case study of competition and struggle between two competitive social actors, Electricity of France (EDF) and Renault. Callon and Latour's study reveals in detail some of the strategic techniques by which actors successfully 'enrol' other actors and other 'materials' (ideas, practices, policies, resources, conventions and the like) and disseminate these consigned ('made durable') materials across a large range of sites. In this way, actors 'grow': for a time, EDF became powerful and Renault 'declined'. However the EDF, for a variety of reasons, was unable to stabilize the asymmetry in power that it had created and it soon 'lost' the power that it had enjoyed for a brief period. It had failed to irreversibly 'macro-structure' the social world; as will be noted in different contexts in some of the later chapters, this is an outcome that, in British social work in the 1980's, some formerly powerful 'professional' social work actors discovered to their cost.

It will be observed later in the chapter that empirical analytical use of the concept 'strategy' is one of the most significant recent transitions in sociological analysis (Crow, 1989; Morgan, 1989). Theorists and empirical researchers associated with what might be termed the 'strategic-contingency' approach in the empirical study of power and social action include Callon (1986), Callon and Latour (1981), Callon and Law (1982), Callon et al. (1983), Callon et al. (1986), Law (1986a and 1986b), Latour (1986), and Barnes (1986). Clegg (1989) identifies (ibid., pp.1-38) the contrast between conventional, 'sovereign' conceptions of power developed in the tradition of Hobbes's Leviathian, and the recent emphasis upon the contingent and 'strategic' nature of power, an approach which owes more to Machiavelli than to Hobbes. Although modern researchers can hardly be said to be the lineal intellectual descendants of Machiavelli(!) there is, nevertheless, an affinity (Clegg, 1989, p.6) between some recent forms of 'power' analysis and (ibid., pp.6-7)

... those of Machiavelli ... (which tended) ... to undercut the sense of a total score in favour of a more contingent and local interpretation ... an analytical focus on ... shifting, unstable, alliances, a concern for ... strategy and a disinclination to believe in any single, originating and decisive centre of power ... Hobbes's representatives have left their mark on ... theory in their insistence on the causal, atomistic and mechanical nature of the relations of power, views which still remain implicit in the insistence on prime movement and first causes in ... views of power.

To say this does not, incidentally, mean that strategic interactions are presumed to develop in a wholly haphazard or totally random way: later, the point will be made that social life is neither 'chaotic' nor structurally predetermined (Layder, 1986, p.378).

For the purpose of empirically investigating patterns of interaction among social actors who are jointly involved in the construction of new policies, or in the routine, ongoing application and reproduction of existing policies, it is useful to think in the terms that these actors comprise an 'actor-network' (Callon, 1986, p.204 and p.218). Social work's actor-network includes the British Association of Social Workers (BASW), social services departments and relevant central government departments, the Association of Directors of Social Services (ADSS), social work training courses, the Central Council for Education and Training in Social Work (CCETSW), and various other social actors such as the Association of Teachers in Social Work Education (ATSWE). It cannot, of course, be presumed that all the actors in a network will formulate the same objectives and interests or will co-operate with each other. It should also be noted that the historical material examined in the previous chapter showed that recent struggles within social work's actor-network embody a number of contingently reproduced continuities with the past: actor-networks have temporal as well as spatial dimensions. In Clegg's (1989) definition 'An "actor network" concerns the interrelated set of entities successfully translated by an actor' (ibid., p.225). In this and the later chapters a less restrictive definition will be employed. The term will be used in a more general way rather than only in the case of a network of actors who have been 'enrolled' by one or more of the relevant actors: in some instances and for certain periods it is empirically possible, for example, that none of the relevant actors has contingently secured a 'dominant' role. In this less restrictive analytic use of the term the question of 'what happens' during the course of social interaction within the actor-network is left open as a separate matter for empirical investigation. Viewed in these terms, the most common feature of an actor-network is that it is made up of a number of actors whose activities interlock around certain focal (e.g. occupational) concerns and activities in ways that to a greater or lesser extent are contingently reproduced temporally and spatially. Although, in the case of social work's actor-network, large numbers of individual human actors are involved, and occasionally some of these may successfully exert powerful influence upon the construction of national social work policies, it is generally social actors who are the more influential in shaping general policy directions. The roles of individual human actors within local sites of (social work) action are not analytically insignificant (Sibeon, 1991) but for the purposes of some of the later chapters concerned with major social (work) policy developments, there will be many occasions when greater emphasis is placed on the roles of social actors and on strategic interactions between social actors and between sites of action rather than on the ethnography of face-to-face interactions among social workers and others 'within' local social work sites.

There are, it may be noted, no valid grounds for supposing that the size or membership of an actor-network is static or structurally predetermined. With regard to the involvement of social actors there are, generally speaking, various contingently reproduced membership parameters: for example, as far as this author knows, the National Farmers Union has no significant role in social work's actor-network. This does not mean that no variations of membership occur. For instance, the central government departments that become involved in various ways in social work matters may vary as duties are re-allocated amongst departments. Another example concerns responsibility for the national system of social work training. This is currently the formal responsibility of the CCETSW but prior to the 1970's various other actors had performed a broadly similar role: also, it seems likely that in the 1990's a new social work training actor (the National Council for Vocational Qualifications) will enter the scene.

Analytic use of the concept actor-network, in the non-reductionist terms defined earlier relating to social action and 'power', will figure in later chapters, particularly chapter seven. It is necessary that one other general theoretical point be clarified here. It is not suggested that an actor-network is an isolated, self-contained entity. Actor-networks are related in complex, diverse ways to conditions of action that are external to the network itself and to the actors involved in the network: but those conditions are not structurally predetermined nor is there any structural predetermination of the relation between those conditions and the outcomes of interactions in actor-networks. In non-reductionist studies of occupations and professions and the construction of policies affecting these, the concept 'actor-network' is analytically highly productive: this, as will emerge in some of the later chapters, is particularly the case in the social work and social policy fields where the construction and application of public policies requires the interlocking involvement of various political, administrative, and professional actors.

When particular actors within an actor-network acquire power, perhaps to the extent of transforming the balance of power within the network, this is a strategic accomplishment. Clegg (1989) observes that 'the central feature of power consists in ... (the) .. stabilizing of the terrain for its own expression' (ibid., p.184). Strategic actors attempt to shape the conditions of action in which they are involved. Actors are not constrained by any mysterious 'structural' forces: no such 'forces' or 'prime movers' exist (Latour, 1986). Rather, actors are constrained, or enabled, by usually unstable and shifting conditions of action which include, among other things, the objectives of other actors and the variable outcomes of actions taken by other previous as well as current actors (Betts, 1986). Actors' capacity to successfully 'manage' (or 'enrol') the conditions-of-action in their own favour is not a structurally 'given' capacity. To reiterate an earlier point, power is an effect not a cause (Law, 1986a) of strategic success in stabilizing the conditions-of-action in one's own favour; in those situations involving conflict, this typically being the case in the construction of social policies that affect political or professional groups, empirical outcomes are '... the result of previous and current contest' (Clegg, 1989, p.200).

The point was made earlier that the conditions of action within which actors operate are not structurally predetermined: they are empirically contingent and often highly fluid, shifting, conditions. They are, nevertheless, always impotant constraining (or facilitative) factors for actors in the particular situations that they are involved in. As Barbalet (1985) puts it, '... power is not reducible to the attributes of agents themselves ... an agent's capability of influencing events, of exercising power to achieve some goal, is ultimately derivable from the relations of social power in which the agent is involved' (ibid., pp.543-4). The forms of knowledge and techniques employed by actors are significant in the strategic acquisition of power, but external conditions are significant also and power, as Barbalet notes, is not 'reducible' to the attributes of actors. To say that neither actors' capacities nor the conditions of action in which they operate are in any way structurally predetermined, is not to imply that actors are unconstrained agents. Actors and social action itself are part of the social relations of power and therefore we '... are concerned with conceptualizing the sites of decision and action (the conditions in which they take place and the obstacles they confront) and the relationships between different sites' (Hindess, 1986a, p. 121). It has already been observed that power, analysed in non-reductionist terms, is an 'outcome' and not a structurally given or fixed capacity of the actor. For this reason, it is necessary in empirical analysis to examine the strategic techniques and contingent processes whereby some actor(s) 'expand' (Callon, 1986) and succeed, sometimes only temporarily, sometimes for relatively long periods, in influencing events across a large number of relevant sites through time and space (Gregory, 1989, p. 188). In describing some of the processes involved in actors' 'expansion' across time-space, Clegg (1989, p.225) observes that

> Episodic power's achievement will consist, first, in constituting a relational field by "enrolling" other organizations and agencies; second, in the "stabilizing" of a network of power centrality, alliance and coalition among agencies within the field; third, in the "fixing" of common relations of meaning and membership among the agencies within that field such that they are reflexively aware of their constitution as a field.

In these processes, the 'central' strategic actor(s) are likely to employ particular techniques. One that will be examined with reference to social work's actor-network in chapter seven, is to try to engineer the conditions of action in such a way as to get other actors to want what the strategic actor wants them to want; sometimes, this involves trying to 'arrange' the relevant social and political terrain in a way that sets up 'necessary nodal points' (Clegg, 1989, p.185) or 'obligatory passage points' (Callon et al., 1986) through which other actors and materials necessarily have to traffic. A rather different technique referred to by Clegg in the previous quotation involves attempting to construct 'common relations of meaning and membership' among a wide range of actors. This is a familiar technique in politics: it will be examined in chapter five with reference to the current disunity in radical social work and the efforts of some actors primarily concerned with class or racism or gender issues respectively, to construct common relations of meaning-and-membership within, and sometimes across, their respective constituencies. In the final section of the present chapter, reference will be made to two specific social work illustrations of actors' use of strategies.

There is another aspect of 'power' that should be mentioned in the context of the present discussion. Power and conflict and the observable exercise of power in concrete situations are often seen as inter-related in the sense that it can be argued power is only real if exercised: an implication is that sociological analysis of power should be confined to investigation of a series of concrete decisions (Dahl, 1958). Other social theorists warn against confining analysis to only those occasions when the exercise of power and the existence of conflict are expressed and observable: powerful groups may exercise power to construct a false, engineered, or manipulated consensus and it has been claimed 'the crucial point is that the most effective and insidious use of power is to prevent ... conflict arising in the first place' (Lukes, 1974, p.123). Lukes's point is widely familiar in sociology, and has been much debated. Certainly it can be argued strategic actors in some circumstances may attempt to forestall conflict or, if it occurs, attempt to smooth things over by such devices as suggesting the issue over which actors are struggling is in fact based on a misconception and that the issue in question threatens no-one. It should not, incidentally, be assumed that only currently powerful policy-making actors are able to secure a 'consensus' that operates in their favour. There are many loci of power, and as argued earlier, power is a contingent 'outcome' of interaction, not a structurally-predetermined capacity of actors. In most circumstances, policy-making actors have to 'negotiate' or sacrifice some of their objectives if faced by anticipated major opposition; and very often '... opposition ... (takes) ... the form of estimates in the minds of policy-makers rather than organized groups treading the corridors of power' (Banting, 1986, p.59). There may be any number of cases where strategic actors invoke the so-called 'non-decision making' strategy and attempt to deflect, redefine, or even promote particular conflicts. Who has not heard, for example, of the idea of deflecting attention away from troublesome issues by giving actors something 'new' but 'innocuous' to fight about amongst themselves?! The debate set in train largely, though not exclusively by Dahl (1958) and Lukes (1974) is involved and protracted. It is sufficient to say here that the idea that power exists in the form of a 'conflict-prevention' capacity should be rejected if by this is meant that the actors involved 'ought' to have engaged in conflict and would have done so had their 'false consciousness' not blocked their perception of their 'real' ('objective') but unacknowledged 'interests'. Actors might or might not engage in conflict for a wide variety of reasons in differential, variable conditions of action. There is more to this debate (see Bachrach and Baratz, 1962; Saunders, 1979) than can be examined here, but in general the debate between Dahl (1958) and Lukes (1974), their respective supporters, and others variously involved in it (for instance Frey, 1971) tends to rest on formulations that fail to pay sufficient attention to a strategic concept of social power as contingently produced and reproduced in shifting conditions of action, and as potentially 'reversible' (Callon, 1986; Callon and Latour, 1981).

Neither the point just made, nor any of the earlier arguments, involve any suggestion that social life lacks any semblance of 'order' or continuity. Clegg (1989) postulates that social life is characterized by '... strategic manoeuvres made in contingent circumstances ... bereft of any overall harmonic ... and ... without the guidance of any overall conductor' (ibid., p.22). This postulate is in opposition to notions of mysterious, hidden structural 'forces' as analytical prime movers. However, to reject notions of a single temporally and spatially omnipresent 'grand architect' is not to suggest that social life is '... just an endless series of contingencies' (ibid., p.7). There are no good grounds for constructing an 'either-or' theoretical dichotomy between, on the one hand, a structural conception of 'rigid' system determination and predictability, and on the other, a conception of social life as a process of endless flux, indeterminacy, or purely random change. Callon and Latour (1981) observe that 'There is no chaos, but no rigid system either' (ibid., p.282). Elias's (1978) figurational sociology theoretically constructs an image of a

40

continuously processual, indeterminate social reality as a series of
'... figurations in constant flux with neither beginning nor end'
(ibid., p.162). Layder (1986) is critical of this model of social life,
and he notes that '... Elias seems to be operating with an illicit
dichotomy between complete statis and complete flux; there are no
intermediary "states" or combination of elements ...' (ibid., p.378).
Layder's criticism is that Elias constructs a theoretical dichotomy
between 'complete statis' and 'complete flux', then opts for the latter.
Anti-reductionist sociology transcends this dichotomy through the
empirical application of a postulate that social life is always
potentially open to change and variability, the extent to which
stability and continuity, or else discontinuity and change, actually
occurs being treated as an empirical variable for investigation. If
relatively stable social conditions persist for long periods, the
conditions in question are not structurally predetermined (Hindess,
1986a, p.123). They are contingently produced and reproduced, and
actors (not 'social structure', or merely taxonomic collectivities) play
a significant role in the production of these outcomes. Social life,
because not structurally predetermined, is always potentially variable
and indeterminate: but many segments of social life do become stabilized
in what is otherwise an 'unstable' and shifting social and political
world.   Clegg (1989) notes '... a theory of power must examine how
the field of force in which power has been fixed, coupled and
constituted in such a way that, intentionally or not, certain "nodal
points" of practice ... (become) ... privileged ... in ... unstable and
shifting terrain' (ibid., p.17). Whether or not any particular
institutionalized 'materials' (ideas, policies, practices, etc.) then
become 'fixed' and further stabilized for long periods is an empirically
open question (Callon, 1986; Callon and Latour, 1981) and not something
that can be theoretically predetermined in terms of an a priori
theoretical commitment to one or the other polar opposites ('complete
statis' or 'complete flux') in an either-or dichotomy. These
theoretical formulations have empirical implications that are too
diverse to explore here, but it is worth noting that broadly analogous
postulates in empirical studies of social policy processes are clearly
discernible in the work of Rein (1976), Elmore (1978), Hjern and Porter
(1981), Barrett and Hill (1981, p.19), and Ham and Hill (1984, pp.106-
7).
    There are a number of reasons - some of which have already been
identified - why anti-reductionist social analysis, though it involves
explicit rejection of 'objectivist' notions that actors' forms of
thought, intentions, and behaviour are structurally predetermined,
cannot legitimately be accused of endorsing subjectivist, voluntaristic
or epistemologically idealist images of actors as unconstrained agents.
There are three main reasons why this is so, these reasons being very
generally applicable to individual human actors and to social actors.
    Firstly, to reject theories that presume actors' forms of thought are
structurally predetermined is not to deny that actors formulate
interests, objectives, and reasons for acting in terms of the cognitive
materials available to them. One aspect of this is the availability to
actors of empirical information. Actors do not 'know everything' and
some events that influence social action and its outcomes may occur
'behind the back' of the actor: an actor may be unaware of historical,
demographic and various other factors that impinge upon the situations
in which the actor may be involved (Duster, 1981, p.113). This is why,
among other reasons, actors may make '... many ... judgements about
themselves and others which turn out to be wrong, partial, or ill-

41

informed' (Giddens, 1989, pp.18-19). Empirical information also has to
be interpreted ('made sense of') in terms of the discourses available to
the actor: these may be 'lay' discourses, academic, professional,
religious, political or any other form of or combination of discourses.
Actors, that is, formulate ideas and purposes in terms of the discourses
available to them, a point developed at some length in social work terms
by Rojek et al. (1988). Hindess (1988) observes that the interests,
beliefs, and desires that '... play a part in an actor's behaviour will
depend on the availability to that actor of the conceptual means of
formulating them' (ibid., p.89). A related point noted in the first
chapter is that knowledge is not always fully explicitly and
discursively held by actors. Knowledge may become tacit, and
unreflectively acted upon. Through its institutionalization and through
various processes of socialization, knowledge in occupations,
professions, or in any other walks of life may by virtue of its regular,
repeated everyday use become 'taken-for-granted' and deeply sedimented
in actors' habitualized, routinized forms of thought and practices
(Berger and Luckmann, 1972, pp.36-38; Giddens, 1982, p.9; Hindess, 1988,
p.48). Discourses are institutionalized constellations of meanings and
practices that, though not every actor will necessarily interpret and
'apply' them in exactly the same way, exist <u>prior</u> to the actor who
becomes involved in them: the social world is not the product of
unacculturated actors. This, though, for all the reasons stated earlier,
does not mean that actors' forms of thought and actions are structurally
predetermined, nor does it mean that in those situations where actors
draw upon discourses in habitualized, 'tacit' ways, that this
constitutes a form of 'false consciousness' in the sense connoted in
reductionist structural theories. Pervasive discourses, that is to say,
are those discourses that have become contingently institutionalized.

Secondly, in rejecting structural theories, anti-reductionist
sociology involves empirical investigation of actors' ways of
cognitively assessing their situation, their decision-making criteria,
and also actors' behaviour and the outcomes of actions, <u>in terms of the
conditions-of-action in which the actors are involved</u>. Actors' forms of
thought and behaviour are not structurally predetermined, nor are the
conditions of action static or structurally predetermined, but these
contingently produced conditions have real existence and may constrain
(or 'enable') actors in diverse ways. Social power is not, in the terms
discussed earlier, reducible to the attributes or intentions of actors
(Barbalet, 1985, pp.543-4). Power is an outcome that emerges out of
(usually) highly complex and variable interconnections between actors'
intentions, decisions, techniques, and actions, and the social relations
of power and conditions of action relevant to the social context(s) of
those actors. The current situation(s) in which actors are involved is
not structurally 'given' and it can, in principle, be 'acted upon' and
changed in various ways; but this is not to deny that contingently
produced asymmetrical distributions of 'power' and resources are very
often already 'in' the situation (Layder, 1987, p.38) as outcomes of
previous and current interactions among actors. Everyone knows that
actors cannot always get what they want. For individual and social
actors alike, there is an obvious but analytically important sense in
which '... choice of strategy is not just a choice between goals, but a
choice between goals <u>set in the context of the means needed to secure
them</u>' (Crouch, 1982, p.139, emphasis added). In any particular
situation, it is possible that not all the actors involved have equal
access to the means and resources necessary for achieving their
preferred objectives, and therefore there are likely to be empirical

instances where actors' '... expressed preferences tend to be confined to possibilities they consider realisable, or to what is available, and do not necessarily reflect ideal notions or objectives' (Watson and Austerberry, 1986, p.149). Another factor in the achievement of objectives is that actors require access to and skill in deploying techniques and strategies relevant to the securing of objectives: although no structural determination is involved, there is no reason to suppose that access to and skill in deploying relevant techniques and strategies are always equally distributed (Hindess, 1986b, p.127) among the range of actors involved in any particular situation(s).

Thirdly, there is another sense in which to reject structural theories is not the same thing as endorsing epistemologically idealist or subjectivist theories about the nature and roles of actors or of social action in general. Non-reductionist sociology, in the ways indicated in the two preceding paragraphs, is based on postulates that direct attention to the empirical investigation of actors' formulations, decisions, and actions in terms of the knowledge, discourses, and means of action available to actors and in terms of the conditions of action in which those actors are involved. Non-reductionist sociology is premised on the understanding that actors' 'definitions-of-the-situation' are not always successfully imposed upon the social world: one specific reason for this, additional to those already examined, is that actions may have <u>unintended consequences</u>. Controversy surrounds empirical uses of this concept, and its potential future analytical significance in sociology (Baert, 1989) is such that separate discussion of it is warranted.

The explanatory significance of the concept 'unintended consequences'

Use of this concept has become, according to Hindess (1986c), a 'banal commonplace' (ibid., p.441) in academic social science. Specifically, this criticism is part of Hindess's critique of methodological individualism in the form developed by Elster (1985). In criticizing Elster's use of the concept, Hindess (1986c) asks 'Why make such a fuss about a few unintended consequences?' (ibid., p.441). Elsewhere Hindess (1988), in criticizing the reductionist presuppositions of methodological individualism, suggests that without the surreptitious introduction of a notion that actors' forms of thought are determined by their social location, it would be an 'absurdity' (ibid., p.25) to argue that an aggregation of unintended consequences '... could explain anything about social structure ...' (ibid.) In the same text Hindess (1988) further observes that knowledge of the unintended outcomes of actors' behaviour does not of itself explain why the actors behaved as they did (ibid., p.106). In more general terms, Hindess (1988) argues that methodological individualism as deployed in recent 'rational choice' theories actually relies on a hidden, underlying postulate of structural determination with regard to actors' forms of thought and preferences. Hindess's general theoretical demonstration of this particular point is illuminating and convincing: this is noted elsewhere (Sibeon, 1991, p.36). However the points to be made here are quite specific. They are that Hindess's criticisms are not reasons for abandoning analytical use of the concept, and that it has major analytical potential that is not acknowledged by Hindess. For reasons that are empirically demonstrated in a case study of social work policy constructions (Sibeon, 1989a), it can be argued the concept has crucial empirical explanatory significance in analyses of the social reproduction or change of social situations, including those situations in which social policies (e.g. social work policies) are constructed and implemented. This is not to say that all unintended consequences have equal significance. Some may be relatively trivial in terms of their consequences for the reproduction or change of social situations; others may have crucial, far-reaching implications. These, however, are essentially matters for empirical assessment in each instance: they are not matters for a priori theoretical predetermination. For the purposes of this chapter, attention will be confined to a number of general theoretical implications that arise from use of the concept in non-reductionist forms of empirical analysis.

Firstly, although Elster (1985) views unintended consequences in terms of a reductionist theoretical framework premised on methodological individualism, use of the concept is not necessarily tied to that framework. Empirical analytic use of the concept requires no assumption that individual human actors 'make society' or that 'social structure' is the aggregated outcome of the preferences and actions of countless individuals: nor is it necessary to suppose that 'constraints' upon individuals' scope for action consist of the outcomes of actions taken by a multitude of other individual actors. Secondly, it is not the case that use of the concept is necessarily tied to any reductionist structural theories premised on the tenets of methodological collectivism. Teleological explanations have no legitimate role in anti-reductionist sociology, but other types of explanation are possible through empirical analytical use of the concept. Application of the concept in social analysis does not require endorsement of reductionist theories which claim that social systems have 'needs' and that unintended consequences perform hidden (or 'latent') functions 'for' social systems (Giddens, 1982, p.10). A related aspect of this point is that use of the concept need involve no reductionist assumption that unintended consequences perform the 'function' of fulfilling 'real' ('objective') structurally-determined 'interests'. It is true that the concept has been used in all of these ways and in social science is commonly associated with them: but it is not necessarily tied to any of them, provided the concept is theoretically re-worked in the terms suggested here. Thirdly, it can be argued that the concept lends itself to incorporation into precisely those forms of anti-reductionist sociology which Hindess himself advocates: his trenchant criticisms of reductionist theoretical applications of the concept are valid, but Hindess leaves the matter there and does not specify possibilities for employing the concept in non-reductionist social analysis. There are signs that recent sociological interest in the concept is increasing (Baert, 1989), although it is also clear that further conceptual and empirical work is required in refining its analytical implications in non-reductionist forms of social analysis: no more will be attempted here than a provisional specification of some of these implications.

In terms of the strategic and contingent nature of social action and the roles of actors, it may reasonably be hypothesized that unintended outcomes perceived by currently powerful social actors (these may include those who initiated the action that led to the outcome as well as second or third party actors) to be in accord with their self-formulated interests and objectives are outcomes that - all else being equal - are more likely to be 'retained', institutionalized and disseminated spatially and temporally across a large range of sites than those outcomes perceived by currently powerful actors to be 'against' their self-formulated interests. The question of which actor(s) is the currently most powerful is, in the scenario just referred to, a

44

contingent variable and no assumption is made that any actors have a structurally-determined capacity to extinguish, veto, or else opportunistically 'grasp' and institutionalize any particular unintended outcomes that come their way. An extension of a point made earlier in the chapter is that some actors may 'fall lucky' and perceive a fortuitous coincidence between an observed unintended outcome of their own earlier actions or of some other actors' actions, and their currently formulated interests and objectives. A special version of this is where an unintended outcome of A's actions fortuitously produces perceived benefits for A in excess of those benefits that could have been achieved had the outcomes intended by A actually come about: though it might not happen as often as actors would like, this is a fairly familiar case of 'all's well that ends well'. In situations where fortuitous coincidences between unintended outcomes and actors' formulated interests occur, analytic use of the concept ('unintended consequences') as a way of explaining actors' retention of those outcomes is crucial in the study of the processes involved in the social production, reproduction, or change of social situations. Nor, in these situations, is any teleological explanation required: it is not claimed that the interests of the actors involved produced or caused the outcome (Betts, 1986, pp.50-51).

Some unintended outcomes can, of course, be very unfortuitous: an actor may make decisions and engage in actions that later turn out to have unexpectedly self-defeating outcomes for that actor. The nature of the outcomes, and how these outcomes are responded to and handled by current and future actors, are empirically contingent and variable matters for investigation, not processes that are structurally predetermined or predictable in advance of their occurrence. Betts (1986) notes that 'Contexts may be built up by a series of unintended outcomes, and an unintended outcome may have the effect of constraining, or enabling, future behaviour, but these are contingent questions' (ibid., p.40). The empirical illustration provided in chapter seven refers to professional(izing) social work actors' strategies that contributed to the emergence of unintended de-professionalizing outcomes arising from the existence of those strategies: but in that illustration, the de-professionalizing outcomes did not just 'happen' for some mysterious, inexplicable reason nor did they happen as an 'effect' of the social totality. They occurred because the outcomes unexpectedly altered the conditions-of-action within an actor-network in which a number of competitive actors were struggling against each other in their efforts to 'define' social work training and practice in particular ways. Shifts in the conditions-of-action had the effect of altering the configuration of power and opportunity within the actor-network; these shifts opened up 'new' strategic opportunities for some actors, and diminished the range of strategic opportunities for others. Specifically, new opportunities were created for particular actors (i.e. the CCETSW, social-services workers, social work employers, and senior administrators) who for some time had been critical of the goals sought by professionalizing social work lobby groups and by 'academic-professional' social work educators. That is, some social work actors were unexpectedly and fortuitously 'enabled' but others 'constrained' in terms of their scope for action in pursuance of their objectives: this happened for specific empirically identifiable reasons that require no reductionist explanation (Sibeon, 1989a).

When the term 'structure' is conceptualized as the current social situation in which actors are involved, there is a sense in which the current situation is partly formed by the intended and unintended outcomes of actions taken by previous, historical actors and also by current actors at an earlier time. These outcomes may, in both the previous as well as current situations, have enabled some actors and constrained others: these will not necessarily always be the same actors, and those constrained in one period may find they are 'enabled' in another, and vice-versa. Without necessarily endorsing the whole of Burns's (1986) conception of 'social systems', there are grounds for concurring with his argument that unintended consequences affect the reproduction or change of social contexts and that this is one reason why social contexts are always potentially unstable (ibid., p.10). Stated in terms of Berger and Luckmann's (1972) dialectical view of 'micro-macro' interconnection, or, too, in terms of Giddens's (1982) concepts of 'structuration and the 'duality of structure', the empirical existence of unintended outcomes and of actors' strategic responses to these outcomes may be regarded as empirically crucial 'complicating factors' in the dialectics of 'agency-structure' (ibid., p.10).

In the analysis of any social situation, the question of 'why' one particular unintended outcome (rather than another) occurred is a matter for empirical assessment on each occasion that the question arises: as observed earlier, this assessment need involve no teleological forms of explanation. Sometimes an unintended outcome(s) will have resulted from miscalculation or lack of adequate knowledge on the part of the decision-making actor, including lack of knowledge concerning previous, existing, or likely future conditions of action relevant to the formulation of objectives, to decision-making, and to the actor's assessment of the probable outcomes of action. Sometimes an unintended outcome is produced directly by the responses and actions of other actors, or sometimes for empirically more complex reasons to do with planned or unplanned 'interlocking' shifts in the relevant conditions of action: some states of affairs may not be 'ideal' for nor have been intentionally planned by any of the actors involved. Nor, to emphasise one particular aspect of a point already made, is any teleological explanation required in those instances where it becomes necessary to explain empirically why an actor chose and/or was able to 'select' and retain one unintended outcome rather than another. Bearing in mind the proviso that power is strategically and contingently achieved, and not a structurally 'given' capacity, Betts's (1986) comment on this point is pertinent. She observes that (ibid., p.63)

> Unintended consequences functional for the more powerful will be more likely to be reproduced, to survive, but a knowledge that they are so functional cannot explain why this unintended consequence and not another. Here, the more powerful are selecting innovations from the range that confronts them, not creating them.

This is to say that actors select from the range of intended and unintended and perhaps also unanticipated 'opportunities' available to them in any particular situation, and the processes involved in this selection can be adequately accounted for in non-reductionist terms that require no recourse to teleological explanations.

In the light of these and the earlier observations there is a good case for suggesting that the concept 'unintended consequences' has a crucial explanatory role in analyses of the reproduction, modification, or change of social situations. There are grounds for re-examining the claims made by Wrong (1979) and others who specify that power refers to intended outcomes. Wrong claims that power '... is the capacity of some persons to produce intended and foreseen effects on others' (ibid., p.2, emphasis added). Power is contingently achieved by individual actors and social actors, but a seriously incomplete understanding of social action is inevitable if the definition of power is restricted to actors' intentions in a way that excludes actors' contingently achieved differential capacities to veto, extinguish, or else select and retain particular unintended 'opportunities' from the range of opportunities that confronts them and other actors in particular situations. The concept has important empirical applications at the level of the middle-range where analysis is focussed on relationships between sites of action (Sibeon, 1989a). The concept has relevance also in micro-social analysis of face-to-face personal interactions within particular sites, and the relation of these to more spatially and temporally dispersed social phenomena: an example is Brown's (1985) study of unintended discriminatory effects upon black people arising from routine 'non-racist' cognitive and practical procedures in the careers counselling service. The concept also has important applications specifically in the study of spatially and temporally widely dispersed materials, as in Pakulski's (1986) study of political events in Poland, and in Skocpol's (1979) account of the Russian Revolution of 1917 which had momentous outcomes that none of the parties involved (including the Bolsheviks who assumed power) had anticipated at that time. As indicated by these examples, the concept is relevant in analyses of events at different 'levels' of social process: for the purpose of analysing the social reproduction, modification, or change of social situations it is a concept that merits much closer theoretical and empirical attention in the 'new' sociology of social work, and in non-reductionist sociology generally.

Actors' use of strategies: social work illustrations

To place in context the empirical illustrations that will be described shortly, a brief theoretical preamble is appropriate. Recent sociological interest in the concept 'strategy' (Morgan, 1989) has intensified (Crow, 1989) to the point where the concept '... is now in extensive use in sociology, and the extension of its use has brought with it new perspectives in several areas of the discipline' (ibid., p.19). Power, it was observed earlier, is not a structurally predetermined 'fixed-capacity' inherent in any particular actors: power analysed in non-reductionist terms (Clegg, 1989) is contingently and strategically achieved, and therefore (ibid., pp.32-33)

> Power is simply the effectiveness of strategies for achieving for oneself a greater scope for action than for others implicated by one's strategies. Power is not any thing nor is it necessarily inherent in any one; it is a tenuously produced and reproduced effect which is contingent upon the strategic competencies and skills of actors who would be powerful.

There is no good reason why actors' accounts should automatically be accepted (by the sociologist or any other researcher) at their face-value. Actors formulate reasons for acting in terms of the means of action and discourses available to them, but the sociologist may also want to examine other discourses and conditions of action not specified by the actor and which in some sense are external to the actor in question. Also, the metier of the strategic-contingency approach is precisely the investigation of actors' 'strategic' accounts: actors' publicly stated accounts (together with those provided to sociological researchers!) may well be strategically intended accounts that are intended to 'translate' other actors. This does not mean that actors' accounts should be interpreted as 'false consciousness' in the sense implied in reductionist theory: for all the reasons outlined earlier in the chapter it is essential in non-reductionist analysis to avoid any '... recourse to devices such as analytical prime movers, or hidden and inexplicable mechanisms of thought control' (Clegg, 1989. p.212). Subject to this important proviso, an empirical understanding of the strategic manoeuvres employed by actors requires of the sociological researcher '... a thoroughgoing determination to follow the actors wherever they go, to uncover what they might prefer to keep concealed, and to avoid being misled by myths' (Callon et al., 1986, p.5).

The illustrations of social work actors' use of strategies described in the remaining pages of the chapter, centre upon social work education as a 'pivotal' institution within social work. Social work education both reflects and influences wider developments across the social work community (Jones, 1979, p.72) and is strategically selected by competitive actors as an institution through which conflicting objectives and interests are 'routed' (Bailey, 1982, p.12). It is empirically and analytically useful to conceptualize social work actors' involvement in policy struggles not only in terms of their location in social work's actor-network, but also in terms of their memberships of social work's competing 'constituencies'. While it is not suggested here that all actors located within each constituency always formulate the same objectives and reasons for acting, or always engage in the same types of action, there tends nevertheless to be some contingently reproduced similarity of objectives and perspectives (Hindess, 1988, p.111) among most of the actor-members of each constituency.

Actors located within what might be called social work's academic-professional constituency tend in the main to be professionalizing actors who in their role as professional educators endorse a broadly based social science model of professional education and professional development (Stevenson, 1971). Social work practice is portrayed as an intellectual activity (Stevenson, 1981, pp.22-22) involving 'intellectual' and 'professional' task-complexity and professional social work practice is said to require 'considerable intellectual ... skills' (Butrym et al., 1981, p.8.) consisting of the application of knowledge derived from '... the behavioural and social sciences ... and ... from social work theory and research' (ibid.). Whether this is an accurate portrayal of social work practice, is, as noted in the previous chapter, highly doubtful. Some actors, particularly social work employers, reject the 'theoreticism' of this professional education model, and also reject the political radicalization of students that is said to be an effect of exposing social work students to a broad 'liberal education' model of professional education grounded in the social sciences.

The professionalizing social work constituency which is composed of actors (such as the British Association of Social Workers) who are strongly committed to establishing social work as a 'profession', is closely aligned with the academic-professional constituency: for example, individual and social actors from both constituencies tend to emphasise the intellectual task-complexity of social work practice and argue for a broad social science foundation of knowledge as a basis for 'professional' expertise. In the late 1970's and throughout most of the 1980's actors from both these constituencies joined forces and fought a running battle against the threat of de-professionalization posed by social work actors (such as the Association of Directors of Social Services) located in what for convenience will be referred to here as the employers' constituency. The nub of these conflicts centred on employer pressures for a reform of social work education in the direction of more practical, less 'academic', and less 'professional' forms of occupational training controlled largely by employers, rather than by professionals or by academic-professionals located in professional schools in higher education institutions. The conflict between these actors became intense (Sainsbury, 1985) and Harbert (1985b), a Director of Social Services whose criticisms of 'professionalism' were noted in the previous chapter, argued that professionals' and academic-professionals' resistance against the reform of social work training rested on professionalizing '... arguments ... (that) ... concentrated not on clients and their needs, but on the extent to which different forms of training might, or might not, confer a higher status upon social work' (ibid., p.15, emphasis added). Harbert suggested professionalizing concerns are '... a sure sign that social work has lost its way. The client has become of secondary importance to professional power and prestige' (ibid.). This indictment was, to say the least, severe, and professional actors, such as Measures (1986) reacted vehemently against his criticisms.

Actors associated with social work's 'technical-professionalist' constituency are ambiguously and contradictorily located in terms of their relationship to the other major social work constituencies identified in the preceding paragraphs. As briefly noted in chapter two, technical-professional actors argue for a type of training that logically requires an occupational in-service training (or 'apprenticeship') model based upon on-the-job training: contradictorily, technical-professionalists are also adamant that training should be in the form of a 'professional' model based in academic institutions, particularly in universities (Davies, 1981c). Like social work employers, technical-professionalists regard academic-professional social work education in the higher education sector as chronically overly intellectual ('too theoretical') and, at least until recently, as overly politicized ('too radical') in terms of its effects upon students' attitudes.

In the major policy struggles over 'professional' social work training that developed after the mid 1970's, the role of the Central Council for Education and Training In Social Work (CCETSW) has been highly significant. The CCETSW, in its role as the national training council with statutory responsibility for validating professional social work training courses, has a relatively 'central' strategic role in social work's actor-network. In chapter seven it will be observed that in the 1980's the CCETSW intervened in social work's policy struggles through the use of 'hard' interventionist, regulative strategies that signalled the CCETSW had visibly 'taken sides' with social work employers and with technical-professional actors. In the 1970's, however, 'power' was roughly equally distributed among the competitive actors involved in these struggles. To have visible sided with actors from any one of social work's major constituencies would have offended actors from other constituencies and thereby have created additional strategic problems for the CCETSW. At that time, the CCETSW portrayed itself as taking a 'neutral' role; its conflict-resolution strategy in the late 1970's rested mainly upon attempts to secure a consensus, or at least, a 'compromise' among the various conflicting parties. This will be returned to shortly.

The assumptions and constructs associated with the technical-professionalist constituency are made explicit in the writings of Martin Davies. Davies departs from the perspectives held by most of the leading 'academic-professional' social work writers. Davies (1985) argues that academic social sciences should have no significant role in social work training or practice (ibid., p.220). Davies (1981a) endorses '... the kind of knowledge of social affairs and the psychology of man that any alert reader of, say, The Guardian or New Society might be expected to have ... to be frank, such knowledge can be learned relatively quickly and painlessly ...' (ibid., p.196). Sociology, in particular, is criticized (Davies, 1982). Davies (1981b) argues that there are grounds for removing sociology from the social work 'professional' training curriculum (ibid., p.19). Sociology is described as a radical left-wing discipline that might '... destroy social work ...' (Davies, 1981a, p.196). Sociology together with disciplines such as social policy and political science have a 'debilitating' impact upon students, and sociologists, in particular, are '... nagging critics of the establishment' (Davies, 1981b, p.20). In Davies's (1981a) text, The Essential Social Worker the following named disciplines, using Davies's own descriptive titles, are either rejected or explicitly marginalized in his model of 'practical' social work training: sociology, psychoanalysis, psychology and learning theory, politics, and social administration. The detailed references to Davies's observations on each of these disciplines are provided in Sibeon (1982, p.132). In Davies's (1981a) view, social work practice requires practical skills, a working knowledge of relevant law and of clients welfare rights, a practical knowledge of the local social environment, and 'good sense, strength of personality, intelligence, flexibility and experience of human relations in general ...' (ibid., pp.196-7).

The strategic role of social work education in the professional socialization of students is regarded as crucial by technical-professionalist actors. In the late 1970's and early 1980's there existed in social work a socially constructed image of '... the evil and corrupting influence of ... sociology lecturers who have laid political hands on the naive enthusiasm ... of social work students in order to lead them away from the path of true professional knowledge' (Clarke, 1979, p.126). In the 1970's and early 1980's social work students were regarded by technical-professional actors as naive novitiates who had gullibly internalized the teachings of radical social science lecturers. The question of whether social work students at that time were actually as 'radical' as technical-professionalists feared is less significant than the fact that this image of 'naive' but professionally 'dangerous' intellectualized student radicalism existed. On the basis of this socially-constructed image of pernicious and widespread radicalism, technical-professionalists sought to 'silence' students' ostensibly radically dissenting voices: students, that is to say, were strategically excluded from the category of actors regarded as having legitimate 'defining rights' in specifying the nature and purposes of 'professional' social work practice and hence of social work training. Davies (1981b) asserted that academic social sciences '... sow irreversible seeds of self-doubt ... in students' (ibid., p.19, emphasis added). Quite apart from the politically radicalizing effects of exposure to social science, some students were said to anyway have professionally 'bad' attitudes. Davies (1981a) argued that many students and newly qualified social workers held professionally-inappropriate radical perspectives, this professionally threatening outcome being '... a function of the personal attitudes of some students and the impact on them of critical literature emanating from the social and political sciences' (ibid., p.195, emphases added). This combination of students' wrong-headed personal attitudes and of exposure to the ideas of radical social science academics, had led to '... the production of practitioners who are in some senses alienated from and hostile to the system in which they are likely to be employed' (ibid.). In this analysis, social work education was criticized as a radicalizing experience that failed to properly socialize students into an acceptance of 'professional' social work's political mores. Davies (1981b) warned against dangers that stem from exposing students to '... critical perspectives' (ibid.. p.19) and he stated that (ibid., emphases added).

> this approach ... sees social work education as an extension of liberal education with the aim of producing critical. questioning, even sceptical graduates ... (and) ... I no longer consider it to be appropriate .... Social work courses are training students for a specific role, usually in the public sector ... those who fund students on the courses have a right to anticipate the end product.

That is, the problem, as Davies saw it, was that students and newly-qualified practitioners were not properly socialized professional 'end-products'. Instead they were left-wing critics who rejected what they mistakenly and subversively claimed was the political conservatism of 'professional' social work and its hierarchical bureau-professional control and 'repression' of clients. From this and Davies's various other statements referred to earlier it is evident that, writing in the early 1980's in the aftermath of the heated political controversies generated during the 'traditional versus radical' debates of the 1970's, Davies's strategic formulation of the means assessed by him as necessary for 'enrolling' (Callon, 1986) social work materials (ideas, policies, practices, etc.) in the direction of technical-professionalism, rested upon a concept of professional socialization based on the strategy of excluding students' 'critical', 'questioning' attitudes and radicalized opinions from the professional activity of 'defining' the nature and purposes of professional social work practice and, thus, of training.

By the end of the decade, Davies (1989) had totally abandoned his earlier critical dismissals of social work students' 'radical' and professionally 'bad' attitudes and opinions. In a seemingly remarkable reversal of virtually all of his earlier critical condemnations of students' attitudes, Davies (1989) stated that the time had come to actively seek (not reject!) social work students' opinions through the use of consultative opinion-survey methods, with a view to students' expressed opinions, attitudes, and political preferences being incorporated into the design of social work training curricula! The earlier fear about students as inadequately professionally-socialized 'end-products' had completely vanished. By this time, Davies (1989) instead of criticizing students' ('radical') attitudes, was arguing for 'organized consumer feedback' (ibid., p.5). In a wholesale reversal of his earlier explicit rejections of the attitudes held by ostensibly 'radical', dissenting left-wing students, he had moved to the diametrically opposed view that in social work training it had now become essential to take steps to ensure that '... the development of vocationally-oriented higher education ... gives ... (students) ... an unaccustomed say in the creation of the product they are consuming' (ibid., emphases added). Within the space of a few years, social work students had been re-habilitated and given new 'defining rights': the previously conferred role of irresponsibly and naively radical 'end-product' was cast aside in favour of a newly conferred role, that of a respectable and responsible 'consumer' of a service. This strategic reformulation, in effect a tactical U-turn, was not unique to Davies and it had by the late 1980's become a strategy also employed by various other actors in their attempts to 'de-radicalize' social work education while at the same time making training more 'practical'. The marginalization of academic social science components of the curriculum would, it was felt, achieve both these objectives simultaneously. By the late 1980's, the CCETSW, in abandoning its earlier presentational role as a neutral arbiter of policy conflicts within social work's actor-network, had moved visibly towards the perspectives of social work employers and of those who advocated technical-professionalist perspectives. Like Davies, the CCETSW had noticed that during the 1980's a shift in student opinion had occurred. Technical-professional actors perceived that the spectre of intellectualized left-wing student radicalism no longer existed in social work, and that the possibility of enrolling students in the cause of technical-professionalism had become a new strategic option. By the end of the decade, many students were demanding very practical forms of training (Twelve Students, 1989). Some academic social work educators reacted against the rise of political conservatism (Jones, 1989, pp.207-8) and anti-intellectualism (Jordan, 1988, p.33) among social work students. For technical-professional actors, however, these contingent shifts in students' attitudes were strategically welcome and strengthened their hand in moving towards the perspectives of employers, who by this time had become a powerful political lobby within social work (see chapter seven). The CCETSW (1987a) stated that 'Consumer research studies by Shaw and Walton, Martin Davies, and Faiers have emphatically concluded that supervised practice on placements is the most useful part of CQSW courses' (ibid., p.6). This recent and unprecedented move on the part of the CCETSW towards the importance of consulting students is now part of the regulations governing the new employer-led Diploma In Social Work (Dip.SW) courses that in the 1990's will replace the existing system of training. Under the new regulations, courses will not be validated by the CCETSW unless evidence is provided of course's responsiveness to '... feedback from students about what they felt and thought about the programme' (CCETSW, 1989a, p.5). This recent emphasis upon student consultation would not have fitted-the-bill at the time when students were '... critical, questioning, even sceptical ...' (Davies, 1981b, p.19, emphasis added). However, as noted earlier in the chapter, the conditions-of-action are not 'static' in social work. Less than a decade after his earlier condemnations of student radicalism and of radical academics, Davies (1989) outlined data from a research programme directed by him, and observed 'The main finding so far as the curriculum is concerned is that most courses ... (concentrate) ... much of their time on the mainstream social sciences of psychology, sociology, and social policy; it was this emphasis that drew some of the sharpest criticisms from students who ... (wanted a) ... practical emphasis ...' (ibid., p.12). It is worth observing that this recent emphasis towards a consumer-led approach makes no provision for including the voices of social work clients as service-users. Davies (1989) states that, compared with students, there are doubts about the capacities of clients to express helpful judgements about the nature and purpose of the training of those who provide services to them (ibid., p.4). Yet clients are the 'ultimate customers'! The nature and purpose of training, and the whole edifice of large scale bureau-professional social work, is supposed to be about them! If a consumer-orientation is desirable and if clients are said to be the prime beneficiaries of 'professional' social work training for 'professional' practice, there are compelling arguments in favour of continuously monitoring the opinions of the clients of social work students (and of qualified social workers) and for responsiveness to clients' assessments of the relevance of social work training-and-practice to their needs as clients. The debate about consumer-orientations will undoubtedly escalate in the 1990's (Bamford, 1990, p.xiv). However, the idea of client-consultation in social work training (and in the design of service-delivery generally) will almost certainly be strongly resisted by professional(izing) social work actors, for reasons that will be examined in chapters five and six.

Another empirical illustration of the strategic roles of social work actors concerns the strategy adopted by the CCETSW in the late 1970's, in its efforts to secure some 'reconciliation' of the conflicting interests and perspectives formulated by competitive social work actors. Heraud (1981) uses the term 'segments' in preference to 'constituencies' and he observes that polarized viewpoints are sometimes 'managed' through the conflict-resolution tactic of even-handedly presenting the viewpoints of all the main actors involved in conflict, in a way that '... appeals ... to a variety of interests and a variety of segmental affiliations' (ibid., p.50). In an actor-network of competitive actors, this strategy may be employed by any of the actors involved, and in this sense 'The appeal to a variety of segmental interests from members of a particular segment is a form of manoeuvre so far given insufficient recognition in the study of segmental behaviour' (ibid.). In what follows, it is proposed to examine the CCETSW's use of this strategy in the late 1970's. In terms of its role as a social actor it was observed earlier that the CCETSW, in respect of social work training and the 'fit' of training to social work organization and practice and to professional(izing) aspirations, has a relatively 'central' strategic role within social work's actor-network.

The CCETSW published a discussion document (Wright, 1977) titled Expectations of the Teaching of Social Work on Courses Leading to the CQSW: Consultative Document 3. For convenience, this will be referred to as 'CD3'. Although written in a personal capacity by Wright, the Assistant Director of the CCETSW, it may reasonably be inferred from remarks in the preface (ibid., pp.1-3) by Young, then Director of the CCETSW, that the document mirrored concerns felt by employers, and also within the CCETSW itself, about the 'theoretical' and also supposedly 'radical' nature of academic-professional social work's social science model of education which had expanded in the higher education sector following implementation of the Seebohm Report's (1968) recommendation for a 'professionalized' social work service.

Although Wright (1977) attempted to 'appeal' even-handedly to a variety of conflicting social work interests, the document (CD3) is an indication that, even at that time, the CCETSW was beginning to move towards the perspectives of employers and of technical-professionalist social work actors. In endorsing the professionally unifying objectives and interests formulated by the professionalizing lobby, CD3 referred to '... professional ... values' (Wright, 1977, p.4, emphasis added) and argued '... being a member of a profession implies shared values' (ibid., p.10, emphases added). However, Wright's support for the social science model of professional development advocated by professionalizing actors and by academic-professionals, was qualified by his simultaneous endorsement of technical-professionalist values. In a way that is similar to Davies's (1981b, p.19) concern about students' as 'end-products', Wright commented '... the purpose of CQSW courses is to produce practitioners with ... a ... system ... of shared professional values' (Wright, 1977, p.10, emphasis added). This was amplified in the statement that (ibid., p.6)

> Social work education is not ... an end in itself. There is some indication at present that the differences of viewpoint are currently immobilizing; for example, it is not uncommon to hear people who might be expected to know better, because they teach and practice it, to say "Social Work? - What is it?" It is the writers view that this has become a trendy negative stance and it is about time it stopped.

This is similar to Davies's (1981b) rejection of critical discourses that '... sow irreversible seeds of self-doubt ... in students' (ibid., p.19). Wright (1977) suggested that 'In the not very distant past sociology had to disentangle itself from being confused with social work - the reverse process may now be necessary' (ibid., p.7, emphasis added). This is similar to Davies's (1981b) remarks about '... the removal of sociology from the curriculum' (ibid., p.19). Davies, however, went considerably further than Wright in rejecting or marginalizing the role of academic social science disciplines in social work training. The de-professionalizing implications of Davies's occupational-training model are seemingly recognized by Davies (1981c) himself who argued '... any suggestion that social work education should be shifted out of the universities should be opposed' (ibid., p.283). Wright (1977), and by implication the CCETSW, seem in the late 1970's and early 1980's to have been more aware than Davies that the only 'rational' educational policy justification for retaining social work training in higher education academic institutions is to argue that the academic social science taught in those institutions is essential to professional practice and therefore an essential ingredient of 'professional' education. Otherwise, there is no legitimate justification for basing social work training in higher education. To be seen to overbalance social work's perennial 'theory-practice' problematic almost entirely in favour of non-academic 'practice' would self-defeat professional(izing) aspirations: likewise, to 'de-radicalize' social work training through the strategy of removing or marginalizing the politically corrupting social science disciplines would, from a professionalizing standpoint, be a classic case of scoring an own-goal. Social sciences may at times be 'troublesome': but to abandon them implies also having to abandon the academic sites in which they are taught. Moreover, the CCETSW was aware that to go down this deprofessionalizing vocational-occupational road would gravely offend then still powerful professionalizing and academic-professional actors. Unlike Davies, Wright(1977) in CD3 stated he (and by implication the CCETSW) did not wish to marginalize disciplines '... like psychology, social policy ... sociology, philosophy, political processes and ... related ... disciplines' (ibid., p.25). However, Wright's and the CCETSW's strategy of appealing simultaneously to a variety of conflicting interests, produces inevitable contradictions. For example, Wright (1977) does not specify how or why these disciplines are 'essential' in professional social work practice and education. Some of the listed disciplines (sociology, social policy, politics, and philosophy) are precisely those implicated by Wright (1977) in an earlier part of the document that referred to 'trendy' (ibid., p.6) intellectualized social science discourses that raised 'immobilizing' (ibid.) questions amongst those who 'should know better' (ibid.). And why sociology, in particular, should remain in the professionally 'necessary' list of disciplines is even more of a puzzle: earlier in CD3, Wright (1977) had argued social work may need to 'disentangle' (ibid., p.7) itself from sociology.

It is the document's strategic objective of 'appealing' simultaneously to a variety of conflicting interests that produced inconsistent and ultimately incoherent presentational arguments. To exclude or marginalize academic social science runs counter to professionalizing and academic-professional interests and objectives. On the other hand, to include these disciplines as having any significant role in training and in practice runs counter to the perspectives of employers (a point that will be returned to shortly) and counter to the technical-professionalist arguments developed by Mundy (1972), Wilson (1974), and later by Davies (1981a) and others. Wright's (1977) tactical 'solution' to this problem of how to simultaneously face in different directions consisted of an attempt to re-define the 'problems' of radicalism in professional social work education as arising not in ('radical')academic disciplines as such but in individual people! Following the listing in CD3 of the 'approved' academic social science disciplines deemed essential as a means of legitimating the argument that social work is a 'profession' based on academic disciplinary knowledge, it is stated that these disciplines, however, happen to be taught by social science academics who as individuals are prone to '... use their clients (their subjects or their students) to sanction their own values ... professional development and ambitions' (Wright, 1977, p.25, emphasis added). Leaving aside this quaint social work reference to subjects and students as 'clients', it may be observed that Wright's (1977) partial endorsement of technical-professionalist perspectives involved a 'solution' that did not go to the 'extreme' and professionally self-defeating point of also endorsing technical-professionalists' arguments that academic disciplines per se should be marginalized to the point of visibly having no significant role in social work: to this extent, CD3, though far more equivocal about the role of academic knowledge than professional(izing) and academic-professional actors would have wished, was an attempt to steer a course that would not provoke outright condemnation from professional(izing) actors. However, placating professionalizing actors in its turn carried the risk of offending the interests and perspectives formulated by other, also powerful, social work actors: here, Wright (1977) turns to the task of 'appealing' to the interests and objectives formulated by social work employers.

The intensity of social work employers' condemnations of social work professionalism in the 1980's has already been referred to. Harbert (1985b) argued that clients had become of secondary importance to 'professional power and prestige' (ibid., p.15) and Jordan (1982) condemned a professional-education model which produced newly qualified agency employees who had been '... disabled by their college experiences' (ibid., p.129). In a way that seems remarkably oblivious to the intellectual incoherence that arises from rejecting perspectives endorsed elsewhere in the document, Wright defended employers' perspectives through an attack on professionalizing and academic-professional interests. Wright (1977) states '... social work courses ... are giving an increasing emphasis to broad generalist education in the social sciences and about social work at the expense of skills based learning' (ibid., p.10, emphasis added). A reason for this is that '... the whole weight of a higher educational institution will tend to support models other than that of practitioner' (ibid.. p.25, emphasis added). To say this offends the interests formulated by professionalizing and academic-professional actors by <u>raising</u> rather than 'damping-down' the professionally-disturbing question of whether social work training properly 'belongs' in academic institutions in the higher education sector. In some other ways Wright (1977), in endorsing employers' views, came dangerously close to an outright rejection of professionalizing objectives, interests, and aspirations: for example, he wrote (ibid., p.10, emphases added)

> ... the growth in claims of professional <u>status</u> has made employers increasingly suspicious that these are <u>more associated with occupational ambition for advancement than with</u> ... <u>skills</u> ... <u>social work has to face up to this scepticism</u> ... (about) ... <u>claims to professional status</u> ...

Statements of this kind are contradictory when compared with statements in other sections of CD3 that refer supportively to other social work constituencies. The CCETSW's conflict-resolution strategy of appealing simultaneously to a variety of conflicting interests produced, in the various ways referred to earlier, a patently contradictory strategy. The CCETSW's strategy in the late 1970's is noted in CD3 itself in a brief but revealing statement that 'Some ... would ... argue the universities are inappropriate places for ... (social work training) .... To some extent the council has to walk a tightrope ... <u>compromising to preclude deadlock in sensitive areas</u>' (Wright, 1977, p.9, emphasis added). The CCETSW did not succeed in breaking the 'deadlock' referred to by Wright: it moved in the 1980's to a much more interventive strategy which, however, may in the future unintendedly produce, in the ways described in chapter seven, the separation between higher eduction and social work training that the CCETSW has struggled to avoid for more than a decade.

There is nothing structurally predetermined about any of the processes described in the preceding pages. Actors' forms of thought and their modes of assessing situations and acting on the basis of their assessments, are framed contingently and strategically in terms of the means of action available to actors (Hindess, 1982, p.507) and in terms of the, usually, shifting conditions-of-action within which actors operate. For example, the CCETSW's strategy (Wright, 1977) in the late 1970's, despite its internal contradictions, rested on the CCETSW's assessment of power configurations within social work's actor-network as it then existed: a decade later, largely through the operation of a number of unintended consequences, this power configuration had shifted and the CCETSW's assessment of this shift led it to develop new strategies. Technical-professionalist actors also responded to 'new' conditions-of-action that emerged in the 1980 s. In the example discussed earlier, the shift in social work students' political attitudes that took place in the 1980's was 'read' by some actors in ways that created new strategic options that involved a virtual 'reversal' of earlier strategies (Davies, 1981a; Davies, 1989; CCETSW, 1987a, p.6; CCETSW, 1989a. p.5). Variations in and even reversals of actors' former strategies are related to changes in the conditions-of-action. As Clegg (1989) puts it '... strategically minded opponents will ... (wait) ... until they have enticed the match into a timing, duration, and a terrain of their own choosing' (ibid., p.221). A regular, ongoing problem, however, centres on the difficulty of strategically stabilizing for long periods the terrain upon which actors operate: this is invariably a problematic matter (ibid., p.212). For instance, momentous shifts in political culture have happened during the last twenty years of British politics. So far as students' and practitioners' politics is concerned there is no automatic guarantee that currently formulated political views will remain constant in the long term. There are also other, more immediate problems facing technical-professionalist actors and also professionalizing actors in general. Currently, professional social work is faced by the increased 'external' visibility of the 'credibility-gap' referred to in chapter two. Disputes over social work education and training have, intentionally or not, amplified and publicized this problem of 'academic-professional' credibility. If social work practice, and therefore training, is seen (by the governing bodies of academic institutions, politicians, client groups, and by governments in their prioritization of resources) as an activity based not on academic social science knowledge but on cultural forms of commonsense and 'practice-wisdoms' (Carew, 1979), the argument for a social work location in higher education is in danger of evaporating into thin air. It is likely that in the 1990's professional(izing) actors will wish to strategically address this problem. One such strategy, discussed in chapter seven, may involve use of the concept theory-practice 'integration' as a way of suggesting that social science knowledge 'is' widely deployed in social work training, but in a 'hidden' (or 'integrated') way. It is also possible that in the 1990's there will be a welter of studies commissioned by professionalizing actors in the hope that these will refute existing empirical studies which reveal that practitioners do not employ formal academic disciplinary knowledge in their practice (see chapter four). However, for reasons that will be examined in chapter seven, there are some doubts as to whether in the 1990's social work will be able to strategically stabilize a set of conditions that might enable it to achieve, after almost a century of struggle towards this end, a socially recognized 'professional' status.

4 Sociology of social work knowledge

In the earlier chapters various references were made to problems arising from conflicting definitions of the structure and forms of social work knowledge. In this chapter attention will be focussed on processes involved in the dissemination of social work knowledge across social space and through time. In the third chapter it was observed that reified, reductionist theories of social structure presume that the form and content of materials, and the uses to which these are put by social work actors, are in some direct or indirect sense 'necessary effects' of the social totality or reflections of so-called 'objective' or 'real' interests. Abandonment of these mystical conceptions of social structure and of social action means that in the sociology of social work attention should be given to empirical investigation of actors' roles and techniques in the construction and dissemination of social work materials across sites through space and time. An anti-reductionist orientation of this kind is beginning to emerge in the sociology of knowledge, where there are signs of a '... shift of emphasis away from macro-level explanation of the relation between social structure and belief ... and towards a middle-range analysis' (Scott, 1988, p.52). This shift of emphasis is formulated on an understanding that materials do not appear 'out of the blue' as a representation of the social totality: in the production, reproduction, or change of materials, the role(s) of actors is crucial.

A core theoretical and also empirical concern in the following pages centres on the distinction between a sociology-of-transmission, and a sociology-of-translation (Callon, 1986, p.196) or of 'transformation'. This distinction refers to continuities ('transmissions') in the dissemination of some particular materials that may travel far across (social work) sites through space and time and with very little if any alteration in the form and content of the material: and to

discontinuities ('transformations') in the sense that some materials may
be radically transformed, or added-to, or even 'dropped' (Latour, 1986,
p.263) by actors during the course of the materials' travel through
space-time. Innovations in social work knowledge, laws, practice
techniques, and organizational conventions, are, in principle, always
empirically possible: but this does not necessarily mean that new
materials are regularly invented or that existing materials are
continuously transformed. For reasons implicit in the historical
overview of social work provided in chapter two, non-reductionist
empirical analysis of the structure and form of materials in an academic
community or profession viewed across large stretches of time-space,
requires that systematic attention be given to the search for both
continuities ('transmissions') and discontinuities ('transformations')
in the spatial and temporal dissemination of materials. As already
observed, the role of <u>actors</u> in these processes is crucial: societies
and other taxonomic collectivities are not actors and such
collectivities do not in themselves have any causal role in the
production, reproduction, or change of social work materials.

The postulate that material (ideas, policies, practices, etc.) may be
'translated' in the sense of its being transformed or modified by
spatially and temporally dispersed actors during the course of its
travel, is developed by Latour (1986). Latour argues that in almost all
circumstances materials are endlessly transformed by successive actors
in actor-chains: in Latour's sense, it would be erroneous to refer to
'it' (or 'the' material) because that which is being continuously re-
formulated is never for long the 'same' material (Sibeon, 1991; 1989a,
pp.11-12). Latour (1986) rejects an ostensive definition of society and
culture (and hence of materials) in favour of a performative definition.
Latour's thesis, as summarized by Law (1986b) is that '... society
should not be seen as the referent of an ostensive definition, but
rather seen as being <u>performed</u> through the various efforts to define it'
(ibid., p.18). Latour (1986) argues that continuities (transmissions)
are not typical: although 'faithful transmission' (ibid., p.267) can
occur, this is empirically rare (ibid.). Latour (1986) observes '...
the spread in space and time of anything ... is in the hands of people
... (who) ... may act in different ways ... letting the ... (material)
... drop, or modifying it, or deflecting it, or betraying it, or adding
to it, or appropriating it' (ibid., p.267). On this view,
'transmission' is extremely rare and if it occurs it requires special
explanation (ibid., p.268). A far more usual occurrence, according to
Latour, is for materials to exist in a constant state of flux and change
(ibid., pp.266-69). In Latour's postulate, material (ideas, knowledge,
practice-conventions, etc.) passes along actor-chains and the various
actors involved may each have different interests, objectives,
priorities, etc., and choose to (and sometimes be able to) re-shape the
material, or add to it, or detract from it, or ignore it, rather than
simply 'enact' it and thereby reproduce it ('pass it on') spatially and
temporally in an unaltered form.

Whether, in the sense just referred to, a sociology-of-transmission <u>or</u>
a sociology-of-transformation ('translation') is the more appropriate
form of analysis, is not a question that can be resolved on any <u>a priori</u>
theoretical grounds. Awareness of the conceptual issues raised by the
distinction is a crucial form of theoretical sensitization that has a
role in informing the design of non-reductionist empirical studies; but
the question of whether, in any particular instances, continuities <u>or</u>
discontinuities are observable in the spatial and temporal 'travel' of
particular social work materials is always an empirical question for

investigation, not something that can be theoretically predetermined in advance of empirical inquiry (Lidz, 1981). Very often, the 'same' material exhibits both continuities (transmissions) and discontinuities (translations or transformations). An example is social work's 'theory-practice' problematic as a particular material. As shown in chapter two, there are some striking apparent similarities and continuities in the space-time dissemination and reproduction of this problematic across a large number of social work education and practice sites since the time of the Charity Organization Society (Jones, 1976). There are also, however, some discontinuities in the reproduction of this problematic: for instance, the theory-practice problematic in modern social work is infused and contextualized by psychotherapeutic concepts (Austin, 1950) which did not exist in social work at the time when the COS's professional(izing) leadership first constructed and then unsuccessfully struggled to 'resolve' social work's perennial theory-practice problematic (Loch, 1877, 1906; Bosanquet, 1900, 1914, pp.404-5).

Scientific knowledge and social work knowledge

The sociology of social work knowledge, at least with regard to the study of material dissemination processes, has much to gain from the sociology of science. This is for two reasons. Firstly, considerably more theoretical and empirical progress has been made in the sociology of science in the study of these processes, this having relevance for sociological investigation of social work knowledge and its dissemination. Secondly, and to say this is not, of course, the same as suggesting that social work knowledge ought to be 'like' scientific knowledge (!), these two knowledge forms are in various respects very unalike and comparing and contrasting them is a useful way of increasing understanding of social work knowledge and its dissemination. In particular, social work knowledge is considerably more indeterminate than scientific knowledge: the latter has a far 'harder' epistemological knowledge-mandate (Halliday, 1985, p.422) when compared with the indeterminacies that characterise the normative foundations of social work knowledge (Halsey, 1984, p.78; Sheppard, 1984, p.28).

In the sociology of science, prior to the development of what Law (1986a) terms the 'new' sociology of science (ibid., p.6), it was observed by Barnes (1974) that 'Transmission of the current paradigm is a key problem' (ibid., p.66). Barnes (1974) rejects notions that knowledge within the scientific community is shaped entirely by a general, occupationally-wide 'logic of evaluation' (ibid., p.63). Professional scientific meanings are shaped in part by situationally-contingent aspects of practice in specific local sites (ibid.) and therefore it is necessary to sociologically investigate the specific local 'context(s) of justification' (ibid., p.59) within which particular knowledge-claims (cognitive 'materials') are produced, or else received from elsewhere and responded to. However, although Barnes (1974) points to a degree of cognitive indeterminacy and local cognitive variability, he also identifies influential, pervasive clusters of institutionalized knowledge and practice that extend across a large number of scientific sites. The transmission of 'validated' scientific knowledge, and of an accompanying socially constructed sense of epistemological certainty or near-certainty about the validity and reliability of that knowledge, is institutionalized through techniques of professional socialization (including the training of science students) which produces a relatively high degree of cognitive and procedural uniformity across the scientific community (ibid., p.66). In a later text, Barnes (1985) relates these observations to empirical investigation of the processes involved in the communication and evaluation of scientific research data (ibid., pp.40-43).

Conceptualizations of the kind referred to by Barnes (1974, 1985) point to the construction and dissemination of materials within a profession as a process whereby actors attempt to 'consign' materials in a particular way, then employ techniques and media (usually written media) for propelling their defined material across a wide range of sites in the hope that the material will become the dominant cognitive mode (or sometimes, the dominant 'paradigm') within the relevant scientific or professional community. Successfully institutionalized (or 'consigned') materials travel far across a wide range of sites, and become '... what everybody is saying' (Callon and Latour, 1981, p.298). This is well understood in the 'new' sociology of science, which is concerned with empirical investigation of the ways in which (given that no actor is 'everywhere') local actors attempt to influence the scientific community from a particular place: actors try to '... make new connections between the 'micro' - and the 'macro', thereby altering ... the social and scientific landscape' (Law, 1986a, p.6). Closely related to this, and in the sense described in chapter three, scientific actors (whether individual human actors or social actors such as academic or research institutes) are strategic beings: this is reflected in the 'new' sociology of science where attention has shifted towards empirical investigation of '... the ways in which actors create and attempt to impose versions of the natural and social worlds upon one another ...' (ibid.). It is also worth observing that the concept 'unintended consequences', which was discussed in the previous chapter, is highly relevant in the study of knowledge production and dissemination processes. Although Law (1986a) does not systematically develop the point, he mentions that Pasteur's work on the anthrax bacillus had outcomes which '... profoundly altered the relationship between French farmers, veterinarians, and scientific laboratories' (ibid., p.6). When Pasteur laboured over his laboratory bench he had not intended nor could he have foreseen the far-reaching effects that stemmed from his research. Unintended outcomes are one aspect of the unpredictability that sometimes surrounds the production, re-production, or change of cognitions and practices: unintended outcomes have real implications for actors and this is one reason why knowledge-dissemination across an academic or professional community is often a highly contingent, variable, and complex process.

Even in science, there are countless situations and periods where some scientific ideas are transformed during the process of their communication across scientific sites (Fleck, 1979; Jacobs, 1987, p.269). Nevertheless, much scientific knowledge is institutionalized and relatively unproblematically circulated across the scientific community. Barnes (1985) in a description that contrasts sharply with most accounts of social work knowledge and its dissemination, observes that in the scientific community (ibid., p.63, emphases added)

New knowledge claims are always assessed in ways which rely heavily upon existing, accepted knowledge. And this existing accepted knowledge is not the personal knowledge of the individual, distilled from his or her individual experience. It is the inherited and shared knowledge of the ... scientific community. Individuals typically acquire this knowledge from teacher or texts, much of it in the course of their training, and they tend to trust it and take its validity for granted. Indeed, <u>if they were to obtain results at</u> <u>variance with the scientific laws, it would probably be the results</u> <u>that they rejected</u>.

In this statement, Barnes notes that scientific knowledge is not 'distilled ... from individual experience '. In contrast, social work knowledge that <u>is</u> distilled from individual experience is generally venerated by social workers and by some social work teachers. Such knowledge is often regarded (for epistemological reasons that are rarely made explicit in social work discourse) as superior to other ways of 'knowing' the social world (Smith, 1971; Shaw, 1975; Timms and Timms, 1977, p.119). Hearn (1982b) wryly comments that '... when one examines the meanings or possible meanings of theory and practice in social work, one can never be quite sure whether asking the meaning of "x" or "y" may begin an infinite regress to solipsism' (ibid., p.98). Social workers' scepticism towards the nomothetic generalizations contained in academic social sciences. and contained in empirical research data on personal and social problems, is fairly well documented. Shaw (1975) observes 'Adhering strongly to a belief in the uniqueness of the individual ... (social workers) ... are reluctant to entertain generalizations .. (these are) ... inferior to the warmth and spontaneity of the social worker's relationship with his client' (ibid., p.151). This cognitive-practico gestalt is almost wholly at variance with that of science. and that of social science. Irvine's (1969) social work objection against academic social science knowledge is that '... science deals splendidly with all that can be ... measured ... but this involves excluding ... the intangible, the imponderable' (Irvine, 1969, quoted in Shaw, 1975, p.152). Irvine seems unaware that the 'imponderables' as she defines them are the <u>product</u> of particular psychotherapeutically-derived social work discourses. In another and different sense, social work's 'imponderables' are associated with protracted debates and disagreements concerning the questions of what social work knowledge 'does' or 'should' consist of. No agreement exists as to whether the cognitive foundations of social work should be academic social sciences (Hardiker, 1981; Stevenson, 1981) or whether these are largely irrelevant or in some ways destructive for social work (Davies, 1981a, 1981b, 1981c). Moreover, those who reject or marginalize the role of social science do not themselves agree on what other forms of knowledge <u>are</u> appropriate for social work. Suggestions have included cultural commonsense and extrapolations from 'life-experience' (Pratt and Grimshaw, 1985); the attitudes, personalities, and personal values of counsellors (Traux and Carkuff, 1967; Garfield and Bergin, 1987); insights acquired from reading poetry, plays, and novels (Morris, 1975; Irvine, 1975; Valk, 1983); forms of understanding derived from direct personal experience of 'oppression' (White, 1972; Priestly, 1975), and 'practice-wisdoms' acquired directly from the practical experience of doing social work (Carew, 1979). This prescriptive diversity and disagreement is, as noted in chapter two, a key factor in social work's failure to gain social recognition as a 'profession'. And of course.there is no possibility of appropriating the whole of the compendium just referred to: to claim that 'everything' is 'social work' knowledge would be puerile.

The politics of social work compound these cognitive indeterminacies. In analytical descriptions of social work politics, significant questions are raised by, for example, each of the different classificatory frameworks offered by Philp (1979), Pritchard and Taylor (1978), George and Wilding (1985), Whittington and Holland (1985), Webb

(1981b), Martin (1981, p.185), Heraud (1981, p.41), and Hardiker (1981, pp.89-99). These writers employ forms of analysis not restricted to the tenets of social work's 'internal' professional discourses, and each in their own way raise analytic questions which illuminate some aspect of social work politics. In contrast, the relationship of political and philosophical welfare values to theories, concepts, and empirical data, is a relationship that is frequently obscured and remarkably simplistically formulated in some professional social work discourses (Timms, 1983). As Hearn (1982b) puts it, 'In social work, theory, concepts and values have become mixed with each other, never to emerge unscathed' (ibid., p.100). A leading professional social work academic, Bartlett (1970) argued not that some accommodation of theory and values is necessary, but that empirical verification of the former should be in terms of the latter! Bartlett (1970) suggested 'The profession needs to examine potentially useful clusters of theory ... but this theory should be examined and tested within the profession's own value-knowledge frame of reference' (ibid., pp.135-6, emphasis added). This remarkably simplistic conflation of epistemological and ontological issues in the construction, evaluation, and application of different forms of knowledge, is in any case pragmatically nullified by the absence of an unambiguous, consensual professional 'value-knowledge frame of reference' as a basis for deciding which knowledge should count as empirically valid. Relatively little is known empirically about how social work practitioners conceptualize these matters, although such data as do exist suggest the conflation evident in Bartlett is not something that is confined to professional leaders: for example, in Waterhouse's (1987) study '... most respondents ... failed ... to distinguish among research findings, factual information, concepts, and values' (ibid., p.13). There are, clearly, a number of research problems involved in designing empirical studies that are capable of providing adequate data on the different forms and types of social work cognitions that 'travel' across the social work community.

A significant empirical difference in the dissemination of knowledge in the scientific and social work communities centres upon professional training and its role in knowledge-dissemination. Cognitive indeterminacy in the wider social work community is both reflected in and reproduced by social work education. In the scientific community '... a reason why natural scientific knowledge is so readily accepted ... is that teachers, having themselves agreed what in their field is reliable and important, and having constructed a curriculum accordingly, generally take care to invest that curriculum with authority' (Barnes, 1985, p.70, emphasis added). This may be contrasted with the use of 'process' perspectives in social work education and practice (Harris et al., 1985). Radical versions of this perspective in feminist social work involve fusing the affective and cognitive components of personal attitudes in womens' consciousness-raising groups. This is said by feminist social work writers to have the beneficial effect for women that it '... validates their subjective feelings, giving them the status of social facts with a legitimacy of their own ...' (Dominelli and McLeod, 1989, p.33, emphases added). Linked to this is the idea that '... evidence as to the nature of social problems ... (accumulates) ... by legitimating the analytical standing of the accounts of those immediately affected' (ibid., p.32, emphases added). There are ontological, epistemological, and practical reasons for concluding that statements of this kind, like Bartlett's (1970) referred to earlier, are an impediment rather than an aid to clarity in the analysis of social problems and of what can be done about them. The immediate point to be made here, however, concerns the role of such statements in the reproduction of cognitive indeterminacy in social work. The 'process' orientation is also a feature of 'traditional' professional discourses in social work education (Greenwell and Howard, 1986). Drawing upon psychotherapeutic ideas, advocates of this approach claim emotionally-linked experiential discussions in small groups enables students and fieldworkers to '... grapple more successfully with their inner experiences of their clients' (Jones, 1982, p.151). Some social work courses give major emphasis to one or another version of the 'process' learning approach. Sargent's (1985) written pro-forma of teaching and learning ground-rules issued to social work students, states that 'We are all learners ... what I know is not adequate for ... you ... we should aim to be ... working towards the formation of a few guiding principles ... planning will be within the broad framework of the syllabus, but anyone can negotiate a change ...' (ibid., p.105, emphases added). Compare this with Barnes's (1985) description of the scientific curriculum (ibid., pp.70-71)

> Typically the curriculum is embedded in a textbook or books which set out the key components of accepted doctrine as the correct way .... Texts are expressly designed to create conviction; they usually present one interpretation only, play down any problems and uncertainties .... The main point is to assimilate the material and become competent in its use ...

What is indicated here is that the role of professional training and curricula is significant in reproducing the cognitive-practico structures of both the scientific and social work communities. The social construction of a relatively high level of epistemological certainty within the scientific community is reflected in, and in turn reproduced by, the scientific curriculum and its institutionalized mode of transmission in the relationship between teachers, texts, and those taught. In social work, the professional curriculum through its 'negotiability' associated with norms of experientialism between teacher and taught in local inter-personal co-productions of knowledge, both reflects and also reproduces the cognitive indeterminacy that pervades the wider social work community.

Oral and written forms of knowledge

Scientific knowledge, though sometimes disseminated through informal channels of communication (Knorr-Cetina, 1982; Jacobs, 1987, p.272), is for the most part disseminated through the use of written media such as textbooks, scientific journals, and research reports (Law, 1986a). This is not so in social work. The point was briefly made in chapter two that an oral culture is more significant in most social work discourses than a written academic tradition. This is partly, though not exclusively, associated with the 'process' learning and practice perspectives referred to earlier. Stevenson (1981) comments that prior to the 1970's, social work teachers '... were struggling ... without a solid body of British ... (social work) ... literature to assist them' (ibid., p.34). However, the availability of written materials does not necessarily mean that they will be read. Social work's normative commitments are, in the main, not oriented to the use of written academic materials. In chapter two, an account was given of this perennial-but-also-contemporary dimension of social work discourse

(Loch, 1877; London University Executive Committee on Social Work Education, 1903; Bosanquet, 1914; Cox, 1982; Satyamurti, 1983; Waterhouse, 1987). Carew's (1979) empirical study suggests that social work practitioners rarely draw upon formal academic knowledge derived from written texts. On-the-job experientially acquired practice-wisdoms (ibid., p.362) are regarded by practitioners as being of far greater importance than written academic or 'professional' knowledge: practice-wisdom consists of '... tried and trusted procedures that are <u>passed from practitioner to practitioner and are reinforced by</u> ... <u>case conferences, and</u> ... <u>through informal discussion</u>' (ibid., p.361, emphasis added). Although Carew, in describing 'practice-wisdoms', does not specify that he is describing an oral rather than written occupational culture it seems clear that it is the existence of the former that he is referring to.

Curnock and Hardiker's (1979) empirically based work is of particular relevance to an understanding of the pervasive 'oral' dimension in the structure and forms of social work knowledge. Curnock and Hardiker's (1979) approach is partly analytic-descriptive, and partly prescriptive in the sense of exhorting that written social work knowledge should be formulated as a basis for 'professional' practice (ibid., p.11). Curnock and Hardiker observe that '... practice theories ... remain in social worker's heads and daily activities, rather than <u>finding their way into the literature</u>' (ibid., p.10, emphasis added). In passing, its worth noting that <u>if</u> this were to happen, Carew's (1979) and others' research suggest it is experiential practice-wisdoms largely untouched by formal academic knowledge that would 'find their way into the literature'. Curnock and Hardiker (1979) note that social science knowledge and social work knowledge differs in the sense that (ibid., p.11)

> ... we can read and learn about social science theories because they are written down and codified, but we cannot understand and develop practice theories if we have to rely on picking them up as we go about our social work practice since they are not written down. Such haphazard and implicit learning is bound to be problematical.

Social work practitioners' knowledge is tacit rather than explicit and '... much of this knowledge remains implicit in social work practice because it is rarely written down' (Curnock and Hardiker, 1979, p.159). An implication of this for the dissemination of knowledge is that '... each generation of social workers has to work out many of its own practice rules for itself' (ibid., p.161). In other words, the possibility of professional cognitive continuity is, in Curnock and Hardiker's (1979) view, jeopardized by an oral culture; they write '... of ... importance for the profession is the fact that accumulated wisdom has not been sufficiently formulated into concepts and generalizations so that it can be fully shared and passed to future generations' (ibid., p.7). Once again, like Carew's (1979) and numerous others', this account of social work knowledge, and by implication, the unresolved question of <u>how</u> social work's indeterminate and locally-produced '<u>oral</u>' cognitions are institutionalized and spatially and temporally disseminated, may be contrasted with the earlier descriptions (Barnes, 1985, p.63, pp.70-71) of the institutionalized use of <u>written</u> media for the dissemination of scientific knowledge across sites of scientific education and practice.

The existence of a predominantly oral occupational culture is not something that is unique to social work: such cultures also exist in other personal-service occupations. A practising psychotherapist, Vance (1968) suggests that in American psychotherapy experientially constructed 'practice knowledge' is circulated almost entirely through a process of oral dissemination. According to Vance, this accounts for the regionalization of psychotherapeutic cognitions and practices: if practice-wisdoms are passed on to other practitioners through face-to-face contacts, cognitive 'regionalization' arises from the fact that, in a country the size of America, the greatest frequency of personal contacts is likely to occur among those psychotherapists living and working in particular geographical regions (ibid., p.117). Voicing his concerns as a practitioner, Vance (1968) is a strong advocate of an oral tradition (ibid., p.115, emphases added))

> Published materials ... are of no help in increasing ones therapeutic skills, and they are of limited value in the initial stages of training. I have no hard evidence that reading has actually harmed beginning counsellors or therapists but I believe it is so. I have certainly had the experience of being forced to uneducate trainees so they would begin to learn from their practicum experience.

Vance's (1968) argument is that '... books concerning theories of therapy are usually directed away from practitioners' needs altogether' (ibid., p.115). The literature on psychotherapy is described as '... a ... nightmare combination of the incomprehensible and inconsequential ... books and journals ... (are) ... suitable for archival use only' (ibid.). Vance (1968) observes that (ibid., p.117)

> Much of the advanced training of psychotherapists consists in sharing experiences with colleagues. I am convinced that the regionalism that exists in theory and practice is determined by the fact that the only really effective channel now available for distributing clinically useful information is word-of-mouth.

In a tilt against academics involved in the academic and therefore written cognitive tradition associated with the college or university part of student training, Vance (1968) states 'To sum up this matter ... let me say bluntly .... Those of us really concerned about training practitioners are living in a world where our skills are transmitted by an oral tradition ...' (ibid., p.115).

Vance (1968), it should be noted, describes a pattern of conflict between academic-professional educators as exponents of a written academic tradition, and field practitioners as exponents of '... an oral tradition' (ibid., p.115, emphasis added). It cannot be inferred that this configuration of 'theory-practice' conflict is a wholly accurate representation of British social work. Social work's oral culture premised on personalized constructions of idiographic 'insights' (Smith, 1971, p.21) is pervasive among practitioners (Kahn, 1954; Carew, 1979; Curnock and Hardiker, 1979) but also among some social work educators in academic institutions, particularly social work teachers who subscribe to 'process' learning perspectives (Barbour, 1985; Harris et al., 1985; Gardiner, 1987b, pp.49-50). This is a matter of degree: no social work academic eschews written professional social work literature. Nevertheless, in British social work it is precisely the existence of a deeply rooted oral culture among many social work academics that has attracted such criticisms as Deacon and Bartley's (1975) suggestion that 'process' learning involves a disavowal of intellectuality and the dissemination of a '... confused collection of social work maxims' (ibid., p.69). Of course, it could be argued that it is possible to focus both on experiential 'process' and intellectual 'content' in social work knowledge-construction exercises: in reality, things do not usually pan out this way in social work's 'process' modes. Timms and Timms (1977) observe that many practitioners and also some social work teachers regularly '... distinguish between intellectual or theoretical "knowing" and real or emotional "knowing" and give primacy to the latter' (ibid., p.119, emphasis added). Simon's (1967) criticism was that the danger in focussing on 'process' learning concepts '... (is) ... that we end up throwing the intellectual content of our course out of the window and remaining on the psychotherapeutic plane' (ibid., p.10). Unlike, then, the situation described by Vance (1968) in American psychotherapy, British social work practitioners but also some social work academic trainers in the higher education sector are 'carriers' of an oral tradition (Barbour, 1985, p.504). This is, without doubt, a significant factor in social work education's tenuous relationship to the academic community and to its 'written' academic culture (Pinker, 1989, p.91).

None of these observations should be taken as an indication that social work's unwritten ('oral') culture is necessarily homogeneous. Although very little reliable empirical data exist on this aspect of social work's cognitive structures it seems probable that a diversity of oral traditions exist within the social work community. For instance, in social work training and practice situations Marxist and feminist versions of social work's oral culture are hardly coterminous with each other or with psychodynamically-derived forms of experientialism. There is also some evidence that the unwritten 'esoteric' psychologistic insights associated with process learning in social work education, drawing on psychodynamic concepts such as 'countertransference' (Jones, 1982, p.151) and the like, may be replicated in some practitioner oral-traditions (for example Gammack, 1982; Kakabadse, 1982, p.147) but not in all. The unwritten practitioner practice-wisdoms reported by, for example, Carew (1979), are, when compared with some 'process' learning constructs in social work education, of a less 'esoteric', more down-to-earth type; this is certainly true of the bluff unwritten extrapolations from very ordinary, practical life-experiences that constituted the cognitive base for practice among the group of social workers studied by Pratt and Grimshaw (1985). Thus, social work's 'theory-practice' problematic is more than a tension between written academic knowledge 'versus' unwritten practice-wisdoms. There are probably also significant antinomies as between the different unwritten traditions and linguistic codes ('theories') that co-exist inside social work's 'oral' cognitive structure. The largely unwritten, unrecorded existence of these linguistic codes means that relatively little is empirically known about them, or about possible cognitive-practico similarities and differences among them.

Paradoxically, an oral culture relies, in part, upon written media for its legitimation. Although the cognitive contents of social work's oral materials are, by definition, not disseminated in written form, it should be observed that an oral culture is re-produced and sustained partly through the use of written media which are designed to legitimize and give credence to the culture (or 'idea') of 'orality' itself. That is, a culture of experientialism (but not its cognitive contents) is itself partly legitimated and disseminated via written media, in the form of written theories which specify that experiential, orally-constructed and orally circulated materials are superior to other (and

67

'written') ways of knowing the social world. Vance (1968), referred to
earlier, argues that the only 'genuinely' practitioner-relevant and
'useful' forms of knowledge in psychotherapy are disseminated almost
entirely by word-of-mouth. His argument is, in effect, a prescriptive
theory. Moreover, he disseminated it in writing: that's how it got to
the writer and then the readers of this book. Still, if the only useful
way of constructing and disseminating practitioner 'insights' is word-
of-mouth, why did Vance not also choose to disseminate his theory by
word-of-mouth? This is a question that will be returned to in the final
section of the chapter alongside some larger questions to do with
strategies of communication. The point to be made for the moment is
that advocates of the culture of experientialism frequently disseminate
their advocacy, and their rationale for preferring orally evolved
cognitions, in the form of written theories which prescribe that
individualized orally-constructed and orally-disseminated 'insights' are
epistemologically superior to other ways of 'knowing'. As just noted,
Vance's (1968) own account is itself an instance of this, as too are
written social work theories which argue that 'process' modes of
learning and practising have affective-cognitive superiority over other
modes (for example Gammack, 1982; Jones, 1982; Greenwell and Howard,
1982). It is entirely possible to disseminate a written theory of (the
desirability of) 'process' and 'oral' modes of knowledge-construction
without specifying what cognitive contents arise out of this mode. When
this individualized or group-based experiential model of learning is
applied in social work eduction, critics have made the point that it is
an approach that '... can ... be ... carried ... to the point where
there is virtually no written syllabus at all' (Haines, 1985, p.127).
Viewed in terms of the controversy that surrounds the 'process-versus-
content' debate in social work (Harris et al., 1985, p.145; Simon, 1967,
p.10) relative unspecificity about content is actually a prime
requirement of the 'oral-process' rubric (Gardiner, 1987b, p.50).
Indeed, Gardiner (1987b) says (or rather, writes) that 'competent'
(ibid., p.49) professional social work knowledge is so individualized
that it cannot be communicated to another: anything that can be
'communicated' is a form of knowledge that is '... relatively
inconsequential' (ibid., pp.49-50). This has an important corollary.
If the accumulated affective-cognitive 'insights' (as outcomes) of
experiential learning were to be formally codified and written down in
textbooks, the experiential mode itself - which rests on a tacit theory
of the 'continuous creation' of a never-ending stream of 'new'
experiential insights - would presumably at some future date become
redundant: in fact it would already have become so, given the length of
time this model has enjoyed a central role in social work. To specify
cognitive contents as having formal nomothetic, generalizable empirical
or theoretical properties of the kind that could be written down in
academic texts and thereby spatially disseminated in written form across
all the relevant sites of 'professional' education and practice, would
be entirely self-defeating for Vance (1968) and for social work
advocates of the 'process' model: this would make the project of
'process' redundant and, in effect, would be a movement towards the
content component in the process-versus-content controversy (Simon,
1967, p.10).
    A different dimension of the point just made is that there may be a
sense in which it is in any case difficult to effectively employ written
media for disseminating experientially constructed affective-cognitive
'insights' across the social work community. That is, it is not clear
how solipsistic cognitions could be meaningfully disseminated via

written academic or professional media. There is a technical hermeneutic difficulty (Bleicher, 1980, pp.1-5) involved in communicating in writing to others the outcomes of episodic, idiographic cognitions produced in particular sites. Reading (1985) in a contribution to the text on 'process' learning in social work education by Harris et al. (1985), describes emotional factors in learning and relates how he held hands with a student to demonstrate '... how much can be communicated through touch .... It was a powerful moment for both of us' (Reading, 1985, p.35). Parsloe (1985) in a critical review of Harris et al. (1985), which contains a number of essays along similar lines to Reading's, referred to the problem of how '... to catch and make explicit the understandings achieved in experiential learning' (Parsloe, 1985, p.159). She observed that for those who, like herself 'did not take part in the action ... if something written is achieved it is difficult to read' (ibid.). To this might be added the hermeneutic complication that Parsloe was only one reader among many: whether the material would have made the same sense to multiple readers scattered across the social work community, is another question. Written materials of whatever kind are always potentially open to multiple 'readings' and interpretations (Ricoeur, 1971). But this is a socially-constructed variable. To anticipate a point that will be returned to later with reference to Schwartz's (1973) concept of 'thematization-thresholds', it cannot be assumed that poetry, laws, mathematical equations, social science data, experiential social work 'understandings', etc., all typically have the same degree of interpretive 'leeway' or will all typically exhibit the same degree of consistency in the interpretation and 'application' of these materials by spatially and temporally dispersed actors.

Advocates of 'process' approaches in social work education and practice tend also to be, contradictorily, advocates of 'professional' social work. This anomaly is evident in Gardiner's (1981a) claim that social work is a profession and that its training system should 'therefore' be located in academic institutions of higher education: this, however, is contradicted by the assertion that professional knowledge cannot directly be '... communicated to another' (Gardiner, 1981b, pp.49-50). This is one particular contemporary expression of 'professional' social work's historically reproduced credibility-gap, referred to in chapter two. If social work does not have, first, an identifiable, distinctive formal written knowledge base, and second, if this academic-professional knowledge is not trans-situational and transmissible across the social work community, it is unclear on what basis any claims to 'professional' status might be sustained. To revert to a previous example, we simply do not know which cognitive social work 'insights' (i.e., social work knowledge) emerged from Reading's (1985) experiential group-exercise which involved holding hands with a student: it is not clear how the claim that such insights are a 'professional' form of knowledge might be socially sustained.

In the oral-process rubric it is not only the cognitive contents of locally produced idiographic, experiential knowledge that are hermeneutically sealed within the sites of their production: so also are the local actors' conceptualizations of the processes that are or might be involved in the construction of these insights and in the activity of 'theory-practice' itself i.e. their conceptualizations of what it means to 'relate' theory-to-practice. Although not all professionalizing social work actors recognize the problems for 'professional' social work just referred to, some do. For reasons that were discussed in chapter two, it may be true that a degree of cognitive indeterminacy is functional for professionalizing actors, so long as this indeterminacy does not 'exceed' what Jamous and Peloille (1970) termed the indetermination/technicality 'ratio'. However, Butrym (1976) argues that professionalism does require an accumulative, written, and visibly transmissible academic-professional knowledge base; therefore professional social workers '... (cannot) ... afford to avoid making and using generalizations ... (that are) ... accumulated ... (in social work) ...' (ibid., p.67). As noted in chapter two, and earlier in the present chapter, there are conflicting and sometimes confused views in social work as to what these generalizations might consist of, where they might come from, how and in terms of which criteria their reliability might be assessed, and how they might be assembled and related to 'professional' practice: to a large extent, therefore, Butrym's statement is more in the nature of a professionalizing aspiration than a currently realistically realizable objective. There is, though, a related issue that should not be lost from sight.Professionalizing aspirations apart, social work's oral tradition raises serious questions about the nature and effectiveness of services offered to clients. Social workers' cognitions and beliefs about people and situations '... often have consequences for their actions and ... shape the decisions they make about their clients' (Hardiker and Barker, 1981, p.1, emphasis added). It is not, therefore, a good thing that relatively little is known empirically about what these indeterminate cognitions consist of, nor how they are produced, evaluated, disseminated and in various ways 'applied' by social workers to the situations of their clients.

The existence of evidence pointing to the pervasiveness of oral traditions in social work does not necessarily mean that all social work materials are wholly idiosyncratic, variable, and 'site-specific'. For one thing, the point has already been made that legitimations of the culture of 'orality', even if not its cognitive contents, are disseminated in both oral and written forms. For another, it is probable that the cognitive contents of at least some social work meanings are disseminated orally in the ways suggested by Vance (1968) and by Carew (1979). Some practice-wisdoms undoubtedly are relatively widespread, collectivized social work constructs that are practised by a large number of social workers across a wide range of social work sites: two examples of such constructs are the 'presenting-problem' thesis (Haines, 1975, pp.39-40) and the client 'emotional ventilation' thesis (Moffett, 1972, p.85). The more general aspect of the point being made here is noted by Giddens (1988), who observes '... day to day talk and conversation, which draw upon a framework of institutionalized discourse and conventions of action, are also the basic means whereby such institutionalized forms are reproduced' (ibid., p.147). It can be said with some certainty that not all social work materials are wholly idiographic, 'site-specific', or solipsistic. Were this not the case, spatially scattered social workers would be virtually unable to speak to each other about commonly understood meanings and activities recognizable to them as something called 'social work': anyone who has attended a social work conference will know that this is not so. Whether this is complicated by a 'regionalization' of oral constructs in the way suggested by Vance (1968) with reference to American psychotherapy, is a hypothesis that merits empirical consideration in the context of British social work. For example, accounts of professional casework in most inner-city social services departments are not in all respects similar to the account in Martinez-Brawley's (1986) paper which carries the title 'Community-oriented Social Work in a Rural

and remote Hebridean patch'. Another probable empirical variation
relates to organizational functions: it cannot be assumed, for example,
that local authority professional caseworkers, community workers, and
probation officers necessarily employ the same collectivized social work
constructs.

A promising empirical conceptualization that may aid the design of
future empirical inquiry into knowledge-dissemination processes in
social work, is derived from Schwartz's (1973) concept of
'thematization-thresholds'. This was briefly mentioned earlier, when it
was noted different types of materials may typically have different
socially-constructed degrees of interpretive 'leeway'. Although
mathematics is not mono-paradigmatic (Hagstrom, 1965), the written
dissemination of mathematical and scientific materials is generally not
as interpretively 'open' as, say, poetry or novels or philosophical
theories; nor as interpretively open as the cognitively indeterminate
forms of social work knowledge referred to earlier. That is,
mathematics has a relatively 'high' thematization-threshold: many forms
of social work materials have a relatively 'low' socially constructed
thematization-threshold and are open to a wide variety of different
local interpretations in particular sites of action. An illustration of
this point with reference to the spatial and temporal dissemination of
material and its 'transmission', or alternatively its transformation
during the course of its 'travel', is the 'passing' by parliament of a
legal statute. For reasons to do with constitutional rights, legal
justice, equity and consistency of application, statutes are a form of
written material that is very tightly-defined and precisely specified,
so as to minimize interpretive 'loopholes' that might otherwise be
misinterpreted or exploited by various actors or 'publics' (Bouchier,
1977) in ways not intended by the law-makers. The originally intended
meanings of laws typically have relative mobility and durability. That
is, a law may travel across sites without much transformation (Latour,
1986) of its originally intended meaning or of its originally specified
contexts-of-application. However, this cannot be empirically known
without investigation of the spatial 'passage' of a law from parliament
to other contexts (including, say, public bureaucracies within which the
law is applied to specific cases) and in this sense the question of
'what happens' to the law during its circulation across sites, and the
uses to which it is put within particular sites, are significant
empirical questions (Lidz, 1981). None the less, for the reasons just
referred to, it seems reasonably safe to assume that laws typically have
higher thematization-thresholds than many other types of materials that
circulate within professional or academic communities.

Various types of materials circulate across local sites in social
work, and it may reasonably be hypothesized that different types of
social work materials have different socially constructed thematization-
thresholds. That is, some materials may exhibit typically higher, or
lower, levels of inter-situational consistency of interpretation and
application than other materials. Statutory social work tasks which,
among other things, involve the practical application of law, are a case
in point. The degree of local administrative or professional 'leeway'
in statutory tasks such as complying with legal procedures in the
process of compulsorily taking a child into local authority care, may be
less than in other types of social work such as 'non-statutory'
psychotherapeutic counselling or family therapy. Sometimes, social
workers draw upon very basic, practical medical information relevant to
the situation of, say, the diet followed by elderly clients; or draw
upon a technical knowledge of the regulations governing clients'

71

entitlements to financial welfare benefits. Technical and 'non-esoteric' knowledge of these kinds, in terms of its consistent application by social workers scattered across a large number of different sites, may have a typically higher socially constructed thematization-threshold than the material deployed in psychotherapeutically oriented casework or groupwork practice. A related point is Hardiker's (1981) suggestion that social work theories exhibit far higher levels of variability and diversity than social work practices, the latter exhibiting greater uniformity: for example, Hardiker's data on probation officers' recommendations to courts concerning offenders, suggest that '... there in fact appeared to be more similarities than differences in the recommendations of probation officers holding different theoretical positions' (ibid., p.86, emphasis added). It is probable that in situations where they have choice in the matter, social workers take care to select different forms of knowledge with different thematization-thresholds for particular and different social work purposes. For example, the 'process' orientation in social work education works upon highly indeterminate personalized experiences and psycho-dynamic insights that have a low thematization-threshold: experiential psychotherapeutic learning models cannot properly 'work' if the group-dynamic 'experience' is focussed entirely on, say, a discussion of the dietary needs of elderly clients or the technical meaning of a social security regulation governing clients' entitlements to financial benefits. For the reasons just indicated, there are grounds for suggesting that in the sociology of social work knowledge, future attention should be given to the empirical investigation of a variety of different types of social work materials that may each have different socially constructed levels of transformability as they circulate across social work sites through space-time and are practically applied within local sites.

Actors' enrolment techniques and use of media

The point was made at the beginning of the chapter that detailed investigation of material construction-and-dissemination processes is an empirical orientation that supplants reductionist structural theories. If the form and content and social reproduction of materials could be simply 'read off' as (direct or indirect) predetermined expressions of the social totality there would not be much point in engaging, in an explanatory sense, in non-reductionist empirical investigation of the processes involved, nor in developing empirical conceptualizations for this purpose. It was observed in chapter three that when power is empirically investigated in non-reductionist terms, it is necessary to '... treat power as an effect of variegated and differentially successful strategies to enrol others rather than as cause of that success' (Law, 1986a, p.5). Actors' strategies (Crow, 1989; Morgan, 1989) play a crucial part in this. The examples provided in chapter three concerned the CCETSW's strategy in the 1970's, which involved 'appealing' simultaneously to the conflicting interests formulated by competitive actors (Wright, 1977), and, during the 1980's, the 'technical-professional' strategy of re-defining the range of actors (e.g. students) granted 'legitimate' defining-rights with regard to social work practice and training (Davies, 1981a, 1989; CCETSW, 1989a, p.5). Using the term 'agency' to refer to actors, Clegg (1989) notes that 'The articulation of interests by strategic agencies is ... the medium and the outcome of unique positioning over the discretion of others' positioning ...' (ibid., p.199). Clegg conceptualizes relationships between actors, and between them and the conditions-of-action, in terms of actors' attempts to construct what he calls 'circuits of power' and 'fields of force': he observes that 'Fixing these fields of force is achieved through enrolling other ... (actors) ... such that they have to traffic through the enrolling ... (actor's) ... obligatory passage points' (ibid., p.212). Of particular relevance to the prominence of oral materials in social work, one feature of Law's (1986a) sociology of (scientific) knowledge is his conclusion that written dissemination is strategically more effective than oral dissemination for securing 'long-distance or 'large-scale' cognitive and practical procedural control within an academic or professional community (ibid., p.33). Words, conversations, and gestures, are important in local 'translations' of other local actors, but conversations '... are not ... especially suited for long distance or large scale attempts at social control' (ibid., p.12). Talk, in the specific sense under discussion here, is not as mobile or as durable a material as texts, academic papers, research reports, and scientific journals: with regard to the strategic use of written media, power is not a cause but '... an effect of the creation of a network of mobile, durable ... (materials) ...' (Law, 1986a, p.34, emphases added). This is not only a question of written material being more mobile and durable than talk as a means of disseminating 'defined' material across sites through space-time: another factor is that writing is a medium which enables scientific arguments to be given formal codification and an elaborated form of expression, presentation, and schematization in a more powerfully convincing, persuasive way than is possible in conversations (ibid., p.14). As Law (1986a) puts it, '... methods for schematizing on paper are more powerful than their conversational counterparts' (ibid., p.15). Actors, to repeat a point made earlier, are not 'everywhere': they are spatially located in particular places. One aspect of actors' strategies for securing long distance cognitive-practico control is the attempt to convert material that is less mobile and durable into material that is more mobile and durable, and it is in this sense that it becomes possible for actors to collapse the 'distance' between sites and thereby '... exert influence upon the world from a particular place' (ibid., p.32, emphasis added). Writing, though, does not always have the intended effects. For one thing, written materials, to become influential, have to be sent to contexts (sites) where their dominance can successfully be exerted on materials that are less mobile and less durable (ibid., p.34). Just as conversations may fail to persuade or inform, so too may written material, and the specific characteristics of the contexts in which both oral and written materials are deployed are crucial to the 'reception' of materials of whatever kind (ibid., p.12). Power is a strategic and contingent outcome, and Law (1986a) does not claim that written materials are invariably or irreversibly effective in translation strategies, but he does claim written materials are relatively more effective (more mobile and more durable, and with greater schematization capacity) than oral materials in 'macro'-shaping the cognitive-practico structure of the scientific community across space and time. This is to say that talk is a strategically less effective medium for disseminating materials in a way that 'consigns' ideas, policies, and practices such that they become dominant across the scientific community.

If Law's (1986a) postulate is accepted as valid and as also having applicability to the social work community, a question arises: does the prominence of an oral culture in social work mean that social work actors who attempt to influence cognitions and practices across the social work community are typically prone to employ strategically ineffective (i.e. 'oral') media? In many respects, social work is 'talk work' (Hearn, 1982a, p.26) and in Law's (1986a) postulate talk, relative to the strategic superiority of written media for disseminating and 'consigning' materials, is a far less effective medium. It seems, however, that despite the predominance of an oral tradition(s) in social work, social work actors themselves recognize and 'endorse' the point which Law makes. Actors strategically select different media (i.e. oral or written) according to the particular objectives the actor has in mind and according to the context and purpose(s) of social (work) action formulated by actors in particular situations. The sheer pervasiveness of an oral culture in social work education and practice is real enough, as testified in the empirical data referred to earlier in the chapter and also in chapter two. However to say that oral media predominate in the routine circulation and dissemination of 'everyday' social work practice-materials, is not to say that social work actors do not also strategically deploy other (and written) media in 'special' non-routine professional circumstances. A hypothesis that warrants empirical attention is centred on the probability that written media are strategically deployed by social work actors in those periods and situations that are not tranquil or routine and which (though this analogy is a loose one) are not the social work equivalents of a Kuhnian period of 'normal science' (Kuhn, 1970, p.5). The use of oral media as advocated by Vance (1968) and by the 'professional' social work writers referred to earlier was, it should be noted, advocated by those writers for the routine construction, reproduction, and circulation of cognitively indeterminate 'oral' practice-materials. The oral form of media appropriate for the purpose of routine pattern-maintenance in a personal service profession is, however, not necessarily also functional in non-routine situations. An example of the latter type of situation is 'crisis-management' during a period of major internal conflict within a professional community, but other examples exist. The empirical illustrations provided in the remaining pages of the chapter indicate that there are grounds for suggesting that written media are accorded special strategic significance by social work actors in those historical periods when actors are struggling hard, against opposition, to establish a particular paradigm ('professional', 'radical' or whatever) for social work; or, after the profession has become relatively well-established, during times of internal crisis and political dissent when professionals perceive that professional interests and professional stability are under threat; or during the construction of controversial new policies and the formulation of professional responses to such policies. Written media are also accorded special significance by social work actors on those occasions when professionals proactively engage in the social construction and dissemination of a sense that massive 'new' or allegedly undetected social problems exist (e.g. 'child abuse' and also 'violence-towards-social workers') and in the construction and dissemination of professionally expansionist claims (particularly in the case of child-abuse) that extra professional resources should 'therefore' be allocated to social work as part of a professionally led repertoire of responses to combat these newly proclaimed social problems. Each of these illustrations will be briefly discussed in turn.

An account was given in chapter two of the Charity Organization Society's political struggles to establish a casework paradigm for social work as an emergent 'profession'; this struggle at the turn of

the century was set in the context of powerful opposition against
casework methods from socialist social reformers who rejected the COS's
political ideology of welfare (Young and Ashton, 1956; Woodroofe, 1962;
Stedman Jones, 1971). Clegg's (1989) observation is relevant here: he
notes that in struggles over policies 'The stabilization and fixing of
rules of meaning ... and techniques ... capable of extensive
reproduction over space and time are the central issue' (ibid., p.241).
For constructing and disseminating its arguments in favour of
professional casework, the COS made extensive strategic use of written
media. Jones (1983) notes that the COS developed a large communication
network for political purposes; he observes that 'Prominent in this ...
network was the Society's monthly journal which contained numerous
articles on how to undertake "good" casework and in particular articles
which established and legitimized the ... underpinning of its strategy'
(ibid., p.83). Conscious that formal academic training would be
necessary to establish the 'professional' credentials of social work,
the pages of the <u>Charity Organization Review</u> regularly commented on
social work education in great detail (Harris, 1989, in Bulmer et al.,
p.41), and in other fields the COS's proactive role in the construction
of 'professional' social work was sustained through the Society's
decision to commit a large proportion of its financial resources to the
production of a prodigious output of written material (ibid., pp.39-40)

> Reports of the COS committees between 1910 and 1912 increasingly
> emphasized the need to ... define ... (social work) ... priorities
> .... Papers written by C. S. Loch, the Secretary, during these
> years suggest that the COS council was mainly concerned with
> publishing non-socialist analyses of social questions and to
> maintain a strong COS presence on the growing number of municipal
> welfare schemes ...

The history of social work, including its recent history, shows that in
periods of major political paradigmatic conflict and turbulence within
the social work community, the strategic use of written media is given
special prominence by competitive actors. This applies to 'radical'
professionals as well as to 'traditional' professionals. During social
work's protracted internal political disputes in the 1970's, the Marxist
'<u>Case Con</u>' journal was an influential medium in the dissemination of
radical social work ideas. Jones (1983) makes the point that 'One of
the most significant of the early developments among socialist social
workers was the magazine <u>Case Con</u>. Formed in the late 1960's, this
magazine constituted an important focus for the increasing number of
radicals and socialists coming into social work' (ibid., p.137). This
early development was followed by a proliferation of radical social work
texts too numerous to list here; these included North (1972), Bailey and
Brake (1975), Pearson (1975), Deacon and Bartley (1975), Statham (1978),
Corrigan and Leonard (1979). It was largely the arguments developed in
these and other radical texts that provoked the emergence and
dissemination of written 'professional' counter-attacks and written
professional defences of traditional casework method, as in the
professional accounts by Munday (1972), Wilson (1974), Wright (1977),
and Davies (1981a, 1981b, 1981c).

Another instance of the strategic use of written media in times of
professional turbulence, and in situations of perceived 'threat' to
particular social work interests and perspectives, is the intense
struggle that developed in the 1980's over social work education and
training policies (see chapter seven). Professionalizing actors and

academic-professionals perceived that a grave danger of de-professionalization was posed by the 'practical' training policies that were being formulated by the Central Council for Education and Training in Social Work (CCETSW, 1982, 1985, 1986) and by social work employers (ADSS, 1986) as well as by some social services lobby groups (Standing Conference Certificate In Social Service, 1985). This struggle may be regarded as a series of attempts to define the nature and purposes of social work training and practice in particular ways, and of attempts by competitive actors to make their defined material 'travel' so as to render less mobile, and less durable, other competing definitions of social work training and practice. The interactions between the competitive social work actors involved in these struggles were articulated through expressions of condemnation, appeal, persuasion, and critique disseminated in written reports, academic papers, working party documents, and articles in journals such as Community Care and Social Work Today which have widespread circulation across the social work community. The intensity and scale of these conflicts, and the written schematization concepts invoked by the competitive actors involved in them, are revealed in, for example, the written accounts by Jordan (1982), Bamford (1984), Harbert (1984, 1985a, 1985b), Parsloe (1984), Pinker (1984), ADSS (1986), and Measures (1986).

It is not suggested that written media have no role in the routine circulation of social work's 'everyday' practice-materials. Rather, the point being made is that social work's ubiquitous oral culture - rather than a use of written academic or professional materials - routinely predominates in practice sites (and to some extent in social work education) and that written media are accorded particular strategic significance by actors in special 'non-routine' situations. Nor, in situations of professional crisis, reconstruction or adaptation, is it being suggested here that oral 'translations' and informal communications have no role. It is probable, for example, that informal behind-the-scenes lobbying within particular sites is a significant medium during the formulation (in committees, working parties and the like) of 'non-routine' new policy materials as well as during the strategic formulation of policy responses to perceived situations of dissent, crisis, or 'threat' of one kind or another; none the less, the outcomes of informal 'committee politics' require the strategic use of written media if these outcomes ('materials') are to be transported within a reasonably short period of time across a large range of relevant sites in the hope that these materials will become influential, pervasive, and 'dominant' within those sites. The two empirical illustrations discussed below, concerning 'child-abuse' and 'violence-towards-social workers', will serve also to indicate that the selection and use of media (whether oral or written) are strategically significant matters in their own right, but are not the only empirical variables that condition the construction of 'new' or non-routine materials: sometimes, highly contingent or 'unique' events or other contextual factors have an impact upon the construction and dissemination of new policy materials. Thus, in focussing on media, it is important to recognize the existence of empirical complexities in the interactions that may occur between actors' selection and use of particular media, the contents of media, and also the contingent contexts of media usage in the social construction of materials.

It is not intended here to debate in detail the extent to which social work concerns with child-abuse may be a professionally amplified 'moral panic' (Cohen, 1980) appropriated by social work actors for the purposes of professional empire-building. Rather, emphasis will be given to

76

media technologies of representation (of 'child abuse') and, in this illustration, to the role that singular or unique events may also play as contingent factors in the social construction of social problems and in the social construction of 'professional' and public policy responses to those problems. Parton (1979) describes how an influential American article on the 'battered child syndrome' (Kempe, 1962) became a significant factor in the taking up of this issue ('child abuse') in a number of British papers on the topic (Parton, 1979, p.436). The notion of child abuse as 'the hidden problem' (ibid.) was amplified in the 1970's by the National Society for the Prevention of Cruelty to Children (NSPCC) which had an important role in the diffusion of a belief that a massive social problem existed (ibid., p.438). These developments were given further impetus by a 'unique' event, the death in tragic circumstances of a child called Maria Colwell and the high level of publicity given to this event. This event and its investigation was communicated to a wide audience in a way which sustained movement towards the construction of a sense of 'crisis' surrounding the topic of child abuse. The death of Maria Colwell was followed by the holding of an inquiry and Parton (1979) notes 'The inquiry formed a regular item in the press and on TV news programmes, so that by the time the report on the death of Maria Colwell was published in September 1974, the issue was established as a major social problem requiring formal interventions' (ibid., p.442). In this empirical illustration ('child-abuse') of the role of written media as a transformational process in the construction and dissemination of a new or 'non-routine' social work material, actors' use of written and other media interacted with a 'unique' event to establish child-abuse, particularly sexual abuse, as a massive 'new' social problem facing the profession, or at least, as a problem said to be new in the sense that it allegedly existed on a major scale that had been hidden prior to its 'discovery' by professionals.

It was not only that the problem ('child-abuse') was 'discovered' by professionals. Perceptions of the nature of the problem itself, and perceptions of appropriate solutions or remedies were also transformed: specifically, these were transformed in the direction of professionalism. There is a sense in which child-abuse became partly de-criminalized and redefined as a professional welfare matter that was shifted increasingly closer towards the domain of professional social work (Hartley, 1982, p.76). Social work responses themselves subsequently became increasingly professionalized. Although this process did not get up a full head of steam until the 1980's, it had begun in the 1970's. It is worth noting that the early stages in the contemporary 'professionalization' of child-abuse policies co-incided with the massive post-Seebohm expansion of social work professionalism in the social services departments. This expansion was reined-in during the public expenditure cuts in the 1980's, and the concept of social work 'professionalism' itself was also under attack (Harbert, 1985a, 1985b; Warner, 1986). By this time child-abuse as a social problem had been 'claimed' by professional social work lobby groups and in the austere social services climate of the 1980's 'child-abuse' offered professional social work an opportunity for professional retrenchment and even expansion in at least one field of professional activity. Social work actors' attempts to professionalize 'child-abuse' policies while simultaneously appropriating a central role for social work within these policies, did not escape criticism. Amidst public criticisms of self-interested professional aggrandizement and the professional 'mystification' of child-care and family issues, some sections of the mass media unfavourably contrasted social work professionals' responses to child-abuse with earlier pre-Seebohm child protection work by the NSPCC. One newspaper (Daily Mail 20 May 1987, cited in Rojek et al., 1988, p.151) commented 'Then the old-fashioned NSPCC officer was usually a burly ex-serviceman speaking a plain language, afraid of nobody, frequently working on instinct, a gut feeling that things weren't right, and with his mind unclogged with the jargon and claptrap social workers get bogged down by'. Professional social workers, in turn, dismiss this older style of welfare work as a hopelessly 'bad' (i.e. 'pre-professional') form of child protection work. Many professional social work actors nowadays argue that the 'intellectual task-complexity' of child protection work, together with the 'professional' knowledge and expertise held by professional social workers, mean that social workers should become the 'lead' agents in society's response to child-abuse as a 'massive' social problem. Following the publication of the Butler-Sloss (1988) Report on child-abuse at Cleveland, the General-Secretary of the British Association of Social Workers (Jones, 1988) made out the professional social work case for 'The ... central role of social workers in responding to child abuse and co-ordinating the role of other professionals. Social workers know about these things ... the complexities ...' (ibid., p.5, emphasis added). This grandiose claim conveniently ignores the existence, described earlier in the chapter, of widespread social work confusion and disagreement as to what the knowledge-base of social work 'does' or 'should' consist of, and is also, it may be noted, a very far cry from the pre-Seebohm days of child protection work. The social construction both of child-abuse as a social problem and of increasingly 'professionalized' policy responses to child-abuse is a distinctive contemporary example of the construction of a 'new' or 'non-routine' social work policy material through professional actors' strategic deployment of transformative concepts that were largely formulated and disseminated through the use of written media.

Another, roughly analogous illustration of the processes described above is the social construction of 'violence-towards-social workers' as a social problem. This refers to verbal or physical attacks by clients upon their social workers. Unreported attacks upon social workers are doubtless not a new phenomenon: however according to Small (1987) the social construction of this phenomenon as a widespread sense of major professional concern was largely sustained through written media (ibid., p.43). As with child-abuse, highly contingent contextual factors played a part. Small (1987) describes how a conjunction of events and circumstances in the period 1985-87 contributed to a major escalation of professional anxiety about 'violence-towards-social workers' (ibid., pp.43-44). Small's analysis indicates that these anxieties about violence had started to develop in the early 1980's and he shows that it was not only the use of written media that transformed an 'occasional concern' (ibid., p.41) into a perception that a major problem existed: in the early 1980's conferences, skills workshops, short courses, study days and seminars on the topic were held in increasing numbers (ibid., pp.41-43). Small's (1987) detailed empirical analysis is a useful indication that the study of actors' transformational concepts in the construction and dissemination of 'new' or non-routine social work policy materials has to refer to an interwoven matrix of actors' perceptions, decisions and activities; to the role of non-written ('oral') communications in the form of, for instance, conferences, seminars, 'skills' workshops and other similar mechanisms that bring spatially dispersed professional actors together in face-to-face situations to exchange and disseminate information and focus their emergent concerns upon a particular 'new' problem or issue; and to the contributory impact of unique events or contingently-related professional circumstances (ibid., pp.43-44). However, Small (1987) highlights the crucial role of written media in social work actors' construction and dissemination of material on this topic in the two-year period after 1985; in describing the role of written media he refers to social work media as having special significance (ibid., p.43)

> Of particular note has been the coverage in Community Care and its six part series on violence beginning on 13 November 1986 and finishing on 11 December 1986. Also in the 11 December issue was an editorial, a page report on a DHSS Conference on violence to staff and a page of news which included four items on, or relating to, violence. This major coverage follows a number of articles throughout 1985 and 1986 ... this preoccupation of the social work press ... as yet has not ... been transferred to the rest of the non social work press.

Small's (1987) study, together with the earlier observations concerning child-abuse and also the previous description of actors' use of written media in the construction of 'professional' politics and policies during times of professional turbulence when social work actors take steps to defend or expand their sphere of influence, are indications that written media have particular strategic significance over and above the routine 'everyday' experiential construction and dissemination of social work's largely orally mediated practice-materials. There are, too, reasons for supposing that even 'new' or non-routine policy materials, if these become professionally institutionalized and internalized within social work's routine practice discourses will in the course of time become absorbed into the unwritten social work codes referred to earlier in the chapter.

It was observed at the beginning of the chapter that the construction and dissemination of social work materials of whatever kind are not structurally predetermined processes, nor reflections of any 'deep' cultural logic, structural 'necessities', or 'objective' structurally determined 'interests'. This is why close empirical investigation of the processes involved in the construction of social work materials, their contents and contexts, and of actors' strategies and use of media for disseminating and in various ways acting upon these materials, are important topics of empirical inquiry in their own right.

5 The politics of social work

Social work politics in the modern era have been reconstructed through two major contemporary developments. The first of these is the 'legitimation crisis' of the modern welfare state. The second, the contemporary construction of radical social work theories of political emancipation, relates to organizational and service-delivery issues and to what Benton (1981) identifies as the 'paradox of emancipation'. Concerning the first of these two aspects of contemporary social work politics, numerous social policy texts have examined various claims about the nature and causes of the 'legitimation crisis': however, social work writing has generally not focussed analytically upon key issues raised by these texts. In particular, social work writers have largely failed to analyse in non-reductionist terms the implications for social work theory, organization, and practice that arise from a large accumulation of statistical and other data on client and service-user experiences and perspectives. It is appropriate, therefore, that in the opening pages of this chapter on social work politics attention should be given not only to theoretical issues but also to empirical data on citizens' and service-users' perceptions of state welfare professionals and the relation of these perceptions to the politics of welfare.

The legitimation crisis of the modern welfare state

The crisis of public confidence in the ability of the modern welfare state to provide effective solutions to personal and social problems is well-documented, although interpretations of the form of the crisis vary. Most analyses concur that the legitimation crisis predates the political ideology of the 'new right' (Levitas, 1986) associated with 'Thatcherite' policies following the Conservative Party election victory of 1979. Brenton (1985, p.134) observes

Labour and Conservative administrations ... have exhibited a degree
of convergence in their support for the voluntary sector. Both
parties have ... endeavoured to cut expenditure on social services.
As a corollary to social expenditure cuts made or attempted, and as
a gesture to mollify adverse public opinion, both parties sought to
make a virtue out of necessity in presenting a glowing case for the
superior advantages of voluntary action of all kinds.

Gough (1980, p.7) comments that '... quantitative attack on the welfare
state was initiated by the Wilson/Callaghan administrations in 1975: the
Conservative policy is simply more (or rather less) of the same'.
Lawrence (1983) identifies social expenditure cuts as an outcome of
political pragmatism that was later reinforced by 'new right' political
ideology (ibid., p.27)

Despite the evidence of a traditional hostility in the Labour Party
to voluntary action, the 1974-79 government was, broadly speaking,
sympathetic to the voluntary sector. This can be identified as a
pragmatic response to the cuts in welfare services, especially from
1976 onwards. If voluntary effort were encouraged it might be a way
of reducing the impact of cuts in state spending or, at the least, a
way of being seen to be doing something to soften the blow. In many
respects Tory policy is a continuation of this with the added
ideological aspect of "rolling back the frontiers of the state".

As well as public and political support for principles underlining the
existence of the voluntary sector as both a cushion against reduced
social expenditure in the face of economic recession and (as will be
shown later) a 'counterweight' against state monopoly of services, the
private welfare sector has expanded considerably, though not as a direct
consequence of Thatcherite welfare ideology. Taylor-Gooby's (1986)
statistical analysis of the expansion of private services in the period
1951-83 reveals a long term upward trend in movement towards the private
sector (ibid., p.230). The data examined by Taylor-Gooby (1986) reveal
no sharp rise after 1979 and he concludes '... the long-run expansion of
private welfare has been little influenced by the policies of the
eighties' (ibid., p.228-9).

In a series of analyses published in the 1980's, Taylor-Gooby employs
data which led him to conclude that (1985, p.20) the notion of '... an
imminent crisis in the welfare state as a response to public opinion and
a watershed in the politics of welfare is mistaken'. This general
conclusion rests partly on data reported elsewhere by Taylor-Gooby
(1983). These earlier data were challenged on statistical grounds in a
paper by Marsland (1984). In a response to Marsland, Taylor-Gooby
(1984) re-asserted the statistical basis for his conclusion that large
areas of the welfare state remain publicly popular, and noted also that
public attitudes towards state services are in some instances highly
ambivalent. He makes reference (ibid., p.89) to an American study by
Free and Cantril (1967) in which a distinction is made between
'ideological' and 'operational' attitudes. Ideological attitudes refer
to approval of disapproval of the principle of state public services,
operational attitudes refer to approval or disapproval of specific
services. The relation between these two attitudinal spheres is often
not consistent (Taylor-Gooby, 1984, p.89) so that is is possible, for
example, to hold a general 'anti-state' ideological philosophy, yet also

place high value upon particular state services. In a later paper, Taylor-Gooby (1986) returned to the question of ambivalence in public attitudes towards public welfare services. His analysis of opinion poll data for the period 1979-83 suggests that the proportion of the population wanting higher public expenditure on health, education, and welfare rose from thirty-nine to fifty-nine percent (ibid., p.229). However these and other data also indicate that large sections of the population do not wish to see a monopoly of state services and '... are in favour of both more state spending and more private welfare' (ibid.). In a reference to supporting data in Harrison and Gretton (1985) this finding is said by Taylor-Gooby (1986) to be unsurprising because '... after all, people may just want more welfare ... and not be too particular as to whether it comes from state or market' (ibid., p.229, emphasis added).

Taylor-Gooby's (1986) analysis of data from a national survey of 2,000 adults contacted in 1984 reveals dissatisfaction with the quality, standards, and level of funding in state services. For instance, occupational pension schemes are seen as superior to the state retirement pension scheme, primarily because occupational schemes are regarded as providing more information to members and give members more scope for collectively influencing how schemes should operate (ibid., p.236), and because the level of provision is regarded as superior in non-state schemes (ibid., p.237). In private health schemes quantity and quality of resources, waiting lists, information provision, and adequacy of consumer complaints procedures were all rated as superior to state health provision (ibid., p.239) and similar views existed in respect of the 'superior' quality, standards, level of resources and user-responsiveness of private education and other private services (ibid., p.238-44). Almost all respondents, however, were strongly opposed to cuts in state services. For state health, education, and pensions the proportion of respondents who wanted expenditure cuts were 4 percent, 3 percent, and 5 percent; for these three services the proportion wishing to see levels of current expenditure maintained varied between 41 percent and 44 percent, and the proportion who wanted increased expenditure on these three services was between 41 percent and 45 percent (ibid., p.241).

Taylor-Gooby's (1986) conclusion is that the private welfare sector is regarded as superior to the state sector in terms of quality of service, level of resources, and consumer responsiveness (ibid., p.244) and on the last of these criteria he notes '... there is strong dissatisfaction with state welfare resulting from the experience by clients of oppression by state professionals and bureaucrats' (ibid., p.243, emphasis added). Equally, there is evidence of a strong body of public opinion in favour of welfare state services being more adequately resourced, made more effective, and democratized to provide greater user-responsiveness (ibid., p.244). Taylor-Gooby (1986) observes that the principle of state welfare is well-entrenched, and further cuts in valued state services are likely to be strongly resisted; he notes '... sentiments that support privatization are real ... (but) ... they co-exist with countervailing sentiments of collectivism' (ibid., p.244, emphasis added).

Less empirically-based analyses than Taylor-Gooby's reveal a variety of interpretations of 'the legitimation crisis'. Levitas (1986) fears that the doctrines of socialism itself are threatened by the persuasiveness of 'new right' ideological rhetoric and 'The electorate has been persuaded to give ... support to a set of extremely damaging policies which are not in their interests' (ibid., p.18, emphasis added). To the extent that interpretations of this kind embody concepts of 'objective' or 'real' but unacknowledged interests, they have no explanatory value. A different emphasis is provided by Deacon (1986) who notes that the state's solution to the problems of social welfare in Britain and other western capitalist societies has been challenged since the mid-1970's in '... a remarkably parallel way from both the right with its case for consumer sovereignty through the market and the left with its case for user control through less bureaucratic, centralised, and professionally dominated forms of provision' (ibid., p.4, emphases added). At least until recently, most of the left-political analyses of the modern welfare state, though containing a wider range of detailed emphases than need be explored here, reflect one or the other of two broad interpretive approaches. The first rests on a view that though it may have a contradictory relationship to capitalism the welfare state is ultimately functional for capitalism, and also - despite the phenomenon of 'new right' politics - commands a high level of public support. Although considerable variation exists as between the form of analysis employed by different writers in this first approach, its major exponents, including Therborn (1984), Offe (1984, pp.153-4) and Taylor-Gooby (1985, p.82) concur that the welfare state is largely intact, well entrenched, and likely to survive its 'legitimation crisis'. The second approach, which takes a less 'optimistic' view of the future of statutory services, rests largely on an (unproven) assumption that there is massive public disaffection from the welfare state and this combined with the continued impact of 'new right' political rhetoric is likely to produce '... a steady, drip-by-drip, attrition of public support for the statutory services ... preparing public opinion for a more severe pruning of the welfare state in due course' (Brenton, 1985, p.151).

Data employed by Taylor-Gooby (1985) indicate that some sections of the welfare state are unpopular, particularly means-tested provision like social security, and council housing, but other sections of the welfare state command widespread public support, in particular education, the NHS, and retirement pensions (ibid., pp.29-32). Riddell (1983) notes that public support for universal state services in health, education, and provision for the elderly, is consistently indicated in opinion polls (ibid., p.138) and public support for the social services was indicated in poll surveys taken before and after the election of the Tory government in⁻1979 (ibid., p.239-40). Empirical data assembled from a wide variety of sources over a number of years point consistently to a high level of public resistance against further cuts in social expenditure. These data lend a degree of credence to a view that the Tory election success in 1979 was partly an outcome of pre-election promises (repeated in countless radio and television broadcasts and interviews and in the national press) in the form of assurances that if elected to office a new Tory government would not dismantle the welfare state (which would be 'safe in our hands') but would 'shake-up' the welfare state, make it more cost-efficient, less bureaucratically and professionally dominated, more effective in its operation, and more responsive to the 'real' needs and preferences expressed by service-users as 'consumers' (Mishra, 1986, pp.6-7).

Mishra (1986) cites Butler and Kavannagh (1984) and others' data on public perceptions of state services and suggests there is no evidence '... that Thatcher won political support and the election (1979) on a platform and an ideology which repudiated the welfare state' (Mishra, 1986, p.6). Though the policy platform of the Tories '... took a strong anti-statist line, it did not go so far as to attack the social services and social expenditure per se' (ibid). During the election campaign

(ibid., pp.6-7)

.. what conservatives promised to cut out was ... wasteful public expenditure ... eliminating unnecessary ... bureaucracy ... making public services more efficient ... unlike the Reagan platform of reducing social expenditures and programmes in the United States, the Thatcher campaign (1979) did not propose retrenching the welfare state.

Mishra (1986) argues that '... it is clear Mrs. Thatcher and the Tories did not fight the 1979 election (or 1983 for that matter) on a platform that was opposed to the mainstream social programmes such as health care, education, and pensions' (ibid., p.7). On the basis of his data analysis, he concludes '... the idea that the Thatcherites campaigned on a platform opposed to the welfare state has no basis in evidence' (ibid.).

Mishra's (1986) central argument is that there has been no public rejection of the principle of state welfare services; what has been rejected by citizens and service-users is '... the actual administration of the services i.e. the form or manner in which the service is delivered' (ibid., p.7, second emphasis added). A distinction between the principle of state social services and the particular form of service-delivery framework through with social services are provided to users is (ibid.)

... an important distinction relevant to the struggle for de-bureaucratizing the services, making them more accountable and bringing them closer to the community. It is a struggle that progressives have been waging within (and without) the welfare state for some time now. But the nature of the "enemy", i.e. the organization and delivery systems rather than the principle of collective provision, has not always been kept clear.

The distinction between '... the welfare state as idea or principle ... and the structure or form in which the idea is realised ...' (ibid., p.10) is in Mishra's (1986) analysis a basis for socialist welfare (ibid., p.8)

... what is involved is both the idea of state responsibility for maintaining minimum levels of living as well as a set of institutional arrangements which translate the idea into practice. They are logically separable and the distinction is important. Surely the left must defend the former while it wages the struggle to change the latter.

In reforming the institutional arrangements of welfare one of the problems requiring solution is '... bureaucratic or professional imposition' (ibid., p.9). Mishra (1986) notes that although opinion polls consistently show public support for the principle (or 'idea') of state social services (ibid., pp.7-8) there is strong empirical evidence that 'many working people ... have experienced ... the social services ... with officials, professionals and others, as negative (ibid., p.8). Mishra (1986) refers to the problems of 'bureaucratic administration ... (and) ... professional dominance ... (in) ... the social services ... (ibid., p.10). He argues for the development of '... less bureaucratic and more self-managed and participatory services ...' (ibid.) which in his analysis are a less 'dominating' and more user-responsive way of responding to an electorate that 'voted with its feet' in rejecting not the general principle of state social services but the particular institutional frameworks and service-delivery systems through which these services are experienced by those who use them.

The politics of emancipation: some problems of theory and of policy

Viewed in the context of the legitimation crisis, social work in both its traditional and radical versions has failed in practical organizational and service-delivery terms to act upon the implications that arise from empirical data on citizens' and service-users' rejections of bureau-professionalism (Collins and Stein, 1989, p.86). It can be argued that for theoretical (Deacon, 1981, p.46) but also 'radical careerist' reasons (Moore, 1976; Parry et al., 1979, p.163; Hearn, 1982a, p.26) radical social work, like traditional professionalism, has strongly resisted '... the transfer of power ... to service-users ... and ... clients' (Bamford, 1990, p.xiv). Closely related to this predilection for professional dominance in the design and delivery of services, there are ground for suggesting that traditional and radical social work theories are in some sense relics from the recent past and an amalgam of 'received ideas' (Rojek et al., 1988, p.162) that are 'isolated' from contemporary developments in social analysis and social research. This cognitive insularity has conditioned the development of social work politics, with some unfortunate consequences. Some of these centre on the idea that the users of services are people who should be 'emancipated'. In the 1970's, radical social work theories of political emancipation coincided with reductionist sociological and other structural theories that were also prevalent at that time: in the 1970's radical social work was, that is to say, not alone in its reified conceptions of social structure and of power and social action. However, the times have changed both in respect of the socio-political context of social work and welfare, and in terms of theoretical developments: social work has not kept pace with these two strands of change. The two most obvious deficiencies revealed in recent radical social work literature are, firstly, that radical social work writers, in the context of the legitimation crisis of social services, have with few exceptions failed to address in non-reductionist terms the critical implications of empirical data on citizens' and service-users' rejection of hierarchical organization and of bureau-professionals' dominance in the design and delivery of services: and secondly, that radical social work theory has remained singularly detached from developments in social science since the 1970's and continues to deploy a reductionist style of thinking that belongs to the past. It is this curiously outmoded way of thinking that produces confused and contradictory 'radical' policy and practice imperatives, some of which are identified by Nelson (1990) and by Ramazanoglu (1989, p.433).

Pierson (1984) refers to simplistic Marxist reductions of political struggles surrounding gender, 'race', generation, and social movements of various kinds to, ultimately, an expression of class struggle. It was observed in chapter two that during the mid and late 1980's radical social work largely abandoned the earlier Marxist concern with class issues and switched its attention to issues of gender and 'race'. Radical social work, in changing the topics with which it is politically concerned, has, however, hung onto the same general processual form of theoretical reductionism that had characterized its 'class-struggle' analysis in the 1970's. Classes are not actors, and 'classes' as such do not 'struggle' (Hindess, 1988, p.27). Nor, for the reasons specified in chapter three, does it make explanatory sense to suppose that any other social collectivities (such as 'society', 'men', 'women', 'black people', or 'white people') can engage in 'struggle'. Possibilities for engaging in empirical analysis of social inequalities, and for constructing political policies in response to inequalities, are obfuscated when the concept actor is '... extended to aggregates that have no identifiable means of formulating decisions, let alone acting on them ... (such as) ... classes, racial or gender categories' (Hindess, 1986a, p.124). Radical social work discourse shows no real signs of recognizing the problems of reductionism, nor, therefore, of addressing them. It was observed in chapter two that in this context of highly problematical theoretical ideas some writers in the radical social work movement are currently engaged in the construction of emancipatory theories that refer to 'alliances' across those sections of the radical social work movement concerned respectively with class, or 'race', or gender issues.

Actors who are adherents of social movements that employ oppositional tactics to secure social change, regularly face the problem of whether or not to form strategic alliances with other oppositional actors (Langan and Lee, 1989b). Some radical actors argue for tactical alliances, founded on some concept of 'unity' that specifies a single-issue emancipatory perspective (based on, say, 'race', or gender, or class) should be avoided in favour of a 'common front' approach that tackles all of the major forms of inequality. The social construction of an 'an-inclusive' approach requires that its advocates justify it by developing supporting theoretical legitimations both as a prior rationale for the approach and as a strategic tactic for recruiting and then retaining an all-inclusive membership. This involves attempting to construct and disseminate some sense of 'commonality' among a range of individual and social actors who might otherwise not 'recognize' a set of common relations of meaning and of membership within a 'new' all-inclusive oppositional political constituency or social movement. However, one of the major obstacles faced by those involved in the construction of social and political commonalities and tactical alliances across political constituencies respectively concerned with class or 'race' or gender, is the countervailing tendency for a similar process of 'commonality' construction to be replicated within each of these constituencies.

Actors located within those specialized radical social work constituencies that give priority to one or another particular form of inequality (i.e. based on social class, or gender, or 'race') tend to exhibit strong concerns to avoid any 'distracting' or splintering tendencies within their constituency. Class-based radicals, for whom the construct 'working class' has privileged ontological and political status and important tactical connotations of class unity and class 'solidarity', have a long history of invoking the 'divide-and-rule' thesis (Jones, 1983, pp.54-9) which specifies that it is in the interests of the dominant class under capitalism to 'distract' or 'fragment' working class solidarity and to 'fracture' the cohesiveness of working class movements along the lines of, say, gender, generation, 'race' and ethnicity or religion. Analogously, feminist social work radicals have a tendency to argue that though the social category 'women' is not in every respect homogeneous, the notion of commonality among 'women' as a social aggregate should nevertheless be central: a fairly representative example of this line of thinking in feminist social work is the claim that '... the . ... needs of women cannot be discussed until we become aware of the commonalities between ... ourselves and our women clients ... between women workers, between women irrespective of age, stage, sexuality, class, race, reproductive history .... These commonalities ... we share as women ...' (Hanmer and Statham, 1988, pp.10-11, emphases added). These reductionist efforts to theoretically construct essentialist 'commonalities' within respectively class-based and feminist radical social work constituencies, and to avoid any internal splintering or political decomposition of these theoretically-constructed commonalities of 'class' and of 'women' respectively, are also evident in the anti-racist social work constituency. Hutchinson-Reis (1989) expresses concern that 'Racism ... has been subordinated to issues of gender or class ...' (ibid., p.168). He concludes that 'Any group of black ... (social) ... workers needs to exist primarily in the interests of black workers, clients and community' (ibid., p.173, emphasis added). Shah (1989) suggests that '... the white feminist movement has ignored ... black women .... The exclusion of black women from feminist theory and practice has helped to marginalize black women ... in social work' (ibid., p.180). These emphases upon the theoretical construction of internal 'commonalities' of interests and purposes within socialist or Marxist, feminist, and anti-racist social work constituencies, each of which in practice accord priority to class or gender or 'race' and are frequently criticized by members of the 'other' constituencies for doing so, pose both theoretical and practical strategic problems for those who simultaneously advocate the construction of 'commonalities' of interests and purposes and tactical alliances across these constituencies. A further complication in this debacle is that the 'memberships' within these specialized constituencies are in any event very visibly internally divided in various ways. For instance, Dominelli and McLeod (1989) note that within the feminist social work constituency there are disagreements as between radical feminists who subscribe to some version of 'patriarchy' as an explanatory concept; socialist feminists who argue against the marginalization of class and who emphasise the point that middle-class women have material resources and privileges not available to working-class women; and black feminists who argue that both radical feminists and socialist feminists have marginalized issues of 'race' (ibid., p.27). It is difficult to avoid the conclusion that contemporary radical social work's theoretical constructions of intra- and inter-constituency essentialist categorizations, 'commonalities', and alliances, have collapsed into a morass of muddled and reductionist homilies.

Theoretical considerations aside, actors involved in 'emancipatory' social movements of whatever kind are always faced with situations that require decisions be made about the problems of constructing strategic alliances (Turner, 1990, p.199). These problems arise, though not always in identical form, in totalitarian societies, in parliamentary democracies, and in situations that involve action through the mechanisms of direct or participative democracy (Lees, 1972, pp.32-52). Oppositional actors and political parties seeking to change the social order are, other things being equal, more likely to succeed in the achievement of their objectives if their political manifesto is widely perceived as a 'catch-all' or all-inclusive political programme that subsumes what would otherwise be a diversity of separate 'single-issue' interests and objectives. There are some limits to this: paradoxically, the more successful a political party or social movement is in attracting and retaining a heterogeneous membership the more difficult will be the problems of internal decision-making and mobilization for concerted political action (Halliday, 1985, p.438). None the less, single-issue political manifestos are in most circumstances inherently problematic. Enrolling others to one's conception of one's own and others' interests is a crucial factor in the contingent and strategic achievement of political power (Callon and Law, 1982). In some sense, the more 'others' there are, and who can be successfully enrolled, the better. This general tendency applies to many forms and contexts of oppositional political practices, including use of the ballot box as a vehicle for social change, involvement in pressure-group activities, or revolutionary activities intended to achieve a mobilization of 'the masses'. Historically, social and political resistance has usually been internally divided and splintered into separate interest groups which, though all of them may desire a transformation of existing social arrangements, have different priorities and concerns. These general tendencies in the politics of social change are noted in Mann's (1986) historical account of why it does not regularly happen that oppositional actors succeed in constructing cross-cutting affiliations and alliances sufficient for social transformation to become a political reality. If in highly unusual situations at particular moments in time a major, rapid social transformation does occur, as in the democratic revolutions in Eastern Europe in 1989 and 1990, it is not only the exceptional nature of such events that is significant, but also their empirically problematic outcomes with regard to the stabilization of any putative social and political 'unity' of interests and objectives in the post-revolutionary period (Williamson, 1989).

It was observed earlier that in the case of social work there are also theoretical obstacles of various kinds which operate to obscure possibilities for developing credible (i.e. non-reductionist) theoretical and empirical understandings of the nature and forms of inequalities and for developing adequate, non-reductionist policy conceptualizations as a basis for formulating practices that might lead towards social change. For example, in those versions of radical social work where anti-racism is accorded primacy, no useful explanatory purpose is served if the analysis is based on the reductionist assumption that '... the fundamental function of a western liberal democratic state is one of control, and that, in facilitating the continuation of a capitalist and imperialist system, racism forms a key mechanism of such a state' (Hutchinson-Reis, 1989, p.165). To refer to 'the state', 'society' or whatever, in these functionalist terms (a style of thinking that was prevalent in social theory in the 1960's and 1970's) is to reify and personify something that does not exist: there are no manifest or latent systemic-needs or structural exigencies, and to suppose social systems have 'needs' is to impose an illegitimate teleology upon them. There are no analytical prime-movers or 'key-mechanisms' in the sense postulated in reductionist structural theories: social phenomena arise from empirically specifiable but diverse, empirically complex and frequently shifting conditions-of-action which are not themselves reducible to any single general principle of explanation (Hindess, 1982, p.498). In other versions of radical social work, analogous reductionisms involving the mere substitution of other structural 'key mechanisms' are evident; thus '...Marxist and feminist ... analysis ... slides into reification: all action is "explained" as a reflection of a giant overarching system such as the class structure or patriarchy' (Rojek et al., 1988, p.160). Reductionist theory per se is inherently flawed, no matter which social phenomena it is applied to: in the cognitively closed circle of radical social work discourse, any disagreements largely centre on attempts to substitute one reductionism for another or else to find ways of combining them.

Reductionist analyses spuriously invoke the concept of 'objective' or 'real' structurally-determined 'interests', and conjure up mystical reductionist images of taxonomic collectivities in the sense of '... classes, societies, men as a collectivity subordinating women as another collectivity, and so on' (Hindess, 1988, p.104). The point was made earlier (and discussed at some length in chapter three) that such collectivities have no identifiable means of formulating decisions, still less of acting on them (ibid., p.105). Merely taxonomic collectivities are not actors: nor do these collectivities or any of their 'members' have 'objective' structurally 'given' interests. Hindess (1988) makes the point that 'There are, of course, actors who claim to take decisions and act on behalf of classes and other collectivities, but the very diversity of such claims is reason to be wary about accepting any one of them' (ibid., p.105). This, however, does not mean that reifications, whether these be the product of reductionist social science or social work discourses or the product of 'lay' actors' reified images of social structure (Berger and Luckmann, 1972, pp.106-9), do not sometimes have social and political significance. Intellectual demonstration that reified accounts of the social world have no theoretical or empirical explanatory value may in some circumstances be irrelevant to the social and political efficacy of those reified accounts in terms of the strategic, political uses to which they are put by oppositional actors. Where some particular oppositional actors impute collective structurally-given 'objective' interests to a social aggregate (a 'class', 'women' as a social category, etc.) and/or to individual 'members' of that aggregate, this may, particularly if the imputations are accepted and acted upon by a large number of the actors who have these 'objective' interests assigned to them, have political consequences and become a relevant factor in political action directed towards social change. Clegg (1989) observes that some actors may be able to '... form a collective representation of "interests". These may then be the basis for policies which contain calculations of the effects necessary to secure these putative interests' (ibid., p.230). Whether, however, it is possible to institutionalize and stabilize the 'objective' ('real') interests and, correlatively, the čommon relations of meaning and of membership imputed to the actors 'assigned' to membership of an essentialist social category defined as relatively unitary, is an ever-present strategic problem for those oppositional actors and radical leaders who base their practice on reductionist social and political theories. Some actors, including those in whose name the struggle for 'liberation' is being fought, may reject a reified representation of their social situation and 'deny' that they share the collective, 'objective' 'interests' and goals assigned to them by radical oppositional leaders or activists.

When this occurs, reactions against the dissenting actors may take an authoritarian form, a possible outcome that will be examined more closely later in the chapter. Rojek at al. (1989) criticize the use of simplistic 'received ideas' in traditional professional social work, but also reject the simplistically authoritarian 'received ideas' embedded in radical social work discourses (ibid., pp.2-3)

As for radical approaches, notably Marxism and feminism, the assumption of collectivism which they make begins to look more and more like a presumption. The problem here is ... the proposition that ... the working class and women have real interests ....

Status and subcultural divisions between these collections of people have turned out to be far more diverse and resilient than was imagined in social work's radical temps perdu back in the 1960's and seventies. In addition, Marxism and feminism have been criticized for nursing a latent authoritarianism which belies their spirit of emancipation. For example, Yelloly (1987, p.19) admonishes Marxist social workers for assuming that there is a "right" construction and the social worker knows what it is.

It is not only the emergence of a modish authoritarianism in radical social work that has come under fire recently. It is beyond the remit of this chapter to trace in detail the conjunctions of intellectual and socio-political circumstances that have led, not only in Britain, to the recent escalation of concerns about ostensibly 'emancipatory' but authoritarian politics: it is sufficient here to note that these critiques are emerging across a number of different political and also academic discourses. In sociology, earlier disquietude surrounding 'the paradox of emancipation' (Benton, 1981) and repression in the name of class-based collectivist principles of 'emancipation' in the Soviet Union is given a renewed and different form of expression by, for example, Ramazanoglu (1989) in her criticisms of feminists' failure to come to terms with the paradox that repression is often purveyed in the name of freedom. Fay's (1987) account of 'the tyranny scenario' (ibid., pp.203-15) very clearly reflects the recent growth of opposition against repressive 'liberatory' political dogma. These concerns, it should be noted, were written before the revolutionary events of 1989/90 in Eastern Europe and it is possible these events will reinforce current academic and political interests in issues of social justice conceptualized in terms of the politics of 'liberation-without-tyranny' (Fay, 1987). This will be returned to later in the chapter: for the moment, other issues require attention as a basis for the later analysis.

Yelloly's (1987, p.19) admonishment of Marxist social workers, is apt. Oppositional actors need to be clear about what it is that they are struggling 'for' and, no less importantly, clear about what it is in the status quo that they are struggling 'against' as a means to securing their objectives. Very often, oppositional theories and practices are directed against something in the status quo called a 'dominant value system'. There is, however, no reliable empirical evidence to support a supposition that particular values or beliefs are 'dominant' and consistently shared by individuals in modern, pluralist societies (Mann, 1970; Abercrombie et al., 1980). Rootes (1981) takes issue with Abercrombie et al. (1980) on the grounds that dominant ideology exists in multiple mediated forms that in an empirical sense are not easily discernible. Here, Rootes is invoking a reductionist assumption that ideas, practices, and values operate 'in the last instance' as a reflection of dominant and 'real' interests, albeit in 'subtle', 'mediated', or 'refracted' form. Rootes's (1981) notion that values and cognitions may cohere and crystallize at different (and sometimes tacit) levels of conceptual consistency and explicitness has potentially useful empirical applications (Sibeon, 1989b, p.39), so long as his framework is shorn of its reductionist presuppositions. Aside from Rootes's (1981) analysis there are some other grounds for predicting that the social survival of theories, world-views and ideologies, is not dependent upon their being internally coherent, logically consistent, or conceptually integrated. Phenomenological sociology and in particular Berger and Luckmann's (1972) work on 'the social construction of reality' refers to actors' involvements in multiple meaning-systems in modern, pluralistic societies. A brief example will make the point. Mannheim's (1972) distinction between 'particular' and 'total' conceptions of ideology (ibid., p.49) is conveniently illustrated in Bernardes's (1985) study of 'family ideology'. In Bernardes's (1985) multidimensional framework, the Mannheimian distinction between particular/total ideologies is juxtaposed with phenomenological and constructionist conceptions of situational and multiple meaning systems (ibid., pp.227-8)

> ... ideology should be conceptualized as being multiple in two senses. Not only is an ideology multi-layered in terms of ranging "vertically" between the "particular" and the "total" but the lived experience of individuals also involves multiple "readings" of an ideology upon any specific "horizontal" dimension at any point between "particular" and "total". Thus, for example, an individual may accept the universal existence of "The Family" ("total family ideology") and yet wish to defend his or her own slightly variant personal "family" circumstances ("particular family ideology"). Further, in any one context he or she may emphasise the joy of parenthood at one moment and then bemoan the economic burden of "family" responsibilities; thus an individual may "read" "family" ideology" in different ways for different purposes.

There is, of course, nothing surprising in this statement. In everyday life actors regularly say 'I am in two minds about this', or say they have 'mixed feelings' about something. What is important is the analytical and ultimately political implications of the point made by Bernardes.

The notion that ideologies and belief systems in society, or within occupations and professions, are not necessarily internally consistent is noted by Levitas (1976) in her sociological analysis of beliefs; she comments that (ibid., p.546)

> Inconsistency is not necessarily a barrier to the adoption of sets of ideas. Since people are quite capable of holding mutually contradictory beliefs, both the questions of adoption and rejection of beliefs must be discussed without too much recourse to arguments about logical consistency, and such arguments must be treated with extreme caution.

Levitas refers to Goffman's observations that involvements in different roles and social contexts entail different behaviours and ways of thinking; and to Berger and Luckmann's work on the pluralization of consciousness, lack of normative consistency, and the 'integration' of beliefs as a fragmentary process linked to modernism (Levitas, 1976, pp.546-7). This processual image of social life is pushed further (too far, in light of the arguments developed in chapter three) in post-structuralist conceptions of the social world as a highly indeterminate and contingent process of flux and variability (Laclau and Mouffe, 1985). In their sociological critique of conventional social work, Rojek et al. (1988) observe that 'We live under modernism. Modernist consciousness is sensitive to the restlessness of life, the ambiguity of meaning, the relativity and diversity of things, the contingencies of action, and the lack of social consensus' (ibid., p.165). The point is well made. Yet the notion that 'a' dominant ideology exists (albeit in a form said to be 'fractured', 'mediated', etc.) as a representation of 'objective' interests, is one that many self-styled radicals continue to cling onto. What some radical social work 'consciousness-raisers' appear to have failed to grasp is that the existence of a very wide diversity of social opinion among 'lay' people, and sometimes the holding of fragmentary and ambivalent viewpoints, is never proof that everyone other than the consciousness-raiser holds mistaken views. Besides which, as we have seen, radical consciousness-raisers disagree amongst themselves; which is to be believed?

Ultimately, radical social work's politics and prescriptions for social change are stymied by virtue of an attachment to mythical images of society that stem from reductionist theory. Reductionist theories, including the essentialist 'categoricalism' (Connell, 1987) that pervades radical social work, feed an inability to grasp the implications of the paradox that social 'order' and the 'stability' of existing social arrangements in pluralist societies is a contingently produced outcome of value-conflict and value-diversity, not a product of social consensus. An aspect of this outcome was described earlier with reference to the strategic advantages of (but problems in achieving) political 'alliances' for the promotion of social change. A corollary of the point made earlier is that 'The stability of ... (a society) ... may depend, not so much upon a consensus concerning particular values or norms, but upon a lack of consensus at the very point where oppositional attitudes could be translated into political action' (Thompson, 1987, p.523). The self-limiting radicalism of single-issue social movements or emancipatory struggles, where groups' pressures for social change focus entirely on a single issue, or else with other issues tacked on as second or third-order concerns regarded as of much lesser importance, is illustrated in the empirical conceptualizations developed in Papadakis's (1988) study of the Green Party in West Germany.

Papadakis's work is also significant for a different but related reason which refers to the previous observation that under the cultural conditions of modernism in western societies, consciousness and ideologies are not necessarily holistic, unambiguous, or unambivalent world-views. Papadakis's (1988) study suggests that social stability is more than a straightforward consequence of the likelihood that oppositional interest groups will pursue sectional interests rather than form alliances or coalitions; and also far more than can be accounted for by erroneous assumptions that society resembles two polarized and homogeneous actor-categories consisting of unambiguously 'radical' critics of the existing social order who are ranked up shoulder-to-shoulder against equally solidaristic and unambiguously 'conservative' supporters of the status quo. Rather, it is '... the considerable ambivalence in public attitudes ... (that) ... has a more powerful impact on the self-limiting radicalism of contemporary social movements than polarization between radical activists and supporters of established ... principles' (Papadakis, 1988, p.442). Sherman (1986) suggests political ideologies have '... a certain untidiness, what Hegal called the interpenetration of opposites ... consistency is rarely the hall-mark of great tides of opinion' (ibid., p.10). Sherman notes that disillusioned socialists in rejecting repressive centralist political controls and the self-interests of state professionals and bureaucrats, may move in any number of alternative directions that have no common denominator. Those who turn away from centralised socialism may be libertarian or authoritarian, free-traders or protectionist, paternalist or laissez-faire, nationalist or cosmopolitan: and conversely (ibid.)

... one can combine full awareness of the market's economic, political and moral shortcomings with profound scepticism regarding intervention by politicians and civil servants on behalf of vested interests. One can quite consistently favour intervention and planning in theory while denouncing all its manifestations in practice.

These and the earlier observations provide pointers to the failure of radical social work politics to come to terms with the dynamics of modernism and modernist consciousness. To the extent that radical social work employs 'theory' this is almost invariably converted into simplistic and reductionist maxims. Moreover, there remains the previously noted problem of authoritarianism. Difficulties of various kinds arise when attempts are made by radical social work actors to 'impose' reductionist sophisms upon their clients, or indeed, upon other social work actors. The reified theoretical presumptions and crude solecisms that have led contemporary social work radicalism towards little more than simplistic authoritarian diktats reflect an attachment to prescribed theoretical dogmas which fail to recognize that '... collectivism is always repressive because it won't tolerate diversity or aberration' (Rojek et al., 1988, p.144) What, other than those noted earlier and in chapter three, are the specific grounds for this verdict? To answer this it will be necessary to look beyond social work, then return to radical social work's microcosmic version of the paradox of emancipation.

The paradox of emancipation

In a critique of Lukes's (1974) three-dimensional view of power, Benton, (1981, p.162) refers to

> ... the ... central problem with which Marxists have been confronted, both in theory and practice, sometimes with disastrous consequences. In its simplest form this is the problem of how to reconcile a conception of socialist practice as a form of collective self-emancipation with a critique of the established order which holds that the consciousness of those from whom collective self-emancipation is to be expected is systematically manipulated, distorted and falsified by essential features of that order. If the autonomy of subordinate groups (classes) is to be respected, then emancipation is out of the question: whereas if emancipation is to be brought about, it cannot be self-emancipation. I shall refer to this problem as "the paradox of emancipation".

This paradox is not confined to orthodox or so-called 'vulgar' Marxism. Leonard's (1984) 'revised' Marxist distinction between action-oriented practice and consciousness-oriented practice (ibid., pp.209-10) is merely a reductionist sidestepping of Benton's 'paradox'. On another front, Althusserian structuralist Marxism involves no more than replacing the old 'kneel and thou shallt believe' by 'indulge in revolutionary practice and thou shallt see' (Gellner, 1974, p.206). Revisionist attempts to purge Marxism of its inherent determinism and reductionism have been tried ad nauseam, and have failed. As Child (1942) put it in reviewing Lukacs's failure to transcend Marxist concepts of economic interests, '... despite his dialectical skill ... Lukacs's theory must be convicted of obscurity, confusion, and incoherence ...' (ibid., p.167). Lee and Raban (1988) advocate retention of 'Marxism's insight into structural determination' (ibid., p.209) in revised, pragmatic form so as to construct '... a version of Marxist theory that is ... fragmented and eclectic ...' (ibid., p.210). It would be better to let go of Marxism altogether: no theoretical re-working can remove its inherent reductionisms, whether in the form of methodological collectivism or methodological individualism (Hindess, 1986c, 1988). Theory, however, is one thing: the relation of theory to political practice is another, and it is through its practical applications that Marxism entered the paradox of emancipation as defined by Benton (1981).

Fay's (1987) historically grounded account of 'the tyranny scenario' (ibid., p.211) refers to situations where repression is imposed in the name of emancipation (ibid., pp.203-15). The scenario described schematically by Fay begins with an outline of the social processes through which, prior to social change, radical activists and leaders develop 'theoretical' rationales for censuring all those who challenge 'the party line': those who are censured may be a majority and include those whose 'liberation' is ostensibly the radical leaders' raison d'etre. After social transformation has been achieved, non-conforming 'ways of thought are forbidden' (Fay, 1987, p.210). Those who reject the imposition of thought-control, refuse to be silenced. In response to this dissent the imposition of tyranny becomes even more widespread, causing some members of the new leadership to have second-thoughts and to express their moral-political concern about what is happening: these leaders are '... removed from the scene as enemies of the revolution' (ibid., p.211). After a period of time, even a few of the members of the remaining, firmly established leadership begin to develop private doubts about whether repression can be morally justified in the name of 'liberation' (of 'the people'). The leaders who harbour these doubts are fearful of expressing them. They realise, too, that they are known as members of a repressive regime and that authoritarian rule unsupported by a majority of 'the people' is always highly precarious; to preserve their own potentially vulnerable position they join forces with the hard-liner leadership in imposing further sets of controls upon citizens, and upon erstwhile democratic-reformist leaders. Until such time as it may be overthrown, the tyranny-scenario ends as '... simply ... played for the benefit of appearance while ... the struggle of maintaining power and control is waged' (ibid.). In an earlier text, Fay's (1975) commitment to issues of social justice and reform did not highlight these problems with the same intensity; by the time of the publication of his later work Fay (1987), though no less interested in social reform, had become altogether more wary of the dangerous paradox which he summarizes (ibid., p.209) in these terms

> Despite all the best hopes, in our century revolutions inspired by ostensible critical theories have often betrayed themselves and those in whose name they speak. They have done so by creating social arrangements which encourage harmful and destructive social relations and behaviour ... by insisting on the self-evident correctness of their doctrines, they have succeeded only in replacing blind obedience to one ideology with blind obedience to another. It is an historical irony of a very disturbing sort that critical social theories promising to set people free often have instead ended up enslaving them.

Fay (1987) does not say that the tyranny-scenario cannot, in particular and unusual circumstances, be overthrown. His concern is to forestall its re-emergence should it be overthrown, but more fundamentally, to prevent it from coming into being in the first place. This requires that actors be encouraged to equip themselves (ibid., pp.13-15) with an analytically and historically grounded political awareness that the tyranny-scenario is endemically latent '... like an incubus ready to be born in the right circumstances' (ibid., p.209). This form of awareness is in Fay's analysis not an obstacle against authentic social reforms and social justice, but on the contrary, a precondition of their practical achievement (ibid., p.215).

Fay's (1987) 'tyranny scenario' amplifies and extends some features of Benton's (1981) 'paradox of emancipation'. Although Fay's (1987) construct is built out of concrete empirical and historical data, it is nevertheless an 'ideal-type' construct (ibid., p.211). Where empirical events identified in the construct do actually occur these will not always be at the 'large-scale' societal level, and even if they do occur at this level they may approximate to Fay's ideal-type construct to a greater or lesser extent. At the micro and middle-range levels of social interactions (e.g. relationships within organizations and between organizations) there are likely to be very many types of situations where expressions of the 'paradox' are empirically of far lesser scale than on the 'macro' canvas described by both Benton (1981) and Fay (1987). Whether episodic 'micro' manifestations of the 'paradox' within political parties, social movements, or within organizations do accumulate and become widely disseminated across larger stretches of social and political terrain, is a contingent empirical variable: no political outcomes are structurally predetermined. One of the concerns expressed by Benton (1981), Fay (1987) and Rojek et al. (1988, 1989) is that at the first signs of the possible emergence of the 'paradox' within, say, organizations or groups involved in the formulation or application of public policies, strong counteractive measures should be taken to forestall a possible escalation of the 'paradox' into a more widely disseminated and institutionalized form (Fay, 1987, pp.212-15).

As observed earlier, critics have suggested that smaller-scale versions of the processes identified by Benton (1981) are becoming increasingly pervasive in contemporary radical social work. Radical social work's reductionist 'theoretical' rationales imply that dissenting social workers or others who challenge the 'correct' theoretical-political doctrine should be censured in some way (Rojek et al., 1989, pp.2-3; Yelloly, 1987). In their account of radical social work, Rojek et al. (1988) refer to a motif which '... creates witch hunts and punishes dissent' (ibid., p.144). Moreover, in radical social work discourses citizens and clients are not regarded as people who should 'control' social services. Clients are 'lay' or 'non-professional' people who are there to have their consciousness 'raised', to be conscientized, rather than to assert their self-determination before the process of consciousness-raising has been embarked upon. In reality most clients do not ask for nor want to participate in such exercises: they have far more pressing self-defined needs, but few institutional mechanisms for expressing them (Collins and Stein, 1989). The fulfilment of human need implies the power to achieve it through access to resources (Taylor, 1989). However, citizens' and service-users' '... exclusion from the political process and control of collective services is associated with deficiencies in both' (Croft and Beresford, 1989, p.16). Rojek (1989) notes that '... self-determination, conceived as the capacity to develop one's faculties and energies freely and fully, remains a major theme in radical writing. Yet ... hardly any social work text has seriously addressed the question

of the organizational form necessary to realise this development in
social work' (ibid., p.175, emphases added).   Self-determination is
precisely the issue addressed by Benton (1981).   There are grounds for
suggesting that the operation of a version of Benton's 'paradox of
emancipation' in radical social work is revealed in the preferences of
'radical' social work writers for hierarchic bureau-professional
organizations that, in addition to perpetuating radical professionals'
formulated self-interests, provide hierarchical sites for reproducing
micro-scale versions of Benton's 'paradox of emancipation' in radicals'
relationships to citizens as clients: some specific organizational
aspects of these processes will be examined in detail in chapter six.
   Radical social work practices in welfare organizations require some
form of 'theoretical' legitimation: an instance of this is feminist
discourse of the kind developed in radical social work.   Ramazanoglu
(1989) in her sociological critique notes that it is not that feminists
regard 'women' as an entirely unitary category, but rather, that
feminism either tends to relegate other dimensions of social existence
as 'secondary' to some essentialist concept of gendered relations or,
where this particular fallacy is avoided, has developed no adequate
conceptual framework for making sense of non-unitariness among 'women'
as a social aggregate, or indeed, among members of any other social
aggregate (ibid., pp.435-7) such as 'black people', 'men', 'classes',
'white people', etc.   Women do not all share the same experiences or
have the same 'interests' and Ramazanoglu's (1989) specification that
class and 'race' are highly significant dimensions of social life
(ibid., p.436) causes her to reject 'bland' (ibid.) feminist concepts of
links between class, 'race' and gender.   This is illustrated by data
from Ramazanoglu's empirical study of shift-working women who are
described (ibid., p.433) as having

> ... quite specific work experiences, but these experiences react
> with their marriages, domestic and social life, and with
> relationships based on class or racism.   Women are not all equally
> oppressed, nor oppressed in the same way.   Political strategies for
> transforming the relations between women and men are, therefore,
> often contradictory.   Feminist claims to improved explanations of
> social life must rest on success in tackling these problems.

With regard to reductionist uses of such concepts as 'patriarchy',
'real' or 'objective' interests, and 'false consciousness', Ramazanoglu
(1989) states that '... most women are not feminists' (ibid., p.435).
It is often claimed that this statement all depends, as radical social
workers are fond of saying, on what "you" mean by the term "feminist":
but the real point is what do "they" mean!   Radical social work
literature contains no definition of the term other than reductionist
definitions.   Ramazanoglu is critical of 'categoricalism' i.e. the
notion that 'men' as a social aggregate oppress 'women' as another
social aggregate.   It was observed in chapter three that such aggregates
are not actors: only actors can do things, formulate intentions, etc.
Nor is it the case that individual human actors and social actors have
'objective' interests: actors' forms of thought, intentions, actions,
and the outcomes of actions, are not direct or indirect 'necessary
effects' of actors' 'membership' of taxonomic collectivities such as
'men' or 'women'.   Ramazanoglu, though she does not directly tackle
reductionism in the sense just stated, writes (ibid., pp.433-4) that

A woman is well aware of her own wedding, but does   not necessarily experience marriage as a patriarchal relationship. A feminist standpoint cannot justify ignoring women's experiences as "real" even where women themselves do not experience oppression. The problem is than how to balance the feminist ... interpretation of theorized, essential relationships, such as the shift-workers' patriarchal marriages, against many womens' lack of experience of their marriages as oppressive.

On the issue of 'unitariness', Ramazanoglu (1989) notes that '... gender is not the only basis of womens' subordination' (ibid., p.435) and she puts the question: is '... a white, middle-class feminist's perspective, which discovers the common interests of all women in sexual politics, as valid as the black, or working-class, or black-working-class feminist's which discovers divisions between women?' (ibid.). Ramazanoglu (1989) refers (ibid., p.436) to Cain's (1986) epistemological postulate that '... knowing from a feminist standpoint is not the same as and indeed precludes knowing from a working-class or black standpoint' (ibid., p.265). Ramazanoglu (1989) concludes that 'feminism cannot afford to ignore the power relationships between women' (ibid., p.437). Her argument is that white middle-class women do not have the same experiences or 'interests' as white working-class women, or as black women, and black middle-class women do not have the same experiences or 'interests' as working-class black women (ibid., p.436). It would be mistaken to uncritically endorse the whole of Ramazanoglu's account. Her account is not in all respects explicitly anti-reductionist in terms of its analysis of power, social action, and the conditions-of-action; and some of her statements require a far more explicit clarification of ontological and epistemological problems surrounding uses of the concept 'real' interests whether ascribed to globalistic social aggregates or ascribed to some cross-cutting combinations that produce various sub-categories such as 'working class women'. Nevertheless, her analysis serves, in the terms just outlined, to raise some important questions about feminist social work theories and political practices.

An underlying theme in Ramazanoglu's (1989) feminist analysis is her critique of white feminists' marginalization of racism, particularly the racism experienced by black women. Concerning employment conditions, black social services staff of both sexes have in general experienced discrimination to a far greater extent than either white women or white men (Hutchinson-Reis, 1989). Simpkin (1989) in a review of radical social work in the 1970's and early 1980's, notes that 'Racism ... had been virtually ignored ... except in so far as racism was linked with the fight against fascism. The fact that there were virtually no black workers in qualified social work escaped the notice of radicals and establishment alike' (ibid., p.170). Two amongst other reasons for, until recently, radical social work's failure to address racisms are the previously noted tendency of Marxist social workers to reduce all forms of inequality to, ultimately, an expression of structural class dynamics; and the tendency among feminist social workers to reduce varieties of social inequalities to, ultimately, an expression of various 'commonalities' and 'real' ('objective') interests imputed to 'women' as a social aggregate (Ramazanoglu, 1989; Shah 1989, p.180; Crompton, 1989, p.581). The problems of Marxist and feminist social work discourses are deeply rooted. In some recent anti-racist accounts of social work and social policy issues there are at least a few indications that the serious flaws contained in other versions of radical social work will not be replicated in the form of reductionist interpretations of the nature of racisms. An example is Gurnah's (1989) largely 'middle-range' account of some specific organizational and other obstacles facing the development of anti-racist strategies. Gurnah (1989) does not fully develop an explicitly anti-reductionist account of power and social action and in places, such as his references to 'petty bourgeois' values and 'neo-colonialists' (ibid., pp.116-17), his assertions make no significant contribution to the development of non-reductionist empirically based conceptualizations of the processes that might be involved in the contingent reproduction of contemporary racisms in (and across) particular sites of action. These criticisms aside, his analysis of specific ideational, organizational, and policy issues in the construction of anti-racist practices is in places incisive and he identifies a range of possible factors (some of which are noted in the next chapter) that may have significance in the design and delivery of public sector services. More generally, however, neither Gurnah's account nor any existing social work account has generated anything resembling an adequate, non-reductionist explanatory interpretation of the various forms of social inequality and their spatial and temporal reproduction. Can the same be said of sociology?

At various points in the earlier chapters it was observed that contemporary non-reductionist sociology, though at an early stage of development, has made important contributions (sometimes in empirical form) to an understanding of issues involved in the analysis of social and political life. Positive contributions are possible, too, in the indirect sense that anti-reductionist sociology is able to expose deficiencies in many existing 'explanations' of social phenomena: in principle, this narrows down the range of credible (i.e. non-reductionist) explanations of phenomena and serves to stimulate a re-direction of energies towards the search for more adequate forms of explanation. However, specifically in the analysis of social inequalities to do with 'race', gender, and social class, some particularly abstruse explanatory problems remain.

An unresolved issue in social science and in welfare politics

It is necessary to critically assess the extent to which modern non-reductionist sociology is likely to succeed in providing theoretically and empirically adequate accounts of temporally and spatially pervasive forms of inequality, including those commonly associated with class, 'race', and gender, without in those explanatory accounts sliding backwards to the outworn reductionisms, reifications, and teleological 'explanations' that have justifiably been rejected in contemporary non-reductionist social science, and in some social policy studies (for example, Barrett and Hill, 1981; Hjern and Porter, 1981; Ham and Hill, 1984, pp.107-8). In the space available for this chapter, it is possible to provide only an abridged treatment of the problems involved in transcending reductionist theories of social inequalities.

A central postulate in anti-reductionist sociology is that there is no structurally 'given' hierarchy-of-sites (or of actors) with those at 'higher' levels always having a structurally predetermined capacity to control all the activities and events that occur in other sites: decisions and actions '... taken within local sites may well be affected by what happens elsewhere ... (but) ... it does not follow that they are determined' (Hindess, 1986a, p.122). The question of which decisions and events in which sites have significant social effects that are disseminated spatially and temporally, is a contingent empirical variable for investigation, not a 'necessary' or inevitable nor even predispositional 'expression' of a structural 'script' (Duster, 1981, p.114). To posit the existence of any such script is patently reductionist. Hindess (1986a) notes that the relations that develop between sites of action are influenced by diverse phenomena that range from legislation to generalized social discourses, conventions, and techniques that sometimes are disseminated across a large number of sites (ibid., p.121). The existence of some patterned regularities and continuities in the contingent construction and space-time dissemination of some particular materials across sites, is acknowledged in anti-reductionist sociology as one empirically expectable dimension of social life. Indeed, anti-reductionist sociology postulates that 'power' as an emergent, contingent outcome of strategic interactions consists, in the case of relatively long-lasting but contingently reproduced asymmetries, of strategic actors' success in 'enrolling' and 'stabilizing' particular relations of meaning, membership, and practice across a large number of relevant sites through social space and time (Clegg, 1989, p.225). In chapter three, the point was made that power is an effect, not a cause, of strategic success (Law, 1986a). The capacity to shape events is not irreversible: the outcomes of most social actions are inherently reversible (Callon, 1986; Callon and Latour, 1981). This is partly because power is not a structurally 'given' or 'fixed' capacity of particular actors. Moreover, neither power, nor a capacity for social action, nor therefore causal responsibility for outcomes, can exist anywhere else other than amongst actors. Hindess (1986a) observes that to impute causal responsibility for social conditions to social aggregates ('society', 'classes', 'men', 'white people', etc.) that do not have the means of formulating or of acting upon decisions is to refer to 'fictitious actors' (ibid., p.116) and this has the two unfortunate consequences of obscuring the social processes resulting in those conditions and of obscuring analysis of what can be done to change them (ibid., pp.116-17).

Underlying the points just made, and for the reasons set out more fully in chapter three, methodological collectivism is reductionist and therefore, in the terms advocated here, is a form of analysis that should be rejected as having no empirical explanatory value. Another form of reductionism is methodological individualism: this is the idea that 'society' should be analysed as the aggregated outcome of the desires, decisions, and actions of countless individual human actors. This type of reductionism has no explanatory value. Individual human actors' forms of thought, objectives, decisions and actions and also the outcomes of their actions are in various ways influenced by conditions that in some sense are external to the actors in question; but these conditions themselves require non-reductionist empirical explanation. Aside from this, there are important actors (i.e. social actors) other than human individuals (Hindess, 1986a, p.114) and the activities of social actors and the conditions within which they operate require non-reductionist explanation. There may be some relatively enduring conditions but there is, as Hindess (1986a) observes '... no need to posit some necessity in those conditions as a precondition for analysing them' (ibid., p.123). Enduring conditions, where these can be empirically shown to exist, are sustained not by some systemic 'needs' of social systems or by any structural necessities but '... because they are situated in complex networks of intersecting practices and conditions' (ibid.).

If, however, the explanatory potential of the 'new' non-reductionist forms of sociology are to be fully realized, it is clear that further work remains to be done in accounting for the contingent reproduction of spatially pervasive and temporally enduring conditions of action. What, in any specific social context, an individual or social actor is able to do is partly a function of relatively indeterminate and (in both a spatial and temporal sense) relatively episodic conditions of action: and partly a function of relatively enduring and socially reproduced conditions of action, amongst which are included contingently reproduced forms of inequality. Recent sociology is better at accounting for the former of these sets of conditions (the 'episodic') than the latter (the relatively enduring). In Clegg's (1989) anti-reductionist sociology, power is analysed in terms of episodic, dispositional, and facilitative forms of power (ibid., p.211). The last two forms of power in particular, but also the first, relate to 'standing conditions' in the sense that what an actor is able to achieve in a particular ('episodic') context is not structurally or historically predetermined, but is nevertheless related to '... the standing conditions of access to means and resources which may restrict or enable the achievement of outcomes' (ibid., p.217). Clegg (1989) is clear that the existence and social reproduction of these standing conditions should not be investigated in reductionist terms: their social reproduction is contingent. Standing conditions are effective when they are 'invoked' by actors, some of whom may be successful in organizing standing conditions in order to realize their constitutive causal powers (ibid., pp.215-17). This model of power is better at explaining in non-reductionist terms how in certain contexts particular standing conditions are reproduced, than at explaining in non-reductionist terms how and why these standing conditions are reproduced across large stretches of space-time.

Organizations are both social actors and sites within which occur 'episodic' reproductions of particular standing conditions that include forms of inequality: although the processes involved in this reproduction are contingent, and not an 'effect' of any putative structural exigency, some organizations may be '... structures of gender, ethnic and class dominancy' (Clegg, 1989, p.196). There are, for instance, some standing conditions that typically condition the reproduction of social inequalities reflected in the division-of-labour in organizations. This raises, if the terms 'class', 'race', and 'gender' are not to be removed from the vocabulary of social analysis, specific and in some sense obvious questions to which there are no obvious or easy answers. For example, why is it that white people in British society generally fare better in organizational divisions-of-labour and in the job market than black people (Dominelli, 1988, p.23)? Why in these respects do men generally fare better than women (Howe, 1986)? Why in these respects do middle-class women fare better than both working-class women (Smart, 1979) and working-class men (Nelson, 1990)? And why, it may be asked, are those who design social services policies almost always middle-class when the clients of social services are overwhelmingly working-class (Jones, 1983, pp.11-12)? Enough has been said earlier to indicate why these examples of relatively enduring standing conditions, and the processes involved in their social reproduction, cannot adequately be 'explained' in reductionist terms. It is not that reductionist accounts are incomplete in some way or that they merely require, to be effective, some theoretical or empirical caveats, re-working or qualifiers added to them: rather, they are accounts that are inherently and irremediably flawed and they therefore should be abandoned in toto as having no legitimate explanatory role in the analysis of social and political life. However, nor, as yet, has recent anti-reductionist social science formulated adequate accounts of how and why it is that some standing conditions and asymmetries of power associated with class, gender, 'race' and ethnicity (Held and Thompson, 1989, p.16) are in some form socially reproduced with such remarkable persistence and apparent regularity across a large number of temporally and spatially distributed sites of action.   Concerning, for instance, the social reproduction of inequalities of class and gender in organizational divisions of labour, Clegg (1989) notes that these are strategically and contingently reproduced through time and space.   He observes 'This is not to say that either class or gender will necessarily function in this way: simply that past sociological observation suggests that it probably will' (ibid., p.198, emphases added).   It is precisely this 'probably will' that requires explanation. As Clegg (1989) puts it, contingency reigns '... albeit with a hegemonic ... cast' (ibid.).   The question of how hegemonic 'casts' might be adequately explained without recourse to reductionisms that belong to a bygone era of social analysis and which are now perceived to have no explanatory relevance, is unresolved in contemporary social science. There is currently very little prospect that radical social work will play any significant role in tackling these issues: the form if not in all respects the contents of radical social work discourse belongs to the 1970's and, for the foreseeable future, is likely to remain within that mode.   Radical social work, that is to say, has failed to even 'see the problem' of reductionism, still less confront the explanatory challenge that exists for post-reductionist social and political analysis in addressing major problems of inequality and related issues of social justice and of reform.

Whether, in social work, clients and service-users should be expected to await these developments, is another question.   The wheels of theoretical innovation and empirical understanding grind slowly, as too does the pace of practical social reform.   In the meantime, in light of the data examined at the beginning of the chapter with reference to the legitimation crisis of the modern welfare state, there may be urgent and compelling reasons for evolving new organizational and service-delivery frameworks that give citizens and service-users a greater say in the design and delivery of social services.   This is, at least, the view of some commentators whose arguments in favour of a radical organizational reconstruction of social work, together with social work rejections of these arguments, will be examined in the following chapter.   As we shall see, there are grounds for suggesting that traditional and radical social work's objections against practical mechanisms that might shift power from professionals to clients are deeply institutionalized 'professional' objections which, to use the terms referred to earlier, are a contingently reproduced part of the 'standing conditions' that have historically governed the typically hierarchical form of the relationship between professional social workers and their clients.

6 Organizational, professional and service-delivery issues

Almost all the topics examined in previous chapters are in various ways given practical expression in the organizational structures and practice frameworks through which services are provided. This is certainly so when viewed from the standpoint of clients and service-users. Social work cognitions, theories, and political values, to the extent that these may be reflected in organization and practice, are directly experienced by clients through social work's institutional mechanisms of service delivery and through clients' experiences of their contacts with social workers. The first section of the chapter will examine the post-Seebohm emergence of hierarchic bureau-professionalism in social work, and the tensions that have developed between advocates of this model and those who argue for looser, more 'organic' organizational structures. This is followed by a review of the decentralization movement which entered the social work scene in the 1980's, and which on current indicators is likely to become a highly contentious focus of social work debate in the decade ahead. The decentralization theme is re-inspected in the last two sections of the chapter with reference to the political theories drawn upon by actors involved in the decentralization debate and with reference to the factors underlying traditional and radical professionals' resistance against organizational change.

The rise of bureau-professionalism in modern social work

The critics of bureau-professionalism referred to later are, in the main, advocates of alternative 'organic' structures. A preliminary clarification of meanings given to this term is therefore appropriate. Most social work references to the term 'organic' are derived in one way or another from Burns and Stalker's (1961) distinction between mechanistic and organistic organizational structures. Mechanistic (or 'bureaucratic') structures are characterized by hierarchical systems of authority and control; and by predetermined allocations of tasks and roles that are predefined by senior managers. Organistic structures are based on the decentralization of authority and a relative absence of predetermined role and task allocations; an alternative emphasis is placed upon processes of adjustment and re-definition of individual roles through informal as well as formal interaction with others, and where individuals' particular expertise and task-interests are 'negotiated' and if necessary 're-negotiated' in the ongoing distribution of tasks (ibid., pp.119-21). Burns and Stalker (1961) argue that mechanistic structures are appropriate in stable environmental conditions where the quantity and nature of demands for organizational goods and services are relatively predictable; conversely, flexible organistic structures are '... appropriate to changing conditions, which give rise constantly to fresh problems and unforeseen requirements for action which cannot be broken down or distributed automatically arising from the functional roles defined within a hierarchic structure' (ibid., p.120). Although critics of social work's post-Seebohm (1968) hierarchical bureau-professional structure advocated various 'organic' alternative organizational forms for the social services, professional(izing) actors rejected these alternatives and endorsed the establishment of large scale 'professional' bureaucracies that were based on the principle of hierarchy.

In the British social services, the creation of the new social services department (SSD's) at the beginning of the 1970's was heralded with professional optimism (Parker, 1971, pp.113-14; Tilbury, 1971). The journal of the British Association Of Social Workers, Social Work Today described social work expectations in its editorial comment of April 1971, and observed '... there is currently much excitement among social workers and expectations are high. It is important that this enthusiasm should be encouraged ...' (Editorial Social Work Today April 1971, p.2). Writing in the same edition of Social Work Today, Richards (1971) in a conference paper to newly appointed Directors of Social Services argued that the prevailing mood of professional confidence was built on a sure foundation that would '... influence ... society as a whole ...' (ibid., p.7). However within a relatively short space of time criticisms of modern social work's bureau-professional 'pathologies' accumulated, a development noted by numerous commentators including Parry and Parry (1979), Clarke (1979), Satyamurti (1981), and Lee (1982). The implications of these criticisms will be returned to later in the chapter.

In the 1970's, bureau-professionalism in a form that was strongly opposed to the organic concept received intellectual support through the academic and management consultancy work associated with 'the Brunel studies' (for example, SSORU, 1974; Billis et al., 1980). These studies have significance, first, because the model of social services structure advocated by them is analytically useful as a comparative framework that may be contrasted with organic concepts, and secondly, their role in the 1970's in providing intellectual support for the principle of social work organizational hierarchy is politically significant. A large volume of research and management consultancy material was produced over a number of years by the Social Services Organization Research Unit (SSORU) of the Institute Of Organization and Social Studies directed by Elliott Jaques at Brunel University. The unit was established through central government funding in the late 1960's to research and advise upon the organizational and management structure of the new social services departments. The research, publication, and consultancy service of the unit was the largest to have been undertaken in the British personal social services (Brown, 1974; Westland, 1974) and the unit's consultancy services and research data were widely disseminated through publications, seminars and conferences attended, in the main, by senior social work management staff and representatives of other bodies associated with the work of the unit and with the social work profession (SSORU, 1974, pp.14-15)).

An objective of the Brunel unit was to engage in 'the ... general dissemination ... of ideas through conference activity, publications, contact with professional and other staff in central government ...' (ibid., p.15). A proactive role in the social construction of modern social work bureau-professionalism is expressed in a statement by the Brunel unit in 1974 that (ibid., p.237)

> ... change ... (is) ... sought at two distinct levels - change in individual departments as a result of intensive project work within them over extended periods of time, and change nationally through the dissemination of ideas in written form and through the national conference programme ...'

The Brunel researchers employed organizational and management concepts developed by Jaques (1975, 1977) in his 'Glacier Project' writings and in the work of his associate, Brown (1960). Many of these concepts (e.g. 'work-stratum levels', 'time-span zones', 'prescribed output') rested on an assumption that a natural hierarchy of work exists in organizations (Whittington and Bellaby, 1979, p.518). This assumption is associated with the concept 'work-strata' (Billis et al., 1980, p.121) which implies that objective, rational criteria are available for constructing a vertical task-stratification model in which definitions of, for example, 'professional work', 'non-professional work', 'more (or less) complex tasks', etc., are logically-defined or 'necessary' categories dictated axiomatically by the functional requirements of the organization and its formal purposes.

A problem in analyses predicated on the assumption of a 'natural' hierarchy of work is their tendency to overlook processes involved in the social production of a 'negotiated order' in which the social construction of hierarchies reflects differences of power, interests, and perspectives among the various social groups involved in their construction. Formalist management concepts of the kind used in the Brunel Studies may be contrasted with Bulmer et al.'s (1986) analysis of organizational decision-making processes and with Hardy's (1981, pp.65-75) analysis of how the two contrasting concepts of organizational 'rationality' and of 'negotiation' are deployed in the study of processes involved in the formulation of social policy.

The organic concept rests on a view that work roles, and task-performances are 'negotiable' within limits that are wider and have more fluid, re-definable boundaries than those connoted in systems predicated upon assumptions that a 'natural' work hierarchy exists in organizations. Whittington and Bellaby (1979) are critical of the Brunel Studies' tacit invocation of the concept 'natural' hierarchy, which in Whittington and Bellaby's view resulted in an aura of 'scientificity' being given to the Brunel researchers' '... ideological justification for hierarchical management structure' (ibid., p.524). Whittington and Bellaby's (1979) thesis is that the Brunel Institute through its publications, management consultancy services and other

methods used for disseminating its organizational perspectives, sought
to provide academic legitimation for a 'natural' hierarchical structure
that was fused to the principle of social work professionalism; this was
achieved through the construction of complex management structures and
lines of accountability designed to accommodate 'professional' social
work in a <u>controlling</u> position in what would otherwise be a
professionally-threatening 'bureaucracy'.

The concept 'bureau-professionalism' as defined in Parry and Parry
(1979, p.43), or 'professional bureaucracy' in Taylor-Gooby and Dale's
(1981, p.206) similar use of the term, is fashioned from an 'either-or'
conception of professionalism <u>or</u> bureaucracy: this takes the form that
if 'ideal-typical' professional autonomy is unattainable in social work,
the professionally unpalatable alternative of 'ideal-typical'
hierarchical bureaucracy is avoidable only through the construction of a
hybrid model of 'professional-bureaucracy'. It was this <u>hybrid</u>
organizational structure that Lee (1982) had in mind in his suggestion
that control of sub-professional 'social services work' by professional
social workers is achieved through a vertical task-stratification model
in which traditional definitions of 'professional' social work skills
('interpersonal' work with clients) are re-defined so as to extend to
the notion that 'professional competence' (in social work) is also
synonymous with the skills required for 'management control' of the
social services as a whole (ibid.. pp.28-9, and p.32). This point made
by Lee will be returned to in the following chapter where it will be
observed that professional actors in the 1980's struggled, against
considerable opposition, to preserve a hierarchical model of social work
education and training that corresponded with and helped reproduce the
hierarchical organizational division of labour that emerged in the SSD's
after the early 1970's.

Whittington and Bellaby (1979) are critical of the 'Brunel'
assumption that ideal-type professional autonomy (identified by the
Brunel researchers with the role of hospital medical consultant) was
unattainable in social work and that professional-bureaucracy was
'therefore' the only alternative to a wholly non-professional
bureaucratic hierarchy; in particular, the Brunel researchers in their
advocacy of professional-bureaucracy failed to evaluate the <u>organic</u>
concept as an alternative solution (ibid., p.514). The Brunel
researchers make note of the organic concept but appear to dismiss it
without engaging in analysis of it. Shortly after the publication of
Whittington and Bellaby's (1979) paper, the Brunel text <u>Organizing
Social Services Departments</u> (Billis et al., 1980) devoted a short
paragraph to the concept, and suggested the literature '... about the
correlations between various kinds of organizational structure and
organizational environment ... (is) ... at broad descriptive or
ideological levels ...' (ibid., p.29). In fact, there already existed a
number of highly detailed American studies of some practical
applications of the concept in welfare organizations (Klein and Snyder,
1965; Litwak and Meyer, 1966 and 1967; Lorch and Lawrence, 1968; Litwak,
1970) and a number of British studies (for example, Cooper, 1975;
Bennett, 1980; Butcher et al., 1980).

Whittington and Bellaby (1979) in their criticism of the Brunel
Institute's 'dismissal' of the possibility that alternative structural
forms (other than professional-bureaucracy) might be possible in the
personal social services, note that (ibid., p.514)

The SSORU findings and recommendations on the personal social
services ... amount to an approval of the principle of hierarchy and

an attempt to discredit alternatives. Such alternatives, not all of them discussed by the SSORU group, were advocated by others ... and most often these were variants of the 'organic' structure described by Burns and Stalker ... (but) ... so resounding was their defeat that little has been heard of them since. The hierarchical principle familiar elsewhere in local government departments was implanted in a variety of ways in the social services departments.

When Whittington and Bellaby wrote this in 1979 the decentralization debate and notions of organic service-delivery frameworks later associated with 'community social work', were still relatively muted. Nor, in 1979, did debate of the 'legitimation crisis' of state social services preoccupy the social work and welfare literature to the same extent as occurred afterwards. It was in the following decade that a new and more 'critical' mood emerged as a challenge against established social work. In public sector services in the 1980's, the idea developed that service-democratization together with an 'organic' concept of decentralization and increased user-responsiveness, might be a viable response to service-users' expressed dissatisfactions with existing methods of service-delivery: in social work, however, this response to the legitimation crisis of the modern welfare state turned out to be highly controversial and, in the ways described later, was strongly resisted by 'traditional' and 'radical' social work lobby groups who remained committed to the hierarchical principle of bureau-professionalism.

Hoggett and Hambleton (1988) in their review of organizational and social policy developments during the 1980's, observe that in public sector services '... decentralization should now be considered a trend rather than a fad ... the ... deep-seated trend towards decentralized arrangements ... now appears to be on the agenda' (ibid.,p.3). Hoggett and Hambleton note that service 'decentralization' and participatory 'democratization' are not the same concepts (ibid., pp.3-4) even though they often co-incide. Although advocates of the one tend also to be advocates of the other, Hoggett and Hambleton's (1988) distinction recognizes that, in principle, decentralization is possible without democratization: decentralization based on a consumerist, user-responsive approach (tailoring services to what clients say they need) is possible while retaining centralised power and authority and without making the organization accountable to the people it serves (ibid., p.3). Decentralization may sometimes of itself create a form of democratization but not necessarily in the 'collectivist' sense of participatory democratization based on specific practical mechanisms that give citizens and service-users a role in the planning and delivery of services. Although this distinction is not analytically unimportant, the empirical reality is that the two concepts are fused together in the local public sector where '... the two aims of decentralization and democratization are inextricably linked' (ibid., p.4).

The Seebohm Report (1968) had stated that citizen '... participation ... provides a means by which further consumer control can be exercised over professional and bureaucratic power' (ibid., p.152, para.493). Social work professionals, however, gave only theorized lip-service to this idea of citizen-participation. When in the 1980's the idea was resurrected in a practical form by the Barclay Report (1982, p.215) it was roundly condemned by a majority of traditional and radical professional lobby groups. Collins and Stein (1989) refer to the failure to develop '... credible participatory structures within the personal social services' (ibid., p.86). They observe that (ibid.)

Very few of the advocates of greater participation in the personal social services make a clear statement of the level of participation or the extent of redistribution of power they consider appropriate, or their underlying rationale. And, in similar vein, some of the other problematic issues are swept under the carpet: the relationship between professionalism and participation, social control and democracy, consumerism and elected representation. These issues will not go away by just ignoring them.

Traditional and radical professionals throughout the 1980's assembled a list of discrete arguments in favour of bureau-professionalism and against the practical implementation of 'participatory' models of service-delivery premised on the democratization and decentralization of services: this list of dissociated professional arguments in favour of the bureau-professional status quo will be returned to shortly.

The decentralization of services

The Barclay Report (1982) argued that too much social work emphasis had been placed on professional casework, and also challenged the assumptions upon which the concept of hierarchic bureau-professionalism had been established. The Barclay (1982) proposals for decentralized 'community' social work were designed to provide practical mechanisms that might '... lead to greater participation from the community ... as partners in formulating policies on social services departments and also in criticizing and evaluating existing services' (ibid., p.229). The Barclay concepts of localism, collective 'patch' methods of working, citizen-participation, and preventive community social work, are noted in Cooper and Denne's (1983) arguments in favour of decentralized 'community' social workers who '... know their neighbourhood intimately and can call upon local helping mechanisms to prevent people becoming ... clients' (ibid., p.17). Community social workers in a preventive role are more likely than distanced bureau-professional caseworkers to have success in minimizing 'the risk of clienthood' (ibid.) by virtue of the decentralized community worker being 'close to the community' and having a close working knowledge of local formal and informal resource networks that can be strengthened and supported to help individuals, families, and other groups (ibid.). Advocates of community social work emphasise that a significant resource may in some circumstances be informal help ('informal care') from neighbours, friends, and family: where this pattern of help exists for an individual, family, or for other groups, it should be supported by community social workers and by the resources of the local social services department (Cooper and Denne, 1983, p.17). The community social work method known as 'social care planning' has a role not only in the preventive sense just referred to but also in the putting together of planned 'packages' of resources for individual clients or groups, these resources being drawn from the statutory sector, voluntary organizations, and also from the 'informal' care sector.

There is, too, a 'social action' component of decentralized community social work which has a political dimension in so far as community social workers may sometimes become 'organically' involved with local neighbourhood projects, local political associations, residents' groups, and neighbourhood pressure-groups of various kinds. It is questionable

whether community social work is as 'left-wing' or as 'radical' as some
professional social work critics have suggested, but this political
dimension nevertheless figured prominently in the initial list of
professional objections against the Barclay Report (1982). Soon after
its publication, Pearson (1983) stated that community social workers
might become embroiled in community politics that '... stir up
antagonisms between local people and the employing agencies of the local
state' (ibid., p.81). According to Pearson (1983), if decentralized
community social workers become involved inappropriately in community
politics this will damage professional social work's public credibility
(ibid., p.81) and reflect a failure to appreciate that '... social work
is neither fitted nor designed for ... vanguard postures' (ibid.).

One of the themes that has emerged from a number of empirical studies
is the accessibility of decentralized community social workers to local
people (Thomas and Shaftshoe, 1983). If this style of 'community'
social work becomes more influential in the 1990's it will, it is worth
noting, require a major change of direction in professional social work
education and training. Stone's (1986) claim that only a relatively
minor change of emphasis will be required, is unconvincing and not
sustained by empirical evidence. The data reviewed by Rees and Wallace
(1982) suggests that social work educators' proclivity for teaching
esoteric, 'rarefied' (ibid., p.166) professional casework and groupwork
theories and methods is '... a major difficulty in encouraging ... (new)
... styles of practice' (ibid.). Beresford and Lyons (1986) show that
community social work requires a substantial re-orientation in training.
A similar observation is made by Sainsbury (1985) who suggests that
community social work requires a more sociological approach (ibid., p.7)
in professional social work education, which is '... still largely
concerned with the production of soloists rather than members of the
chorus' (ibid.).

The authors of the Barclay Report (1982) had reason to anticipate
strong professional criticism and this seems to be reflected in the
report's strategic use of presentational arguments. A strategy
available to actors for the 'translation' and 'enrolment' (Law, 1986a;
Callon et al., 1986) of new materials is to present a case for change
while arguing that 'in reality' it does not involve any major departure
from existing practices, other than an extension or amplification of
some aspect of already-existing practices. A variant of this is where
proposals for change are said to be merely a logical, if belated,
putting into effect of a long-established policy. A strategy of this
kind was one of the presentational arguments employed in the Barclay
Report (1982) which suggested the proposal for decentralized community
social work was merely a way of giving effect to an unimplemented
intention of the Seebohm Report (1968). In fact, suggested the Barclay
Report (1982), its recommendation for community social work was doing
'... little more than repeat the recommendation of Seebohm' (ibid.,
para.13.18, emphasis added). This presentational ploy did not wash with
professional social work lobby groups. Whatever the stated intentions
of the Seebohm Report (1968) concerning citizen-participation and
community involvement in the provision of services, the expansion of
post-Seebohm professionalism was in real terms based almost entirely on
professional casework and groupwork theories and practices implemented
and managed through the hierarchical principle of bureau-professionalism
(Whittington and Bellaby, 1979).

It was noted earlier that professionalizing actors in the 1980's drew
up a lengthy list of reasons for rejecting the Barclay Report's (1982)
proposals for decentralized community social work. Pinker (1983b)

argued that '... social work is professional casework' (ibid., p.68, emphasis added). He challenged the report's emphasis on social care planning and stated that 'social work ... and casework are virtually synonymous' (ibid., p.69). In Pinker's (1983b) view, support for community social work comes from two opposed political ideological positions. The first reflects a right-wing belief that community social work will reduce public expenditure through increased reliance on informal care (ibid., p.74). The second reflects socialist motives for community work, and the Barclay Report was '... influenced by fashionable opinion in favour of egalitarian forms of community action and participation' (Pinker, 1983b, p.74). Pinker argued that the 'real' issues of how to use highly specialist professional knowledge and professional skills are left unaddressed when '... intellectuals and activists who are largely middle-class condemn the elitist nature of professionalism and the status of "esoteric" knowledge ...' (ibid.). In reality, it is mainly clients who condemn the elitist nature of professionalism, a point that will be returned to later.

The relationship between political ideologies and organizational and practice prescriptions is more fluid and complex than implied by Pinker. Community social work is a practical expression of arguments for service decentralization and democratization. Decentralization, though, is supported by radicals associated with the 'new urban left' (Weinstein, 1986) and by welfare pluralists who have little in common with the radical socialism of the new urban left nor, of course, with the 'new right' whose politics are expressly rejected by welfare pluralists (Hadley and McGrath, 1984, p.15). The point here is that there is no straightforward or invariant relationship between, on the one hand, political values, or indeed formulated occupational-professional interests; and on the other, advocacy of any particular organizational and practice framework. So far as professional self-interests are concerned, the association between professionalization, casework method, and bureau-professional organization, although close, is nevertheless a socially constructed and contingent association. In principle, alternative methods such as 'social care planning' could be professionalized, rather than dismissed as an 'anti-professional' community-based activity. There is nothing inherently 'non-professional' about social care planning. This has strategic implications for professional(izing) actors. If there are strong indications that at some future date a version of community social work such as social care planning will, despite professional resistance, be 'imposed' upon conventional bureau-professional social work there may well be strategic advantages to be gained if casework-oriented professionals 'drop' their resistance against social care planning, re-define it, and incorporate ('enrol') it into 'professional' social work. A strategy of this kind is evident in Bamford's (1990) professional text on the future of social work. Sometimes, rather than continue to reject innovations as inherently 'anti-professional' and then risk being left out on a limb if resistance fails (not to mention the difficulty of having to 'reverse' all ones' previous 'professional' arguments against the innovation) it is better to 'enrol' new, potentially professionally threatening policies and to attempt to do so on the most favourable (i.e., 'professional') terms possible. A strategy along these lines is particularly appropriate for professional social work. To define 'professional' social work exclusively in terms of casework and inter-personal groupwork skills without extending the repertoire of 'professional' skills to include social planning functions is to court the danger of remaining forever an 'incomplete profession' (Gilbert and

Specht, 1977) and even more threateningly, to risk social planning functions being removed entirely from the domain of 'professional social work' and taken-over by other occupational, administrative or professional groups. If this happened, it is possible that professional casework itself would be re-defined as a kind of 'second-tier' activity that should be controlled by those responsible for the 'larger' social care planning framework within which casework would be merely one component: far better, from the standpoint of professional social work, that 'social work' be re-defined to include having charge of this planning function. This form of strategic professional manoeuvre, however, was not the initial response of social work professionals to the Barclay Report (1982). In the early 1980's, it seemed to professionalizing actors that the possibility still existed of 'locking' social work into the professional modus operandi of the previous decade.

Shortly after the publication of the Barclay Report, Cypher (1983), the General Secretary of the British Association of Social Workers issued the following statement (ibid., pp.3-4, emphases added)

> If community social work becomes the vogue .... There is the real issue of who will take charge and develop those things like knowledge, values, and skills lying at the core of social work. For in the cause of flexibility and relevance social work practice does have an inbuilt tendency to fragment ... why community social work ... why not community social service or community social care?

Cypher (1983) argued for 'increased professional autonomy' (ibid., p.4) in the face of what he regarded as Barclay's 'anti-professional' (ibid.) recommendations. Cypher, in the statement just quoted, also evidenced concern about professional 'unity' (will professionalism 'fragment'?) and professional control ('who will take charge?'). In his statement he also emphasised a hierarchical organizational distinction in the social services departments (SSD's) between 'professional social work' and 'social services work'.

It was observed earlier that the Brunel studies lent academic support to professional(izing) arguments that a 'natural' hierarchy of work exists in social services departments. In reality, a hierarchical distinction between professional social work and social services work is socially constructed by actors. It has already been noted that Pinker's (1983b) rejection of the Barclay proposals rested on a view that social work is professional casework (ibid., p.68). One of Pinker's (1984) reasons for rejecting 'Barclay' community social work was that it failed to make '... a distinction between social work and social services' (ibid., p.6, emphasis added). Pinker objected that the Barclay proposals were an attempt '... to combine social work and social service roles and tasks ...' (ibid.). As noted earlier, professional actors' struggles in the early and mid-1980's to preserve this vertical task-stratification model in the SSD's centred upon professionals' and academic-professionals' rejection of proposals to blur this distinction in social work education and training. As Parsloe (1984) observes, these struggles surrounding the 'fit' between training and the reproduction of a clear hierarchical demarcation line between a casework-led professional social work and very practical 'sub-professional' social services work, were closely enmeshed with professionals' simultaneous resistance against the Barclay Report's (1982) proposals for community social work.

Pearson (1983), it was observed earlier, suggested community social work would damage the public credibility of professional social work.

Pearson (1983) stated that although an element of 'community involvement' is appropriate, social workers should not abandon 'their conventional styles of work' (ibid., p.85) and it '... would be foolish and irresponsible to take social workers further down the de-skilling avenue in the name of a misconceived egalitarianism' (ibid.) Davies (1983) stated that community social work is '... politically dangerous and likely to lead to widespread disquiet about and reaction against social work' (ibid., p.30, emphasis added). In contrast, Bolt (1984) in a description of a community participation experiment in Handsworth reported that service-users' satisfaction with service provision had been significantly increased through their direct involvement in the planning of services. Cooper and Denne (1983) in their account of community social work at Wakefield concluded it is not community social work, but rather, casework professionalism that damages the public credibility of social work: they stated that 'A marked failure of social work with individual clients is the lack of any ... measure of effectiveness. This ... is the cause of public incredulity, even scorn' (ibid., p.18). Cooper and Denne's observations are consonant with the data on service-user perspectives discussed in the previous chapter with reference to the legitimation crisis of state social services. Moreover, far from improving, public perceptions of conventional professional social work services, according to some surveys, had become even more highly critical by the late 1980's (King, 1989, p.16).

Another of Pinker's (1983b) numerous objections against the Barclay proposals for community social work was that constructing 'linkages' to informal care networks would place increased burdens on women as informal carers (ibid., p.71). Of the other critics referred to earlier, Cypher (1983) of the British Association of Social Workers, in rejecting Barclay's 'anti-professionalism', also expressed doubts about '... the existence of informal care networks' (ibid., p.4). Pearson (1983), whose other objections (including professional 'de-skilling') against the Barclay Report were noted earlier, stated that community social work '... will mean placing even more burdens on the unpaid domestic labour of women' (ibid., p.82). Professionals' rejection of community-work on the grounds that it would have bad implications for womens' roles in informal care give the impression of being ideologically appropriated and strategically inserted into a catalogue of other unrelated arguments in favour of retaining the bureau-professional status quo; but this is not to say that this particular argument does not merit serious scrutiny (Lawrence, 1983, p.27).

The Barclay Report (1982) recognized that the bulk of social care is provided by informal carers (neighbours, friends, and especially family and kin) and recommended that social work should therefore in future become more directly concerned with supporting carers than it traditionally had been (Hadley et al., 1987, p.7). Bulmer (1986) notes that the 'The ideal of domiciliary care proclaimed by the vast majority of those actually and prospectively in need of care is in effect a blunt preference for the family' (ibid., p.233). Formal statutory and voluntary organizations provide a far smaller proportion of 'care' than the informal care sector. In describing the extent of informal care, Bulmer (ibid.) observes that

> Something like nine-tenths of the care given to those who in various
> ways cannot fend for themselves in our society is given by spouses,
> parents, children and other kin. If any policy for informal care is
> to be relevant to the actualities of need and provision it must
> begin with relations and the problems and possibilities of

supporting the bonds of kinship.

The Barclay Report (1982) specified that statutory services should have a 'lead' role in the planning of social care. The report notes that some care-services can properly be provided only by statutory services; and in circumstances where informal care networks can be supported the report observes (Barclay Report, 1982, quoted in Social Work Today The Concise Barclay, 1983, p.21) that this support is also ultimately a responsibility of statutory agencies

> Some of the ideas about the capacity of the community to care are confused by a failure to distinguish types of care which can be provided by social networks from those which need to be provided either jointly or entirely by statutory agencies. We think it is vital that a social services department should retain the ultimate responsibility for seeing that social care networks are maintained.

These points are sometimes misunderstood by critics of community social work; nevertheless, there is a possibility that an emphasis upon 'interweaving' formal and informal care sectors will have the effect of increasing the burden on women as unpaid, informal carers. This is related, of course, to cultural assumptions concerning women as 'natural' carers: cultural assumptions of this kind exert 'moral' pressures upon women as having a so-called natural 'duty' or 'obligation' to provide care in the domestic sphere. Drawing upon Graham's (1983) analysis, Finch (1984) refers to the familiar distinction between caring as an expression of love and as a form of labour. Caring about (someone) is not synonymous with caring for (someone) and the former can exist without being expressed as the latter (ibid., pp.14-15). It is not sexist if those women who freely choose to care 'for', say, elderly parents or a dependent spouse or child do so in the knowledge that adequate statutory support exists as an alternative to informal care; and if, having decided to be informal carers they are properly supported by adequate statutory resources designed to 'help the helpers'. However in Finch's view none of these forms of support are likely to be available in adequate form (ibid. p.16) and the possibility of women exercising 'free' culturally unconstrained choices on whether or not to express their care 'about' in the form of caring 'for' is unattainable (ibid.). Because Finch sees no non-sexist alternative to institutional care she concludes that '... the residential route is the only one which ultimately will offer us a way out of the impasse of caring' (ibid.). Sufficient empirical evidence exists (for example, Finch and Groves, 1983) on the roles of women as informal carers to justify some of the concerns expressed by Finch and others. However, Finch's (1984) either-or polarization of institutional 'versus' community care fails to recognize that pragmatic policy options may be available. For example, informal care exhibits regional and local diversities (Pahl, 1984) and policy-prescriptions should also acknowledge that relatively little is known about the contribution of men in the domestic sphere (McKee, 1982). Nor is much known empirically about the motives and perspectives of carers; even less is known about the numbers, identities, and perspectives of 'non-carers', these being '... those who said "no"' (Ungerson, 1987, p.143).
Harris (1985) in a paper titled 'End Points and Starting Points' is critical of Finch's (1984) analysis and he suggests patterns of informal care are more variable than the archetypal situation of a woman looking after her elderly mother; he refers, for example, to the care of

discharged married women mental patients, disabled younger wives, and the care of elderly parents without daughters or married sons (ibid., p.117). Harris refers to research undertaken at the University of Wales at Bangor and cites data that indicate '... the majority of daughterless non-dependent elderly people who need help to live alone rely on sons rather than daughters-in-law' (ibid.). These data also indicate (ibid.) that

> ... where these non-dependent elderly have both sons and daughters the child living nearest tends to be relied upon regardless of sex. It is ... possible that if and when such non-dependent elderly mothers become dependent, the cultural taboos discussed by Ungerson (1983) may result in daughters and daughters-in-law becoming more involved in caring. But this does not mean that sons drop out of the picture. Nor is it necessarily such a distasteful prospect to daughters and daughters-in-law that "the residential" alternative becomes the policy of first choice.

It could, of course, be argued that the men reported in Harris's data who cared 'for' had greater choice than women, who may feel under stronger cultural compulsion to provide care; or that the women and men in Harris's data had no unconstrained choice if formal care resources in Wales are deficient in quantity or quality; or that the particular types of care provided by men and women itself reproduces the sexual division of labour in society. However the point about such issues is precisely that considerably more work needs to be done by way of careful empirically based evaluation of them: too often, debate of these issues slides into simplistic, dogmatic assertions.

The existence of empirical variability in patterns of informal care raises a question mark against '... the crude ways in which the "domestic labour debate" has sometimes been approached since the late 1970's, with a dominant tendency to assume that all domestic work always falls to women as their responsibility ...' (Pearson, 1989, p.30). Subject to this caveat, issues of gender are undoubtedly important in the debate of community social work policies for 'interweaving' and resourcing combined patterns of formal and informal care, and it is possible to agree with Finch's (1984) own suggestion that it '... is ... important to go on studying the impact of such policies upon women (and indeed upon men) ...' (ibid., p.6). Then it might be possible to properly evaluate Pinker's (1983b) assertion that one amongst numerous other 'professional' reasons for rejecting community social work in favour of the existing bureau-professional casework model is the burden that '... would fall largely on women in a community based model of welfare' (ibid., p.71). Similarly, it might then also be possible to better evaluate radical professionals' objections, especially feminist objections, against decentralized community social work.

It is essential that such evaluations should include data on actors' own constructions of meanings surrounding such concepts as 'care about', 'care for', 'choice', and 'non-sexist' community care. In her empirical study Ungerson (1987) was '... struck by two quite different types of carer, particularly among the women: those for whom caring was truly grim, and those for whom it seemed to bestow a certain satisfaction, even, in one or two cases, an extraordinary kind of joy' (ibid., p.144). Ethnographic data on relationships between professionals and carers are another significant resource for policy development purposes. Lewis and Meredith (1988) in their study note that the relationship between professional and carer '... is not the usual one of client and professional; the professional helper <u>must work out how to supplement</u> <u>rather than direct</u>' (ibid., p.157, emphases added). Lewis and Meredith (1988) argue both for a major re-orientation of professional perspectives and for adequate resources to be provided for carers: they observe 'Our evidence suggests that carers do <u>want</u> to care, but that they also need considerable support to enable them to do so' (ibid., p.158, emphasis added). However, do such carers have 'wrong' or 'incorrect' motives and attitudes? Should they simply be given what they 'know' they need: or should their 'consciousness' be 'raised' by feminist social work bureau-professionals? For the reasons discussed in the previous chapters, major empirical and theoretical (not to mention moral and political) problems arise if it is suggested by feminist social workers or others that the expressed preferences and preferred actions of carers should be regarded as 'false consciousness' or as an expression of some putatively 'real' ('objective') structurally-given interests of 'men', or of 'women', or of any other merely taxonomic collectivities. Traditional and radical professionals' resistance against the 'transfer' of power to clients and service-users is manifested in virtually all areas of professional activity , including the one under discussion here. The Barclay Report (1982) as part of its advocacy of service decentralization and democratization, argued for a transfer of power from professionals to, among other citizen groups, informal carers, this being achieved through the construction of specific practical mechanisms aimed at '... allowing informal carers and communities <u>direct influence on how resources are used</u>' (ibid., p.214, emphasis added). The report advocated that social workers and social work managers have a duty to account for their decisions and actions to 'clients' as conventionally defined by professionals, but '... <u>also</u> to informal carers with whom they are in partnership' (ibid., p.215, emphasis added). These issues together with the government's proposals for community care (Caring For People, 1989) indicate that more data are required for policy formulation purposes; but assessment of these issues should not be in terms of the dogmatic assertions that have sprouted up around the 'domestic labour debate' nor in terms of traditional and radical professionals' ideological defences of hierarchic bureau-professionalism as an organizational form for the personal social services.

Another familiar professional objection against decentralization and against 'community' social work is the allegation that decentralization policies rest on a 'romantic illusion' concerning the social structure of communities (Cypher, 1983, p.4; Pinker, 1983b, p.74; Pearson, 1983, p.81). There are adequate grounds for suggesting that these objections are little more than another ideological plank in professionals' social construction of legitimatory theories in defence of the organizational-professional status quo. This statement requires explanation in terms of its larger context. Some of what have been called the 'classic' empirical community studies of the 1950's and early 1960's are reviewed in Frankenberg (1966). There is not the space to review these studies here, but it may be noted they were followed by a period in which British sociologists showed relatively little interest in this field of research. Bulmer (1985) describes the recent resurgence (ibid., p.430) of empirical sociological interest in community studies. Unlike the earlier social anthropological tradition a significant feature of recent community-studies research is its applied perspective, and in particular, exploration of the relation between social networks, 'neighbouring', and patterns of formal, informal, and neighbourhood care. This empirical and applied orientation is described in detail by

Bulmer (1985) who observes recent community studies 'lie on the boundaries between sociology and social policy' (ibid., p.433). Another characteristic of recent work is the shift away from abstract theoretical attempts to define 'community'. This shift involves an abandonment of 'the metaphysical problem of community' (ibid., p.434) in favour of detailed empirical investigation of actual patterns of social relationships and networks of interaction and, as just noted, the relationship of these to 'care' patterns. In rejecting theoretical, abstract and 'metaphysical' ways of thinking about 'community' as a concept, Bulmer (1985, p.434) observes

> To be sure, the existence of ties between neighbours remains empirically problematical, and ... in certain settings, for certain sections of the population, ties between neighbours are slight or relatively unimportant. Ways of life indeed do not coincide with settlement patterns, but in studying neighbours one is not studying settlement patterns but social networks and the ways in which people construct their primary group relationships.

A fuller account of the relatively recent empirically based and also 'applied' reorientation away from mystical, reified conceptions of 'community' is provided in Bulmer's (1986) text Neighbours: The Work of Philip Abrams. Another useful illustration of such an approach, in which empirical data are related to social work and social policy issues, is the 'Glengow' study reported in Cecil et al. (1987) and in Offer et al. (1988).

Recent community-studies data suggest that British sociology in the 1960's and 1970's, in reacting against 'romanticized' illusions about older patterns of community life, had through neglect of empirical inquiry gone 'too far the other way', almost to the extent of supposing that primary group relationships are no longer a significant feature of contemporary social life. This 'over-reaction' is indicated by recent research. For instance, in Wilson and Pahl's (1988) research their respondents regarded their involvement with 'family' as a major part of their everyday lives: it is mistaken to assume 'family' is synonymous with 'household' or with any particular household-type and in Wilson and Pahl's study respondents used the term 'family' to include people who would be regarded in some conventional sociological definitions as 'kin' (ibid., p.236). With regard to social networks in general, Bulmer's (1985) data review indicates that 'A variety of variables - social class, sex, age, stage of life cycle, mobility experience, type of neighbourhood - influence the actual patterns of neighbourly contact and involvement, but there is no evidence that neighbouring has ceased to be a significant relationship' (ibid., p.434).Harris's (1985) data, referred to earlier in connection with Finch's (1984) work, indicates that social class rather than only gender is a factor in mens' involvement in local networks and in 'neighbouring', and he rejects Finch's view that it is mainly women who are 'attached' to local place (Harris, 1985, p.119). Harris observes that the notion that where people work is more salient than where they live is a middle-class notion bound up with occupational and geographical mobility in the advancement of middle-class careers (ibid.). He observes that for very many working-class people 'Attachment to place is very powerful ... working class careers are quite different from ... (middle class) .... Promotion, if it occurs at all, is within a particular work place and involves little or no geographical mobility' (ibid.). Contemporary social life is not, of course, a network of happy relationships among proverbial 'urban villagers': and sometimes, for some groups in some locations, social networks are mutually protective responses to forms of social deprivation. But equally, the distorted images of working-class neighbourhood life held by some 'remote' middle class bureau-professionals is an indication of the sheer 'distance' that exists between traditional and radical professionals and the realities of 'everyday' patterns of life and networks of family and primary-group relationships in many working-class areas. Not everyone lives the same kinds of lifestyle as middle-class professionals! Professional objections against decentralized 'community' social work, in so far as these objections refer to everyday social life among 'ordinary' ('non-professional') people, are founded upon empirically uninformed assumptions that have served as professional ideological justifications for retaining the hierarchical bureau-professional model of organization and for prioritizing 'interpersonal' rather than collectivist, community-based forms of practice.

Another argument in the professional compendium of objections against decentralized 'community' methods of working, relates to 'statutory' social work tasks. In social work, statutory control or protective functions may involve a local authority taking into care a child who is in moral or physical danger, or may entail compulsory hospital admittance under the relevant mental health legislation if this is judged necessary in an individual's own interests or for the protection of others. The Brunel Studies, referred to earlier, argued that statutory social work functions are '... most readily undertaken within the framework of a hierarchically organized agency service' (SSORU, 1974, p.279). Some writers give greater emphasis to the collective, organizational decision-making aspects of such work: others emphasise the individualized 'professional' aspects, as in Henkel's (1984) comment that work of this kind requires individual professional judgement and should be based upon individual professional responsibility (ibid., p.24). Professionals have for some years argued that statutory responsibility means that community social work is either unworkable or undesirable (for example, Pinker, 1983b, p.73). This ignores the fact that the bulk of the work undertaken by social services departments (SSD's) is not 'professional social work', as conventionally (i.e. professionally) defined, but 'social services work' as defined in the hierarchical distinction between these two types of work formulated by, for instance, the British Association of Social Workers (BASW, 1977, p.16, para.3.11 and p.18, para.3.14). The SSD's, as their title suggests, are social services departments in which most of the tasks undertaken consist of social services work. described by the Brunel team as the provision of 'basic services' (Billis et al., 1980, p.88). These services are provided by social services workers, not professional social workers, to a very wide variety of client groups (ibid., p.87). This is reflected in the fact that most of the employees in the SSD's are social services workers, not professional social workers. In view of the relatively tiny proportion of the total range of SSD task-performances, functions, and services classifiable as 'statutory social work' it is not clear why 'professional' statutory social work tasks (not that all professional social work is of this type) should be cited by professional social work lobby groups as a 'necessary' reason for retaining the conventional hierarchic bureau-professional organizational form across the whole of the social services, and as an argument against proposals for decentralizing the social services. Even if it were assumed that a different organizational matrix is appropriate for each 'function' or category of task-performance, it would not be logically necessary to have a single matrix ('bureau-professionalism') to encompass them all, still less would it be necessary to have an all-encompassing organizational matrix tailored to a particular activity ('statutory' social work) that in reality is a very small fraction of the total range of functions, services, and task-performances undertaken by the social services departments. There is, furthermore, some doubt as to whether professionals' arguments against community social work hold water even in those situations that do include the performance of 'statutory' social work tasks. Bailey and McGrath (1984) provide an account of a community social work scheme at Macclesfield in which 'statutory' child-care work is successfully integrated into community social work (ibid., p.19). Bennett (1980) describes his involvement in a decentralized, community-based social services project and comments that prior to this experimental project the professionals to be involved in it were sceptical and 'we were used to throwing out phrases like "statutory work" ...' (ibid., p.161). In fact, says Bennett, work 'with individuals and families continued and statutory obligations were fulfilled' (ibid., p.164) at the same time as the project moved towards preventive community work based on the involvement of clients and local residents in the planning and provision of services. Commenting on Bennett's work, Jordon (1982) observed that in this instance a decentralized, 'community' approach '... has not precluded ... good practice in statutory tasks; rather, it has enabled more informed and coherent policies to be developed' (ibid., p.110). The professional argument that 'statutory' social work requires the retention of a bureau-professional hierarchical structure which locates professional social workers in a controlling position over social services workers, and that the existence of professional 'statutory' tasks means that service decentralization and community social work is unachievable, is an argument that collapses immediately it is put to any serious scrutiny.

Much the same can be said of the arguments examined in the preceding pages where it was observed that social work professionals in the 1980's compiled a catalogue of unsubstantial rationales for retaining the bureau-professional status quo and for struggling against the movement towards community social work and the decentralization and democratization of services. These rationales included: the criticism that community social work is politically 'radical' and will therefore undermine professional social work's public credibility; the objection that community social work involves professional 'de-skilling' and fails to preserve the post-Seebohm hierarchical organizational distinction between professional social work and social services work; the view that community social work will necessarily and inevitably place an improper burden upon women as carers; the professional claim that advocates of community social work hold to abstract, 'reified' assumptions about working-class social networks; and the familiar professional objection that decentralized 'community' approaches to social services work are incompatible with the 'statutory' element in professional social work. Another of the professional objections referred to earlier, and which tacitly underscores many of those just mentioned, was the explicit argument that professional social work is casework: this merits separate comment with reference to an issue of professional strategy that was briefly touched upon earlier in the chapter.

The government's community care proposals for the 1990's are, if they are implemented, likely to involve styles of practice not dissimilar in form to the Barclay Report's (1982) concept of social care planning (Simpkin, 1989, p.171). Cypher's (1983) implied suggestion that the

Barclay 'community approach' is 'social services' work that is inherently intellectually 'less complex' than 'professional social work' was tacticly highly problematic by virtue of making it more difficult at a later date to, in Callon's (1986) term, 'enrol' community social work and social care planning as a 'legitimate' integral part of 'professional' social work. This strategic difficulty also attends Pinker's (1983b) argument that 'social work is professional casework' and, in the early 1980's at least, his implacable professional resistance against the idea that community social work is or may become a legitimate part of professional social work. Professional power, it was argued in chapter three, is, like other forms of power, a contingent and strategic 'outcome' of interactions among actors in particular and usually shifting condition-of-action. In Callon and Latour's (1981) sociology of translation, social actors that wish to 'expand' (or at least, not be diminished in size) have to find ways of 'consigning' threatening materials and 'Only thus can one "grow"' (ibid., p.284). There are grounds for predicting that in the 1990's an increasing number of professional(izing) social work lobby groups will develop strategies intended to 'enrol' community social work and social care planning by means of extending definitions of social work's 'professional' skills repertoire to include casework and other interpersonal skills and skills in social care planning. It is likely that, in effect, a 'new' social work professionalism will be constructed: this will almost certainly be established by the end of the decade. It is highly probable that this development will involve reproducing in a different form the existing hierarchical division of labour in the SSD's; it is likely that the 'new' type of professional social workers involved in social care planning will control the activities of, to use Cypher's(1983) terms, 'community social service' workers and 'community social care' assistants. The new 'hierarchical' training strategy currently being formulated by the Central Council for Eduction and Training In Social Work (CCETSW, 1990) appears to be closely geared to this future professionalizing objective (see chapter seven). In his text The Future of Social Work, Bamford (1990), the former assistant General Secretary and later chair of the British Association of Social Workers, argues that professional social work, for its survival as a 'profession', should recognize the political reality of the movement towards a pluralistic mixed economy of welfare and towards the more collectivist, less casework-dominated approaches associated with social care planning; and should recognize also the political force of the movement towards increased responsiveness to consumer choice. One of Bamford's central concerns is that, in facing these challenges and in responding to them, social work should retain a strong 'professional' identity. In his review of Bamford's arguments, Philpott (1990, p.27) comments

... inspection, quality assurance, registration, and strategic planning will emerge as the leitmotifs of the born-again SSD, where social work will lay claim to exclusive skills ... what's interesting is ... (Bamford's) ... conclusion that in a world of variegated welfare and a dramatic assertion of consumerism emerges a stronger and more distinct professional identity.

Philpott's observations, however, should be viewed in terms of a broader context that includes, among other things, the recent history of social work. Accommodative professional re-orientations of the kind proposed by Bamford (1990) will undoubtedly gather strength in the next few years. But this will not in every respect be a smooth or unproblematic process; its context is the legacy of political scripts that throughout the 1980's infused social work actors' construction of the decentralization-and-democratization theme and its relation to welfare politics. Whether in the 1990's professional social work actors will re-define or abandon all or some of these political scripts, remains to be seen.

Theories and politics in the social construction of service decentralization and democratization

Reflecting the pro-decentralization ethos prevalent among large sections of the Labour left, Tony Benn wrote 'In the light of our experience of state authorities in various forms, the democratic left would want to emphasise self-management and the decentralization of initiative and control to protect us from the abuses of central power' (Tony Benn, MP, quoted in Murray, 1983, p.12). This left-labour perspective is noted in Beresford's (1983) comment that one of the methods of decentralization, patch social work, places emphasis upon a transfer of power to local residents and this '... is one of the unstated reasons for objections raised <u>against it</u> from the right' (ibid., p.18, emphasis added). However, in another, jointly written paper (Beresford and Croft, 1984a) a different emphasis is given by Beresford who says one of the reasons the right <u>is for</u> 'patch' decentralization practices as advocated by welfare pluralists is that these practices will lead towards the goal of further privatization of services (ibid., p.31). So far as most of the leading proponents of welfare decentralization are concerned, an increase in privatization (or else a wholesale handing-over of services to the voluntary sector) is said to be no part of the decentralization movement. Hadley and McGrath (1984) indicate that community social work is not '... compatible with the proposals of politicians of the right to dismantle the statutory welfare services and hand them over to voluntary organizations and the market' (ibid., p.15). In theories advocating welfare decentralization the dominant ideological basis for these theories is welfare pluralism, based on the concept of a 'mixed economy of welfare' which rejects state service monopolization and argues for a combination of state, voluntary, informal, and (to a lesser extent) private care sectors. Hadley and Hatch's (1981) development of the welfare pluralist concept in their influential <u>Social Welfare and the Failure of the State</u> moved beyond academia after its publication in 1981 and their text gained endorsement by politicians belonging to the Conservative Party, the Labour left, and the Alliance parties (Beresford and Croft, 1984a, p.19). A recurring theme in modern welfare pluralism is not that there is no role for state services but that these services should be complemented by an increasing emphasis upon 'voluntary and community based alternatives' (ibid., p.21) and on processes of 'interweaving' (Howe, 1983, p.82) resources between formal, informal, and voluntary care sectors. In arguing for a mixed economy of welfare with a plurality of resources to complement state services, more emphasis is given to the statutory, voluntary and informal sector and to the 'interweaving' of services between these than to the private ('commercial') sector. The last of these compared with other sectors is given relatively little attention in Hadley and Hatch (1981) who suggest the private sector might have a role in the mixed economy of welfare <u>provided</u> it is 'subject to safeguards to maintain the quality of service and ... does not have a <u>detrimental</u> effect on <u>other</u> sources of welfare' (ibid., p.p.99-100, emphases added).

Hadley and Hatch (1981) express doubts about whether an expanded private sector should have an enhanced role in welfare pluralism; they suggest there is an antithesis between the values and objectives of social services, and the 'commercial sector' (ibid., p.100). This perspective is taken further by some welfare pluralists, such as Gladstone (1984) who suggests the commercial sector has no place in a welfare pluralist model committed to social justice. Welfare pluralist's rejection of or ambivalence towards the private sector appears to be one reason for the support of welfare pluralist concepts from the Labour left; another is the pluralists' arguments for shifting power and resources away from an emphasis on bureaucratic and professional forms of 'domination' and towards an emphasis on increasing the power and involvement of citizens and service-users. However, Beresford and Croft (1984a) suggest the 'respectability' (ibid., p.31) of welfare pluralism, which 'includes voluntary, community ... and statutory provision and the possibility of alliances between them' (ibid.), does not alter the probability that 'The welfare right is only interested in pluralism in so far as it means the profitable predominance of the market' (ibid., emphasis added). This leads Beresford and Croft to a critical interpretation that welfare pluralism, whatever the actual motives of its proponents, will have the effect of opening the door to the privatization ideals of the 'new right' (ibid., p.25). Whether this will happen is open to question. Indeed, in another paper Beresford and Croft (1984b) in endorsing some aspects of welfare pluralists' arguments for community social work, stated that 'There are already many critics on the right wing waiting on the sidelines to see community social work and patch fall on their face' (ibid., p.21). Nevertheless, their views about the possible, if unintended, 'privatization' effects of welfare pluralism are of some interest, not least because they are views that are readily appropriated by professional(izing) social work actors in defence of the bureau-professional status quo.

In general terms, Beresford and Croft's (1984a) prognosis is not supported by empirical data on public perceptions of the welfare state. In chapter five, when examining data analysed by Taylor-Gooby and others on the legitimation crisis of the modern welfare state, it was noted these data suggest the long-term trend since the early 1950's towards greater privatization has been largely unaffected by Tory policies in the 1980's (Taylor-Gooby, 1986, pp.228-9). These data also show that there is popular support for both public and private sectors, reasons for support of the latter including quantity and quality of service and 'user-responsiveness' (ibid.); that there is widespread public opposition against further cuts in valued state services (ibid., p.241); and that the principle of state services is widely supported, it being primarily the particular institutional frameworks of services and the methods of service-delivery that are rejected (Mishra, 1986). It was also noted in chapter five that this last point is given special emphasis in Mishra's (1986) analysis of data on the legitimation crisis: in his analysis it is not the principle or the 'idea' of state welfare that has been rejected by citizens and service-users, but 'bureaucratic or professional imposition' (ibid., p.9) which many service-users have experienced as a 'negative' (ibid., p.10) barrier against 'less bureaucratic and more self-managed and participatory services' (ibid.). These data and the interpretations of them just referred to, qualify Beresford and Croft's (1984a) largely unsubstantiated prognosis that 'welfare pluralists ... cannot escape opening wider the door to privatization by the support for the commercial sector inherent in their advocacy of a plurality of sources of welfare' (ibid., p.25). As already noted, welfare pluralists do not advocate privatization; most welfare pluralists are ambivalent in their attitudes toward the existence of the commercial welfare sector and argue for 'safeguards' against it (Hadley and Hatch, 1981, pp.99-100), in some cases are explicit in rejecting private welfare entirely (Gladstone, 1984), and in virtually all cases reject 'new right' welfare politics (Hadley and McGrath, 1984, p.15). Welfare pluralists' main emphasis is upon 'interweaving' the different care sectors in decentralized models that construct closer interrelationships between statutory, informal, and voluntary care in a way that also maximizes user-choice and user-participation in the design and delivery of services.

So far as public opinion is concerned, the data referred to above suggest that by far the largest section of mass opinion is opposed <u>in principle</u> to further cuts in state services: this majority in Taylor-Gooby's data (1986), depending upon which particular services are being looked at, are in round figures between 80 per cent and 90 per cent of the population (ibid., p.241, Table 7). However, like Mishra (1986), Taylor-Gooby (1986) refers to empirical evidence showing strong dissatisfaction with state welfare resulting '... from the experience by clients of oppression by state professionals and bureaucrats' (ibid., p.243). Hypotheses that an inevitable effect of welfare pluralism will be to open the door to wholesale privatization, or produce public disaffection away from the <u>principle</u> of universal public social services in a way that permits future governments to impose large scale social expenditure cuts are, at the very least, unproven. It could equally well be argued that welfare pluralism may have some success in tackling what recent empirical analyses suggest may be one of the major underlying causes of the legitimation crisis of the modern welfare state. That is, these analyses suggest it is citizens' experiences of monolithic, controlling state services dominated by bureaucrats and professionals that has contributed to the long-term expansion of privatization and to increased interest in the voluntary sector since the early 1950's. Statham (1984, p.127) makes the point that

> ... paternalistic and elitist approaches ... made privatization easier. Services were devised and provided by experts for people, they were not negotiated, there was formal but not direct participation. The negative experience of this type of welfare accounts for the failure of the Labour movement and local people to fight against cuts.

Although most of the available empirical evidence on public attitudes towards welfare bureau-professionalism broadly supports Statham's statement, difficulties of various kinds attend the question of whether social work actors (whether 'traditional' or 'radical' professionals) will willingly 'surrender' power to citizens and endorse those forms of decentralization and democratization that require a major shift away from the hierarchical principle of bureau-professionalism.

Professional resistance against change

Simpkin (1989) in a comment on the emergence, in the early 1970's, of post-Seebohm 'professional careerism' in the new social services departments, notes that '... while the BASW professionals prepared to take their seats alongside doctors and lawyers in public estimation, they were also jockeying for jobs in a new hierarchy' (ibid., p.162). In chapter five, it was noted that as well as 'traditional' professionals a majority of 'radical' social work professionals and radical social work writers also support the principle of hierarchy as an organizational form for the social services. The emergence of 'radical careerism' was discussed in chapter two with reference to various critics of this phenomenon, including Hearn (1982a) who referred to the failure of radicals to specify identifiably 'radical' models of organization and practice, and to radicals' as well as traditional professionals' concerns with career advancement in large, hierarchical 'professional' bureaucracies. Lee and Raban (1988) note that left-wing theoretical welfare critiques of 'heavily bureaucratic structures and practices, overall paternalism, and professional self-interest' (ibid., p.220) became criticisms that in the 1980's were re-expressed by the Conservative government which in its appeal to voters successfully capitalized on '... the majority of the working class's negative experience of welfare provision and delivery' (ibid.). This, together with data showing widespread public support for the principle (or 'idea') of the welfare state, implies that, short of attributing 'false consciousness' to voters and service-users, there is something seriously 'wrong' with welfare bureau-professionalism per se as a framework for providing social services and that this is a crucial factor in citizens' and service-users' rejections of hierarchic bureau-professional methods of service-delivery (Mishra, 1986, p.7).

If, as seems to be the case, the 'legitimation crisis' has an important message for social work, this has largely not yet been heard, still less acted upon. In practice and organizational terms, Marxist social work has failed to specify and press for an organizational form that might give practical effect to Marxist social work theories of client 'emancipation' (Rojek, 1989, p.175). It is difficult to find any practical 'radical social work' specifications of the precise institutional or else community-based mechanisms through which citizens and clients might be given a direct say in the planning and provision of services. Leaving aside radicals' rhetoric about 'consciousness-raising', 'conscientization', client 'emancipation' and the like, many radical social work writers appear not only to accept the principle of hierarchy as the dominant organizational form for social work and social services, but also propose policies which have the effect of nurturing this principle of organization. In feminist social work, Hanmer and Statham (1988) do not propose a decentralization and democratization of services (Hoggett and Hambleton, 1988, pp.3-4) that would involve rejection of hierarchic bureau-professionalism as an organizational form: instead, they propose that the social work hierarchy should be retained but with the proviso that women should be substituted for men at the higher echelons. This 'substitution' principle involves replacing predominantly male senior managements by increasingly female managements (Hanmer and Statham, 1988, p.108). In order to achieve this objective, it is argued that mechanisms should be established for decreasing the number of men and increasing the number of women employed '... in higher levels of decision-making hierarchies in social work' (ibid., p.139, emphasis added). Here, it is fairly obvious that the principle of hierarchy is left intact, in favour of a preoccupation with the question of who should occupy the top positions in the hierarchy. Dominelli and McLeod (1989) leave the principle of hierarchy entirely unchallenged in any fundamental or practical sense, and indeed, argue for a hierarchical organizational structure '... in which women can rise through the ranks more quickly ...' (ibid., p.139). Dominelli and

McLeod, like virtually all radical social work writers, repeat the familiar rhetorical radical denunciations of hierarchical organization (ibid., p.125) then leave the matter there: they do not proceed to offer any specific policy, organizational, or practice prescriptions for the decentralization and democratization of services in ways that might in real, concrete terms 'transfer' power from professionals to citizens and service-users. Instead, Dominelli and McLeod (1989) attempt to legitimate the principle of hierarchical organization and of 'professional' bureaucracy. They state that '... feminist workers are ... interested in establishing themselves within bureaucracies, including taking up managerial positions' (ibid., p.43) and a crucial objective in feminist social work's 'struggle' is that of initiating '... positive action programmes to promote women's entry into the senior management in greater numbers' (ibid., p.122). This way of thinking is conspicuously detached from the debate about de-hierarchicalization (Howe, 1983) and the decentralization and democratization of services (Hoggett and Hambleton, 1988). And also conspicuously detached from contemporary anti-reductionist social and political analysis. That is, precisely whose interests would be served by feminist positive action programmes of the kind just referred to? These cannot be the 'real' ('objective') structurally 'given' interests of 'women' as a social category in general or as a client group, nor the 'objective' interests of individual women clients; neither social aggregates of this kind or any individual human actors possess such 'interests'.

Where hierarchical bureaucratic structures are the dominant organizational form in social work, there are no valid grounds for the continuation of those hierarchies in which men are overrepresented at the higher levels. This is not to say that those hierarchies should be retained and perpetuated with equal representation of women at the higher levels. Of course, if social work hierarchies are structurally 'necessary' and immutable facts of life rather than actors' constructions, then the feminist social work arguments just referred to would have much substance; if a hierarchical organizational structure containing a lot of top jobs is said to be immutable (e.g. a 'necessary effect' of the social totality) there is no point in trying to change this organizational form and every point in ensuring women get a fair share of the top jobs within it. Claims that hierarchical bureau-professional forms of organization and service-delivery are for some reason historically or structurally 'inevitable' may safely be dismissed as, in many instances, an ideological legitimation purveyed by those who currently do or prospectively might benefit most from their existence. Organizations are contingently produced and contingently reproduced or changed. Social work bureau-professionalism as an organizational form did not even exist prior to its construction in the wake of the Seebohm Report (1968)! Nor can it be claimed that bureau-professionalism magically appeared 'out of the blue' in the early 1970's or brought 'itself' into existence(!) as a structurally predetermined 'expression' of the larger social system. It was observed in chapter three that there are individual human actors and social actors; but no other actors. Only actors can 'do' things, formulate intentions, or formulate a sense of having 'needs': further, actors do not have 'objective' interests. Therefore, bureau-professionalism in social work is not structurally-predetermined; it is not a 'necessary effect' of the social totality nor an 'effect' of the supposed 'actions' of any social aggregate (a 'class', 'men', or whatever) nor an 'effect' of any teleologically adduced structural 'needs' ('the interests of capitalism', 'the interests of patriarchy', and so on). As Whittington and Bellaby (1979) have empirically demonstrated, hierarchic bureau-professionalism was socially constructed in the 1970's by professional(izing) actors who struggled hard to establish and legitimate this organizational form in various ways and who vigorously defended their legitimations when these were challenged by other actors: when these legitimations were again challenged, in the 1980's, by advocates of service-decentralization and democratization they were, as we have seen in the present chapter, even more vigorously defended by bureau-professionals. Nor do any convoluted social work arguments about bureau-professionalism being an irremovable fixture of Thatcherism hold any water! The construction of social work bureau-professionalism, and indeed its 'golden period' of expansion and consolidation, occurred in the decade prior to Thatcherism. Then after the 1979 election, the Tory government soon revealed that it was no supporter of professional social work bureaucracies (Mishra, 1986, pp.6-7; Lee and Raban, 1988, p.220).

To say that social work and social services bureau-professionalism is a contingently produced and actor-reproduced organizational form, rather than a structurally predetermined or immutable 'necessity', is to say that this organizational form is in no sense structurally inevitable. But even if not inevitable, perhaps it is desirable? Another way of looking at this is to ask: who needs 'hierarchy'? Or more precisely, who needs hierarchy in the form that this principle of organization has come to be associated with 'professional' social work bureaucracies? Apparently citizens and clients do not: this is indicated by the previously mentioned data on client and service-user rejections of hierarchic bureau-professional systems of service-delivery in social work and the personal social services (see chapter five). Perhaps, then, it is the bureau-professionals themselves who stand to gain most from the continued existence of hierarchical professional bureaucracies? This possibility is raised by Moore (1976, p.10), Parry et al. (1979, p.163), Hearn (1982a, p.26), Lee and Raban (1988, p.220), Jones (1989, pp.208-9), and Simpkin (1989, p.162). Reference was made earlier to Hanmer and Statham's (1988) hierarchical 'substitution' principle: this reduces to the prescription that '... ultimately one of the changes must be a reduction in the number of men in senior management and the increase in the number of women' (ibid., p.108, emphasis added). Surely this cannot be an 'ultimate' objective of the personal social services? To a hard pressed, down-and-out client whose immediate concern may be that he cannot eat because his social security giro cheque is a day late, prescriptions of this kind are likely to sound suspiciously like a professionally self-interested attempt to replace one managerial-professional elite with another. Clients want, and increasingly are demanding, far more than the social work equivalent of a cabinet re-shuffle. Dominelli and McLeod (1989) ask '... what about affluent male social work managers enjoying the prestige and material rewards of their status? Surely, it is not in their interests to support a feminist approach to working relations?' (ibid., p.154, emphasis added). To the client waiting for his giro cheque, or the young black unemployed person, or the teenage mother struggling in the face of poverty to make ends meet, it does not matter very much whether 'the prestige and material rewards of their status' are enjoyed by affluent male managers or by affluent female managers substituted in their place: clients of the social services have other immediate and more pressing concerns, none of which involve much sympathy for the plight of 'affluent' managers of either sex. This is because 'In the main, most clients of social work are working class and poor' (Jones, 1983, pp.11-12). And on those rare occasions when clients are given an opportunity to state their views (as in public opinion surveys) about professional social work bureaucracies and social services organization, there is, as noted earlier and also in chapter five, overwhelming evidence that their views are more consonant with those formulated by advocates of service decentralization and democratization than those formulated by professional actors who argue for retention of the hierarchic bureau-professional status quo in professional social work and the social services. With regard to the 'substitution' principle promulgated in professional feminist social work discourse, none of the empirical data on the legitimation crisis, and on client rejections of hierarchic bureau-professional systems of service delivery, contain an inkling that social work clients demand this substitution principle or consider it will help them get more or better welfare.

For some years, most of the major professional social work lobby groups (whether 'traditional', or 'radical' in the form of Marxism and feminism) have struggled to defend the post-Seebohm professional-organizational structure and its practice concomitants against criticisms from service-users and from advocates of service decentralization and democratization. It is an indictment of social work that anti-racist concerns have only recently received attention within the radical social work movement(s). However, the recency of this development is also an opportunity to avoid replicating the failure of other ostensibly 'emancipatory' motifs. Marxist and feminist social work has largely turned out to be a mixture of simplistic reductionist theories; dogmatic, authoritarian impulses; radical careerist ambitions; and encrusted practices predicated upon a commitment to the perpetuation of monolithic, centralised 'professional' bureaucracies that give citizens and clients little say in the planning and delivery of services. Some anti-racist welfare workers and writers appear to be aware of some of these problems. An instance is Farrer's (1988) account of the decentralized work-methods employed by black youth and community workers in Leeds. Farrer rightly observes that community participation centred around 'organic' organizational forms is not a universal panacea: nevertheless, the political reference points of the radical black community workers involved in these 'organic' structures preclude any desire to replicate the practice-assumptions of conventional hierarchic bureau-professional structures. The organizational forms described by Farrer are considerably more informal, 'looser' and less structured than in, say, most community social work projects. Farrer (1988) refers to the grass-roots philosophy of practice employed by these community workers and notes that (ibid., p.113)

> Their critique of hierarchy and the commitment to remaining organic to their communities ... combined with tactical requirements ... make for an acceptance of the obvious deficiencies of operating with a very loose structure. These deficiencies are often overcome by the close personal networks that operate within the communities ...

Broadly analogous to some of the points made in Farrer's analysis is Hutchinson-Reis's (1989) observation that 'In respect of black social workers, a major concern must be in maintaining the respect of our own communities whilst functioning from a position of relative advantage. If this is not achieved, we will lose all perspective of the struggle and the support of black people generally' (ibid., p.171). Gurnah (1989) comments that '... white ... professionals always assume they know what the communities want and need, despite all the contrary advice given them by the communities themselves and black professionals' (ibid., p.120). Little is gained if the voices of local black communities and black professionals diverge. One of Gurnah's (1989) concerns in the promotion of effective anti-racist welfare strategies based on community support is to avoid the emergence of '... black careerism. Black staff being supported by the community will not be judged by their rhetoric, but by their ability to secure new resources ... for direct provision to the black communities' (ibid.. p.124). Community support may in turn increase the probability that black staff will be in a stronger position to secure organizational and policy change: as Gurnah observes '... the support that black workers receive from the community makes them not only stronger, but more independent and effective in the system' (ibid., p.123).

One of the most radical of recent proposals for decentralization and democratization in professional social work and the personal social services. is Rojek's (1989) 'self-management' proposal which involves shifting power from professionals and professional managers to local citizens and service-users and also to social services workers who are not professional social workers. Rojek (1989) anticipates that his proposal for a radical deconstruction of hierarchic professional bureaucracies will be strongly resisted by professional social workers, and he comments (ibid., p.187)

> Given the long and difficult struggle by social workers to gain recognition for their professionalism, this is understandable. However, when all is said and done, we have to ask ourselves who is social work for? If clients and unqualified staff feel that their talents, energies, and ideas are monotonously ignored, who can be said to be the gainer?

Resistance against change is sometimes strategically re-formulated by professionals in a way designed to imply that the only or main groups responsible for the ascendancy of bureau-professional pathologies in modern social work organization are not the professionals themselves, but administrators and 'bureaucrats'. This ignores the fact that social services departments are a 'hybrid' organizational form, a fusion of 'bureaucracy' and 'professionalism'. They are 'professional' (or professionalized) bureaucracies. There are no grounds for supposing professionalism and bureaucracy are necessarily antithetical, least of all in social work (Parry and Parry, 1979, p.43). One factor in the demise of an oversimplified professional/bureaucratic analytic dichotomy in organizational theory was the accumulation of empirical data in a number of studies pointing to an 'accommodation thesis', as in Benson's (1973) and Davies's (Davies, 1983, in Dingwall and Lewis, pp.177-94) sociological accounts of the mutual accommodation of 'professional' and hierarchical 'bureaucratic' norms. A large number of American and British studies extending across a number of years indicate fairly consistently that professional social workers are in general normatively committed to the principle of hierarchical organization: see Wilensky (1964), Hefferman (1964), Billingsly (1964), Scott (1965), Varley (1966), Aiken and Hage (1966), Kakabadse and Worral (1976, p.7), Williamson (1978), and Whittington and Bellaby (1979, p.528).

The core of Rojek's (1989) proposal is that members of the community, clients, and basic grade social services staff and ancillary workers should not simply be 'allowed to speak' but should be practically 'enabled' by means of specific organizational mechanisms that involve a transfer of power. Rojek's argument is that '... it is not enough to let ... (these groups and individuals) ... speak. They must be given real power in the planning and administration of care' (ibid., p.180). In some respects, suspicions that modern bureau-professional social work may be little more than an unpractised 'emancipatory' rhetoric are a contemporary expression of long-standing concerns. In a reference to the work of Lansburg, who became leader of the Labour Party in 1931, Holman (1989, p.22) writes

Lansburg noted in his time that middle-class socialists - far from making way for people from his class - often exploited poor people by coming to work amongst them and using that experience to obtain top posts for themselves. Fifty years later, the same kind of socialists still keep power away from those who have not had their advantages. An alternative is the practice of vacating whereby the privileged deliberately make way for others. Already examples exist at neighbourhood level ... (in) ... community projects .... Now it needs applying to larger organizations ...

Just as professional actors' legitimations of the professional status quo should be critically assessed, so also should radical proposals for change. There are, of course, problems in overcoming professional resistance against change if radicals' programmatic ideas are such as to realistically have very little chance of ever being implemented. Rojek (1989) in his proposal for organizational change recognizes that all radical proposals for a transformation of the status quo are prone to sceptical dismissal (ibid., p.187). However, although change may seem threatening it also opens up new possibilities. Radical reconstruction as part of the movement towards service decentralization and democratization '... may be unsettling, but it can also be challenging and exciting ... (it) ... shakes the sediment in the glass and gives social workers opportunities to break free from encrusted, authoritarian influences' (ibid., p.177). For this to become a reality it would be necessary for traditional and radical professional social work lobbies to breakaway from the patterns of bureau-professional retrenchment and resistance against change that emerged in the early years of the post-Seebohm era and which strengthened and solidified in the 1980's in the ways described in this chapter.

7 Social work education and training

Since the time of the Charity Organization Society (Urwick, 1904) social work education has been regarded as a 'pivotal' institution within the social work community (Seed, 1977, pp.53-76). Jones (1979) observes that social work education is viewed by social work leaders '... as one of the crucial places where the social work perspective is established and sustained' (ibid., p.72, emphasis added). What, however, is the social work perspective? It is precisely because there is no internal consensus available for specifying the nature and purposes and methods of social work, and because competitive social work actors have always regarded control of education and training as crucial to the achievement of their attempts to impose their own definition of 'the' social work perspective, that social work education has for almost a century been a key institutional arena through which competitive actors 'route' their formulated interests, perspectives, and objectives (Bailey, 1982, p.12; Henkel, 1984). In the sociology of professions, empirical attention is regularly focussed on investigation of '... the relationship between education, practice, and the organization of occupational groups' (Atkinson, 1983, p.234, emphasis added). Control of this relationship is regarded by social work actors as an essential element in the achievement of professionalizing objectives. Throughout the 1970's, following the Seebohm Report's (1968) recommendations for a fully 'professionalized' social work service, social work education became more closely associated with the higher education sector (Pinker, 1983a, pp.151-2). Related to this, Dingwall (1974) makes the point that for semi-professional occupations such as nursing or social work, entry to what is often publicly perceived as the 'prestigious' university sector of higher education is regarded by professional leaders as crucial to the achievement of 'professional' status: this point will be discussed later in the chapter.

The structure and form of social work education is related to the organizational division of labour in social work and the personal social services. A significant factor in the 'crisis' over social work education that developed in the 1980's was the introduction in 1975 of a binary system of social work education and training (CCETSW, 1975). In 1975 the Central Council for Education and Training in Social Work (CCETSW) introduced a new 'sub-professional' qualification, the Certificate in Social Service (CSS), that was designed to be a second-tier social services qualification alongside the already existing first-tier professional social work qualification, the Certificate of Qualification in Social Work (CQSW). The CSS was intended as a less academic, less 'professional', and more practically based vocationalist qualification than the CQSW. The CQSW qualification was strongly supported by professionalizing actors such as the British Association of Social Workers (BASW), and was largely though by no means exclusively controlled by academic-professionals in the higher education sector. In contrast, the CSS courses following their introduction in 1975 were provided by colleges of further education, and the administrative arrangements and regulations for the CSS were such that social work employers and organizational managers had (relative to the 'professional' CQSW courses controlled largely by academic-professionals in the higher education sector) a far greater influence upon the CSS curriculum, methods of training, and the assessment of students.

The CSS was highly attractive to social work employers; they were able to shape its curriculum and ensure it had a very practical emphasis. Some higher education social work academics condemned the CSS as a narrow form of employer-controlled 'training' rather than, as in the case of the CQSW, a more broadly social science based form of professional 'education': one academic critic described the CSS as '... no more than a glorified form of in-service training' (Jones, 1979, p.88). Many professionalizing actors, however, enthusiastically welcomed the new binary system because it served to reinforce the organizational division of labour in the social services departments (SSD's) predicated on a socially constructed hierarchy of work: this hierarchy rested on the formula that 'CQSW work' ('professional social work') was more professionally and intellectually complex than 'CSS work' ('social services work'). The BASW (1975, p.18) applauded the CCETSW's introduction of the new binary system which, in the mid-1970's at least, seemed to offer professionalizing actors an opportunity to symbolize and reinforce a rigidly demarcated hierarchical organizational division (Lee, 1982) between 'professional social workers' ('CQSW workers') and 'social services workers' ('CSS workers'). The British Association of Social Workers was keen to preserve this hierarchical division of labour (BASW, 1977, p.16, para.3.11; p.17 para.3.12; p.18, para.3.14). However, the new binary system had professionally unintended consequences: it set in train a series of contingently produced outcomes that, far from assisting social work professionals' long standing quest for 'professional' power and status, had highly threatening de-professionalizing outcomes. These outcomes, it should be noted, are an empirical illustration of the arguments developed in the third chapter concerning unintended consequences as crucial 'complicating' factors in the contingent reproduction or change of social (work) situations (Baert, 1989; Sibeon, 1989a).

The de-professionalizing consequences stemming from the CQSW/CSS binary system were associated with unexpected shifts in the distribution of power and strategic opportunity within social work's actor-network. These professionally unanticipated shifts occurred in three interconnected ways. Firstly, once the CSS schemes in the further education sector had come into existence they became a new and highly positive comparative 'reference group' for employers. The new CSS training schemes created what employers regarded as an increasingly visible dichotomy between the 'practical relevance' of the CSS in the further education sector, and the 'remote' academic-professional 'intellectualism' of the CQSW curricula in the higher education sector. Not only did social service employers have a large measure of control over the 'practical' CSS occupational training schemes. The availability to the employers of the new CSS qualification also provided employers with an opportunity to redefine 'the social work task' in terms of practical, occupational competence (as defined by employers) and, more importantly, an opportunity to give practical effect to this redefinition of the 'social work' task: accordingly, employers began appointing (Carter, 1985, p.27) newly qualified CSS holders ('social services workers') to posts that prior to 1975 had been the exclusive preserve of CQSW holders ('professional social workers'). Needless to say, this organizational blurring of the hierarchical division between 'professional social work' and 'social services work' was strongly condemned by professionals: this will be returned to shortly. Secondly, the introduction of the CSS had the professionally unanticipated consequence of bringing into existence a new pressure group. This new pressure group consisting of newly qualified CSS holders and their trainers in the further education sector joined forces with the employers in demanding that, in recognition of the newly emergent role-blurring in the SSD's whereby some CSS holders were now performing the same organizational tasks as 'professional social workers', those staff who were CSS holders should in future have the same title, status, pay and promotion prospects as CQSW holders ('professional social workers'). Thirdly, the newly created corps of CSS holders formed an alliance with employers in arguing (for example, Standing Conference CSS, 1985) that the reality of the newly emergent division of labour in the SSD's arising from the role-blurring between the two 'levels' of work, meant that the hierarchical distinction between CQSW work (professional social work) and CSS work (social services work) was no longer relevant and that the CQSW/CSS two-tier system of training should therefore be replaced by a new single system of training that would fuse the CQSW and CSS into a single new qualification. In effect, this was a demand for a major reform of the whole of social work education, including the CQSW, in a new and more 'practical' vocationalist direction modelled on the CSS occupational 'apprenticeship' pattern of a more employer-controlled, less academic and less 'professional' form of training. It was also, as just noted, a demand for recognition that 'professional social work' was no longer dominant in the SSD's, or at least, that its organizational 'power' had diminished.

A consequence of these interconnected developments was that in the 1980's power contingently shifted away from academic-professional and professionalizing actors, and towards employers, social work managers, and the newly created CSS lobby. In the 1970's, in the sense described in the last part of the third chapter, 'power' had been roughly equally distributed within social work's actor-network: the 'deadlock' that this had produced was broken in the 1980's. Partly in response to this contingent shift of power, and partly because the CCETSW itself was becoming more convinced of the need for reform leading towards less 'esoteric', more practical occupational training, the CCETSW increasingly aligned itself with the perspectives of employers and of social services occupational groups. The CCETSW therefore embarked on the task of formulating proposals for replacing the CQSW/CSS binary system with a new single qualification that (ostensibly at least) would recognize the organizational erosion of the distinction between professional social work ('CQSW work') and social services work ('CSS work'). The CCETSW's various proposals, which differed in detail in ways that need not concern us here, were set out in three key reports (CCETSW Paper 20.1, 1983; CCETSW Paper 20.3, 1985; CCETSW Paper 20.6, 1986). These proposals generated conflicts on a scale that led Sainsbury (1985) to suggest that the social work community had become intractably internally divided and was in danger of splitting apart for reasons primarily to do with internal conflicts rather than to do with any 'external' factors such as government policies (ibid., p.9). The BASW, having previously praised the CCETSW's introduction of the CSS and the resultant binary training system, roundly condemned the decision to phase out the two-tier system. Bamford (1984), then chairperson of the BASW strongly attacked the CCETSW for having '... the arrogance to ... phase out CQSW/CSS ...' (ibid., p.21). The employers, in contrast, were understandably gratified at the new training scenario that was emerging. Harbert (1984), a Director of Social Services, reiterated employers criticisms of 'status professionalism' and declared that CCETSW's paper of 1983 (Paper 20.1) was '... the most important document to be produced on the social services since Seebohm' (Harbert, 1984, p.21, emphasis added). Another Director of Social Services, Warner (1986) stated that resistance against reform emanated from '... a shrinking cadre of professionals' (ibid., p.15) who were attempting to 'insulate themselves from ... the reality of 1980's style social services' (ibid.). Academic-professionals and other professionalizing actors were alarmed at what seemed to them to be a determined attempt both to de-professionalize social work education and, in organizational terms, to 'reverse' the process of professionalization in the SSD's that had been set in train in the early 1970's. The Association of Teachers in Social Work Education (ATSWE) condemned the CCETSW's proposed reform of training (ATSWE, 1984, p.2) and Bailey (1984, p.59) stated that the proposal to organizationally and educationally fuse together 'CQSW work' (professional social work) and 'CSS work' (social services work) was untenable. Pinker's (1986) academic-professional response to the CCETSW's proposal of 1986 (CCETSW Paper 20.6) for a single new employer-led qualification called the Qualifying Diploma In Social Work (QDSW), was that the time had come '... to stop this initiative in its tracks' (Pinker, 1986, p.21, emphasis added).

The CCETSW was the central strategic actor in these policy struggles. Government departments exerted some influence, but they stood largely on the sidelines and most of the action was played out within the social work community itself at the middle-range ('organizational') level through strategic interactions among the major competitive actors in social work's 'actor-network' (Callon, 1986, p.204 and p.218). As Jones (1989) observes, '... the principle target was the CQSW ... much vilified by many employers and a terrain the government ... was content to see fought over' (ibid., p.205). In the 1970's, the CCETSW had adopted a less interventionist, 'impartial' posture and had attempted to secure some compromise among the relevant actors; this rested, in the ways described in chapter three, upon the strategy of appealing simultaneously to a variety of conflicting interests (Wright, 1977). This earlier strategy, in the perception of the CCETSW, had fitted the circumstances of that time (ibid., p.9). In the mid and late 1970's, power was relatively more equally distributed in social work's actor-network and the previously described contingent shifts of power and strategic opportunity were outcomes that developed some years later. The CCETSW in its earlier strategy had attempted to placate employers' technical-training demands while simultaneously 'appealing' to the interests and objectives formulated by professional and academic-professional actors. These professionalizing objectives rested, in effect, on the reproduction of 'indeterminate' professional knowledge in social work education and on professional control of practice. Professional education was highly relevant to these concerns, for reasons that are not unique to social work. In the sociology of professions, a number of studies have indicated that '<u>professional</u>' <u>curricula embody the difficult-to-achieve objectives of 'containing' or</u> <u>'masking' internal occupational or professional conflicts while at the</u> <u>same time attempting to formulate a 'public' presentation of a cognitive</u> <u>structure that is relatively indeterminate, esoteric, and distinctive to</u> <u>the profession as a whole.</u> Drawing upon the work of Bordieu and Passeron (1977), Atkinson (1983, p.239) notes that professional curricula

... promote the appearance of consensus while actually enshrining sectional interests and perspectives ... curricula ... incorporate - while often masking-intraprofessional interests, as well as reproducing the esoteric expertise which is held to be the preserve of the profession as a whole. Relatively little attention has been paid to this aspect of professional curricula.

This strategic approach involving the use of professional curricula in the reproduction of professional interests can, however, 'break-down' if, in the perception of powerful 'non-professional' actors, the indetermination/technicality ratio (Jamous and Peloille, 1970) is exceeded by professionalizing actors and/or by their academic-professional associates: this is precisely what happened in British social work in the 1980's.

In the early 1980's it was becoming increasingly apparent to the CCETSW that its earlier 'softly, softly' strategy was unlikely to produce any tangible shifts of emphasis by professional and academic-professional actors: or at least, it was becoming clear that these shifts were unlikely to be voluntarily undertaken on the scale demanded by employers, by the expanding CSS lobby, and, by this time, by the CCETSW itself. Moreover, as already noted, power and strategic opportunity was shifting towards employers and towards occupational groups associated with social services interests rather than professional social work interests. The new organizational role-blurring and personnel policies of the employers were major factors in the CCETSW's perception that a professional/sub-professional organizational demarcation line buttressed by the hierarchical CQSW/CSS binary system was rapidly becoming an anachronism that was increasingly harder to defend. To resolve matters, it was perhaps inevitable that the CCETSW had to 'come out' and say where it stood. Although the loci of power and influence were shifting, actors from each of the major social work constituencies continued to engage in seemingly irreconcilable conflict (Henkel, 1984, p.17). Professionals and professional educators were increasingly portrayed as self-interested groups who were remote from the 'real' questions of how to gear a training system to practical, effective forms of service to clients. Some employers, it was noted earlier, had started to use terms like 'status professionalism', and 'a shrinking cadre of professionals'. Amidst the heightened conflict and controversy surrounding the CCETSW's announcement of its QDSW scheme in 1986, the chairperson of the CCETSW began her paper with the words 'In any profession, education and qualifying training are the gateways to life chances in prosperity, social power and prestige' (Cooper, 1986, p.18). A leading member of one of the CCETSW's working parties (Parsloe, 1984) rejected professionals' and social work educators' 'misguided' efforts to turn social work into a profession along the lines of medicine and law, and she suggested it was time that social workers and their educators abandoned the terms 'professional' and 'clients' and instead thought of service-users as '... partners and ... citizens' (ibid., p.110).

The employers' 'victory' in the form of the QDSW announcement in 1986 received a temporary set-back when the government, partly on the grounds of financial cost, rejected the CCETSW's proposal for a new QDSW qualification based on three-years of practical training (as compared with two-year training for the existing CQSW courses, except for social science graduates on shorter one-year CQSW courses). The CCETSW responded by assembling another proposal (CCETSW Paper 30, 1989) for a two-year Diploma in Social Work (Dip.SW) which, though of lesser duration, implemented virtually all of the QDSW objectives for 'practical', employ-led training schemes. By 1990 the first crop of Dip.SW schemes had been established in a small number of locations and by the mid-1990's these new training schemes will have been completely phased-in as a replacement for all existing CQSW and CSS courses (CCETSW, 1990, p.22).

The CCETSW had established a localized committee infrastructure to govern the local administration of the QDSW schemes. The infrastructure had a key role in these developments and therefore was retained for implementing the proposals for the Dip.SW schemes. This infrastructure consists of a network of local committees, curriculum groups, working parties, etc., containing representatives from, in particular, local social work employers and local academic institutions involved in social work training. For all institutions involved in social work training, participation in these committees was made mandatory by the CCETSW. The underlying rationale is based on a concept of 'enforced partnership' designed to administratively consolidate the contingent shifts of power and strategic opportunity described earlier. In the future these local committees will, if they wish to have a role in social work training, have to jointly agree a local training curriculum; agree upon criteria (within the broad, national parameters framed by the CCETSW) for assessing the practical competence of students; and agree upon methods for jointly monitoring and evaluating the new Dip.SW training schemes in their geographical area (CCETSW Paper 30, 1989). Local academic institutions and social work employers (designated by the CCETSW as 'joint programme providers') who are involved in training have to furnish evidence to the CCETSW that they have collaborated in the ways just referred to and come to some agreement about their local training scheme: without this evidence of local agreement, the Dip.SW scheme in question will not be validated by the CCETSW. Social work academics, understandably so in light of the conflicts referred to earlier, regard this local committee infrastructure with suspicion and, shortly after its announcement, argued that its constitutional and membership arrangements should not be overly weighted in favour of employers (Report of Joint Working Party, 1986, p.6, para.28). Academic-professional actors are, however, currently showing signs of acknowledging their declining influence and of recognizing that, if their courses are to be validated by the CCETSW, they have no option other than to participate in the new local committees established by the

CCETSW to control the pattern of social work training within each local region.

For academic-professional actors, who in the main are strongly committed to the professionalization of social work, the prospects for the 1990's are far more bleak than in the professionally-expansionist era of the 1970's and early 1980's. Power has contingently shifted to actors for whom professionalization is not a major objective. It is possible that the power given to employers and other 'non-professional' groups in the new committee system will result in a form of training which marginalizes academic disciplinary knowledge to the point where the retention of social work training in higher education becomes problematic. For professionalizing actors there is, though, no currently realistic alternative to participation in the new network of committees which are, so to speak, a case of 'better something than nothing'. A location in the higher education sector is widely regarded as the sine qua non of a 'profession'. Social work educators, as a consequence of their strong commitment to the professionalization of social work, are predisposed to ultimately concur with virtually any system of training that ensures the post-Seebohm expansion of social work training courses in the higher education sector is not jeopardized. This ultimate fall-back position is a consequence of higher education being an 'obligatory passage point' (Callon et al., 1986) for professionalizing actors, even if this means concurring with a reshaping of social work training that moves so far away from academic knowledge that no logical ('rational') educational policy criteria remains as a justification for social work's continued association with higher education. There are, however, other features of these developments that require analysis arising from the local committee network established by the CCETSW as a delegational policy-implementation strategy.

Some problems and issues in a policy-implementation strategy

In the construction of new social policies, not only in social work, delegation to local actors is always necessary. This is partly for the technical reason that the local details-of-application cannot always be predefined and calculated from 'the centre': and partly for the political reason that - particularly if conflict is anticipated - delegation has strategic advantages for the policy-entrepreneur (in this instance, the CCETSW). Delegation is necessary both in order to be able to put policy into practice across a large number of local sites and to retain an element of control via some form of 'feedback' to the centre from the delegated sites (Barnes, 1986, p.84). Rules laid down at the centre, however, including new rules of policy, procedure, and rules relating to imposed or else jointly agreed feedback or 'reporting' mechanisms, are not absolutes and when it comes to their detailed local specification and application, subversive or 'deviant' interpretations of them by local actors are nearly always possible (Strauss, 1978). Therefore there is in these circumstances a general predisposition on the part of 'central' or policy-making actors to enrol other, preferably 'trustworthy' and 'authoritative' local actors (e.g. social work employers) and get them to act as 'relays' to pass on the new policy material to other relevant local actors whose commitment to the new policy may be suspect. When it set up its new local committee infrastructure in the mid-1980's as an administrative conflict-resolution strategy the CCETSW was, in effect, creating a network of mutually antagonistic committee memberships, and the CCETSW was well aware that some of the participants (specifically, those associated with academic-professional interests) could not be relied upon to perform the role of faithful 'relay' actors: the social work press had, for instance, given widespread publicity to Pinker's (1986) call for sabotage of the CCETSW's policies. The CCETSW's perception of this mood of strong dissent among academic-professional actors was a key factor not simply in the creation of a network of local committees for implementing the new training policy, but also a factor in the 'constitutional' committee regulations framed by the CCETSW (see CCETSW, 1987b) in its efforts to retain an element of control over the operation of these committees and over the range of possible local outcomes that might emerge from the 'negotiations' taking place within them.

The possibility of multiple or, from the standpoint of the 'central' actor, deviant interpretations arising at the local level is especially marked in social work by virtue of the ambiguities and cognitive indeterminacies that characterize not only social work education but also the structure and forms of social work knowledge and practice (see chapter four). For example, the code of social work 'values' set out in the regulations for the new Dip.SW is more than vague: it is a confused 'semantic muddle' (Jervis. 1990, p.22) and doubtless will provoke controversy and confusion in the local committees. Cognitive and practical indeterminacies are, however, by no means confined to social work and therefore delegation, particularly when ambiguities and conflicts of various kinds exist, is in general a way both of seeking clarifications of the indeterminacies that may exist in a social policy and of 'resolving' conflicts of purpose and of interpretation (Rein, 1976, p.22)

> ... one usually finds that the ... objectives ... of social policy are open to many interpretations. Ambiguity seems to be essential for agreement. When the purposes of policy are unclear and incompatible, each successive stage in the process of implementation provides a new context in which further clarification is sought. One of the consequences of ... (initiating) ... ambiguous and inconsistent ... (policy) ... is to shift the arena of decision to a lower level. The lack of consensus is resolved at the level of everyday practice, through the concrete actions taken by administrators and practitioners.

This reference by Rein to 'everyday practice' has some wider implications for the everyday practices of the local committees established by the CCETSW.

In the absence of consensus in local actor-networks involved in the detailed formulation and application of a social policy it is likely, because both the acquisition and reproduction of the 'power' of the central policy-making actor is a strategic, contingent outcome of interaction and not a structurally 'fixed' or 'given' capacity of the actor, that the policy-making actor will rarely be wholly 'sovereign' (Law, 1986a, p.6). A performative rather than ostensive concept of social action and power (Latour, 1986) leads to the view that '... those subject to power will tend to frustrate the realization of the others' capacities and detract from their intended effects' (Barbalet, 1985, p.539). Much of what happens in the social policy field is produced emergently at the middle-range level of interaction between social ('organizational') actors; for this and the other reasons identified earlier there are grounds for predicting that the intentions of policy-making actors such as the CCETSW will rarely be wholly achieved. They may be 'more-or-less' achieved, but some accommodative shifts and adjustments are usually necessary; in most situations '... the power of an agent will be less than the capacities ... (the agent) ... mobilizes in attempting to achieve an intended outcome' (ibid.). In similar vein, Clegg (1989) observes that '... rarely will intentions be realized, if we mean by intention the outcome projected by the agent at the outset' (ibid., p.208). Some commonplace social science assumptions about power and delegation are challenged in Barnes's (1986) rejection of conventional sociological definitions of authority as power 'plus' consent, legitimacy, or institutionalization (ibid., p.180). Barnes argues that power is synonymous with discretion: authority is not power 'plus' other things. Authority is something 'less than' power because authority is power 'minus' discretion. Agents with power are '... agents with <u>discretion</u> in directing routines, who act not in response to predetermined external signs but on the basis <u>of their own judgement and decision</u>' (ibid., p.182, second emphasis added). An actor that possesses only authority may have directive capabilities, but not on the basis of discretion: it is in this sense that '... whereas a power directs a routine with discretion, an authority directs it without discretion' (ibid.).

Although, as observed earlier, delegation is necessary in the policy-application and policy-monitoring process, an implication of Barnes's (1986) analysis is that local actors (or local committees) should be 'authorized' but not 'empowered'. Barnes notes (ibid., p.184) that from the standpoint of the central policy-making actor, to delegate discretion (and thus power) may amount to a loss of discretion (and thus power). In order to construct, disseminate, and practically implement a new social policy across a large number of local sites, some delegation is inevitable and unavoidable; but in most circumstances, it is authority not power that should be delegated. Even where this is done, however, a regular problem for the 'central' actor, particularly where policies involve (as in social work) endemic cognitive-practico indeterminacies or are the subject of conflicting interests and objectives, is the problem of how to prevent delegated 'authorities' turning themselves into 'powers'. Strategic calculations therefore have to be made by central policy-making actors: such calculations are formulated in contingent and often empirically shifting conditions-of-action.

There may sometimes be occasions when central 'powers' discover it is convenient to deny or at least 'play down' the fact that they have power, and to call it 'authority' instead. There are grounds for interpreting the 'soft-pedal' strategies of the CCETSW in the 1970's in these terms which involve a self-representation as a 'mere' authority attempting to 'appeal' to and 'reconcile' the conflicting interests formulated by powerful but mutually opposed social work actors (Wright, 1977). In the 1970's, the CCETSW's approach to conflict-resolution involved a self-portrayal as a piggy-in-the-middle buffeted by conflicting demands upon itself. When power is more or less equally distributed among powerful but competitive actors, the 'central' or policy-making actor may find it convenient to '... walk a tightrope ... compromising to preclude deadlock in sensitive areas' (ibid., p.9). This strategy, as noted earlier, did not 'work'. Later, by which time power had contingently shifted and become asymmetrical within social work's actor-network, the CCETSW, although not wholly 'sovereign' nor a holder of 'perfect' power in Barnes's (1986) sense of total discretion, flexed its statutorily conferred powers of discretion in formulating national social work training policies and moved to the 'harder', more interventionist and controlling policies referred to earlier. In doing so the CCETSW signalled that henceforth it was, in Barnes's (1986) terminology, to be regarded as a 'power' and that the other relevant actors were but delegated 'authorities' within a newly created network of local committees.

In the late 1980's the CCETSW continued to talk about 'partnership' between academic-professionals and employers: it had not entirely abandoned its earlier strategy which had been largely based on appeals and exhortations that the competitive actors should themselves 'negotiate' a settlement and then give practical effect to this in their policies and practices. However, this earlier strategy was not overly relied upon. The CCETSW, it seems, had 'learned from experience'. Specifically, it enforced a concept of 'partnership' by means of creating a localized committee structure together with a new system of regulative controls. In a situation where competitive actors are assembled into committees to jointly formulate, implement, and jointly monitor local training schemes that (subject to any 'legitimate' concessions to local needs and circumstances) faithfully and consistently embody the CCETSW's national policy priorities for social work training, centralized regulative, co-ordinative, and 'feedback' mechanisms are from the CCETSW's standpoint indispensable: they are techniques for minimizing the possible disjunctions between initial national policy-intentions and local outcomes discussed earlier with reference to Barbalet (1985), Clegg (1989) and Barnes (1986). They are also techniques for administratively consolidating ('institutionalizing') the contingent shifts in power referred to earlier. Clegg (1989) observes that 'All forms of standardized reporting, co-ordinating or control mechanisms, within a circuit of social integration, will tend to reproduce existing configurations of power within a given ... field' (ibid., p.227). This can also apply in situations of conflict rather than of integration and such mechanisms are, in Barnes's (1986) terms, a necessary means of preventing 'authorities' turning themselves into 'powers' and subverting policy at the local level.

Very often, external control mechanisms are backed up by sanctions in the sense that conformity to the 'central' actors' rules-of-procedure is necessary to retain the official approvals required for continued organizational survival (Clegg, 1989, pp.227-8). In a significant departure from earlier practices, the CCETSW ruled that it '... will only consider for approval Dip.SW programmes submitted jointly by educational institutions and social services agencies' (CCETSW, 1989b, p.22, section 3.1.1, emphasis added). Courses will not be validated unless academic institutions and social work agencies as 'joint programme providers' (ibid., p.5) join together to furnish documentary evidence to the CCETSW of 'joint' written agreements on curriculum content; selection and assessment of students; methods of training; and on arrangements for 'joint' continuous local monitoring and evaluation of each local Dip.SW scheme (ibid., p.22). The outcomes of these various local agreements will have to be submitted in writing to the CCETSW for its approval, and the findings of the continuous 'joint' local monitoring of schemes will in the future also have to be regularly reported to the CCETSW together with reports on any other matters requested by the CCETSW (ibid., p.30, para.3.7.3.2).

These recent regulations associated with the new local committee infrastructure signify an increasing tendency towards the bureaucratization of social work training: it is possible that in the future the role of the social work educator will be less that of an 'academic' and more akin to that of a college-based local government training officer or training administrator. Later, the point will be made that these developments are likely to significantly increase the administrative and external liaison workloads of social work educators, with a reduction in the time available for intellectual work such as research: this may cause some higher education institutions, particularly those that define research as a crucial part of their academic role, to withdraw from social work training. Another aspect of the new regulations may also raise a question mark about the continued involvement of some academic institutions. A significant departure from existing training arrangements is that student assessment will be undertaken by a joint Assessment Board which will include external assessors appointed by the CCETSW (CCETSW, 1989b, p.27, para.3.4.6.4). The 'joint programme providers' for each Dip.SW training scheme will be required to appoint two external examiners from a CCETSW approved list; these examiners will be paid by the CCETSW and be involved in the Assessment Boards and report to the CCETSW on the adequacy and operation of courses (ibid., pp.27-28). The question of whether all academic institutions will accept these and the previously mentioned additional curbs upon educational autonomy is likely to become increasingly significant in the 1990's. It will be noted shortly that the possibility of some academic institutions in the higher education sector withdrawing from social work training has recently become a topic of debate in social work and academic circles. This potentially de-professionalizing outcome of policies constructed by the CCETSW as a response to the protracted struggles of the 1980's over social work education and training, though its amplification as a focus of concern is recent, has a number of antecedents in the recent history of social work.

Higher education and social work training: the marginalization of academic disciplinary knowledge

Professional arguments for a location in higher education tend to refer mostly to universities, rather than to polytechnics. It is doubtful whether this is for reasons to do with academic excellence. No evidence exists to suggest that the quality of teaching or research across a wide range of disciplines in polytechnics is in any sense 'inferior' when compared with universities; it is just as likely that in some disciplines, particularly those of an 'applied' type, polytechnic standards are superior. Nevertheless, popular images exist of universities as the relatively more prestigious higher education institutions and, as noted earlier in the chapter, this may be a factor in professionalizing actors' perception of universities as key locations for professional training, particularly in the case of professionalizing occupations ('semi-professions') such as social work (Dingwall, 1974). This point will be returned to later and for the moment discussion will centre on the higher education sector in general.

In the future, vocationalist 'social care' training is likely to expand in colleges of further education (CCETSW, 1988, pp.2-3). It is the future of 'professional' social work training in higher education that is relatively less secure. The Association of Teachers in Social Work Education (ATSWE) observed that '... for the first time in its history ... social work education is entering a phase of significant and painful contraction' (ATSWE, 1986, p.85). In 1988 the CCETSW voiced concern at proposals to close social work courses at the University of Newcastle and the University of Wales at Cardiff (CCETSW, 1988, p.7). Gardiner's (1987a) concern about '... the survival of social work education' (ibid., p.55) rested on his view that social work should be regarded as a 'professional' activity (ibid., p.53) and that social work professionalism is threatened by recent developments which raise doubts as to whether it will be possible '... in the end, to ensure that we can maintain the activity of social work education ... within higher education' (ibid., p.55). These professional(izing) anxieties about the future of social work training in the higher education sector stem partly from professional leaders' concerns about the possible reactions of the governing bodies of academic institutions to pressures for very practical, 'non-academic' forms of social work training. These pressures are being exerted by social work employers; the CCETSW: some 'technical-professionalist' social work lobby groups; social services occupational groups; to some extent the government; and more recently, social work students. There are signs of growing restiveness in some academic institutions of higher education about the marginalization of academic knowledge in social work training: these academic concerns have a very long history (for example, London University Executive Committee on Social Work Education, 1903) but they have been amplified by recent developments. There are also recent academic institutional concerns about the implications for academic values and educational autonomy arising from employer-led Dip.SW training schemes with significantly increased employer control over social work curricula, teaching methods, student assessment, and course evaluation.

It should, however, be noted that the CCETSW, despite its decision to abolish the distinction between the CQSW ('professional social work') and the CSS ('social services work') in favour of a new single award (the Dip.SW), has in reality not wholly abandoned its earlier strategy of responding to employers' demands for 'non-academic' vocational training while simultaneously keeping social work's professional(izing) and therefore 'academic' torch alight. Professional and academic-professional actors were, it was observed earlier, resolutely opposed to the CCETSW's proposals for a single training award that combined professional social work and social services work: but in fact, the CCETSW's movement towards a single award has been more illusory than 'real'. The earlier hierarchical distinction has been reconstructed, but not abandoned. That is, 'social services' work (or 'CSS work' under the old system) has been redesignated as 'social care' work (CCETSW, 1990) that will in future be geared to 'sub-professional' vocational qualifications provided by the further education sector and linked into the new National Vocational Qualifications (NVQ) framework of awards. The qualification proposed for 'professional' social work is the new Dip.SW taught in higher education academic institutions: the CCETSW explicitly states that the Dip.SW in the 1990's will '... become the professional qualification for social work' (CCETSW, 1990, p.22, original emphasis). The CCETSW's strategic reconstruction of social work training policies seems designed to offer benefits to employers, in ways that will be discussed shortly, while also reproducing professional social work interests in terms of the hierarchical division of labour in the SSD's: moreover, academic-professional interests have not been entirely forsaken by the CCETSW. In its reconstruction of social work training the CCETSW indicates that its proposals for the 1990's rest on a 'continuum' of education and training for social work and the personal social services (CCETSW, 1990, p.22). The term 'continuum' is a misnomer. In reality, the CCETSW's proposals are for a hierarchy of training at three 'levels' that reflect and in future will (unless other factors intrude) reproduce most features of the existing hierarchical task-stratification model in the SSD's. The first level is 'sub-professional' vocational training in 'social care', based in the further education sector with the training system largely controlled by employers and validated by the CCETSW in conjunction with the National Council for Vocational Qualifications (NCVQ). The second level is intended for 'professional social workers', based on the new Dip.SW schemes provided in the higher education sector on the basis that these schemes will be validated by the CCETSW. That is, the Dip.SW is intended to be at the level of basic, qualifying 'professional' training in 'social work'. As already noted, this level through the new local committee infrastructure and the concept 'joint programme providers' also involves a strong element of 'practical' employ-led training, or at least, a far greater emphasis upon this than under the CQSW system. The significance of this point will be returned to shortly. The third level is 'post-qualifying' training; it is clear that the CCETSW has the interests of 'professional social work' in mind at this level of training and 'The establishment of an advanced award in social work in the early 1990's ... (is) ... one of CCETSW's objectives' (CCETSW, 1990, p.25, emphasis added). In short, the CCETSW's (1990) planning objectives rest on the argument that 'Together these three elements - vocational qualifications, Dip.SW, and one or more post-qualifying awards - offer the kind of framework the personal social services will need in the 1990's' (ibid., p.5). It is evident that many aspects of the binary CQSW/CSS hierarchical system of training and its filiation to the hierarchical division-of-labour in the personal social services, are being preserved in these policies for the 1990's though in a modified three-tier form and through the use of a new nomenclature in which 'sub-professional' social services work is re-designated as vocational 'social care' work.

The CCETSW's (1990) proposed 'training and education' hierarchy seems designed to satisfy employers demands for occupational and vocational 'practicality' in two key respects. Firstly, at the first-tier level, through the CCETSW's involvement with the NCVQ in expanding the number and range of practical 'social care' vocational training schemes in the further education sector. And secondly, at the second-tier and 'professional' 'social work' level, through the Dip.SW local committee infrastructure which shifts power to employers. These two policy strands of the CCETSW's movement towards an endorsement of demands for increasingly employ-led forms of less 'professional', more practical 'non-academic' training are, however, balanced against the CCETSW's simultaneous efforts to strategically nurture professionalizing aspirations, even if in a more diluted form than had been possible in the 1970's. Professional and academic-professional actors were aware by the mid-1980's that they had 'lost' the struggle that they had waged against the CCETSW, the employers, and social services occupational groups. The ostensibly 'professional' Dip.SW is intended as an employer-led form of practical training, administered and controlled through the local committee network established by the CCETSW. The Dip.SW is in most respects a 'victory' for the employers; but it is nevertheless a qualification that the CCETSW hopes will also as far as possible perform a professionalizing function. Social work's 'heady' professionally expansionist post-Seebohm era of the early 1970's is unlikely to return: but professionalizing actors evidently believe that it might, none the less, be possible to salvage 'something' from that era. The Dip.SW is regarded by the CCETSW itself, and by professionalizing groups who currently perceive that there is no realistic 'academic'-cum-'professional' alternative to the Dip.SW, as social work's future professionalizing mainplank: hence the CCETSW's (1990) statement that '... the Dip.SW will set the standard of professional social work education and training well into the next century' (ibid., p.21, emphasis added). There is also an important sense in which professionalizing aspirations are strategically reinforced by the existence of the <u>third</u> ('post-qualifying') level in the CCETSW's proposed hierarchy of training for the 1990's. In the future it is at least possible that the employers will (through their roles in the new committee infrastructure governing Dip.SW courses) shift the Dip.SW so far away from academic disciplinary knowledge as to negate the credibility of any claims that the Dip.SW is a 'professional' qualification; or perhaps even to cause academic institutions to withdraw from the Dip.SW programme. If the Dip.SW is 'translated' by employers into a vocational form of occupational apprenticeship, claims to a 'professional' status for social work might <u>then</u> be sustained by encouraging increasing numbers of Dip.SW holders to 'step up' to what the CCETSW (1990) describes as its new post-qualifying '... advanced awards in <u>social work</u>' (ibid., p.25, emphasis added). The third-tier, 'advanced' social work awards should - on the face of things - convince any sceptics who harbour doubts as to whether social workers in the new 'practical' training scenarios of the 1990's should be regarded as 'professionals'. These third-level awards, to state the matter another way, seem intended as a reserve standby that may, if necessary, be widely deployed by the CCETSW to 'rescue' professional social work from any potentially de-professionalizing outcomes that emerge at the second-tier level of the new employer-led but putatively 'professional' Dip.SW schemes.

Whether the CCETSW will succeed in its strategy of trying to unproblematically satisfy demands for practical social work training while simultaneously reproducing professional(izing) interests and objectives, is open to question. As just noted, the new regulative local committee infrastructure governing the Dip.SW may mean that academic-professionals will 'lose control' of the Dip.SW in the sense that social work employers will 'convert' it into a 'non-academic' and therefore 'non-professional' vocational qualification. However, while this outcome is probable it is not inevitable, and an outcome in the opposite direction is in principle possible. In the perhaps unlikely event that it is professional lobby groups and academic-professional actors who succeed in retaining a high degree of control over the Dip.SW, or more precisely, a degree of control regarded by employers, by the CCETSW, and by social services (or 'social care') workers as unacceptable, it is possible that the social work community within the next decade will undergo a process of conflict analogous to that which occurred in the late 1970's and early 1980's. This statement requires explanation.

Earlier in the chapter it was observed that the introduction of the CSS in 1975 provided a new and positive comparative reference-group for the employers. Employers were able to control the CSS schemes in the further education sector and the employers contrasted the practicality of the CSS schemes with, as they saw it, the 'professional intellectualism' of the CQSW courses provided in the higher education sector. The employers began appointing CSS holders (social services workers) to posts that previously had been the preserve of CQSW holders (professional social workers). This organizational role-blurring, together with the emergence of a new pressure group reflecting the interests of CSS holders, contributed to the previously described contingent shifts of power within social work's actor-network and to the development of pressures leading to the introduction of a single qualification to replace the binary CQSW/CSS system. The Dip.SW is the new 'single' award culminating from these developments. It is, though, a single award in name only and as observed earlier the CCETSW's proposed hierarchy of training for the 1990's is, in effect, a reconstructed three-tier version of the two-tier CQSW/CSS binary system. Under the previous system, the employers regarded academic-professionals' 'control' of the CQSW as unacceptable. Although unlikely under the new 'committee' system of regulations governing the pattern of future training, it is at least possible that in the 1990's academic-professionals will manage to retain control of the 'professional' Dip.SW programmes to an extent that employers regard as unacceptable: in this event, by which time the CSS will have been abolished, the employers may move increasingly towards the first-tier in the CCETSW's new education and training 'continuum' and define the 'sub-professional' employer-led vocational 'social care' qualifications in the further education sector as the main and also most practically relevant form of training for 'social work' (as defined by employers) in the organizational context of the personal social services. If, in this scenario, employers promote holders of these 'social care' vocational qualifications to posts that professionalizing actors, together with the CCETSW, regard as the rightful preserve of 'professional' Dip.SW holders, there will almost certainly be a repeat performance of the protracted conflicts that infused the CQSW/CSS binary system.

For the reasons that power, social action, and the conditions-of-action are contingent, the possible future scenario identified above is only one amongst others. It was observed earlier that a more probable scenario is that under the new local committee arrangements and administrative regulations it is academic-professionals who will 'lose control' of the Dip.SW to social work employers and to other groups committed to vocational styles of training at what is ostensibly a 'professional' level of training. If this occurs, and providing academic institutions in the higher education sector do not withdraw from basic, qualifying 'professional' social work training, the Dip.SW will probably remain in place although in reality this will be in the form of a vocational type of training that is academic-professional in name only. As suggested previously, social work educators, given their professionalizing concerns, are more than likely to concur with this outcome. These developments may be further reinforced by a related possibility. It was mentioned earlier that the National Council for Vocational Qualifications (NCVQ) will in future be involved with the CCETSW in planning and validating the first-tier vocational 'social care' qualifications in the further education sector. There are, however, some current indications that the NCVQ will also extend its control 'upwards' to the 'professional' Dip.SW level of training in the higher education sector. Given the strongly vocationalist, practical-training and employer-led 'apprenticeship' principles of the NCVQ, this may have the effects predicted by Jones (1989) who suggests that (ibid., p.215)

> The extension of the NCVQ framework across all levels of social work training and education will ... consolidate the influence and control of employers ... reducing the power of ... (social work) ... professionals and its roots in liberal higher education. There will undoubtedly be ... hiccups in this transformation. Some

institutions of higher education may for a variety of reasons, such as a commitment to liberal education ... refuse to participate.

However, professionalizing actors, including social work academic-professionals, are predisposed to retain at any cost a foothold in higher education as an 'obligatory passage point' for the achievement of a professional status for social work. In part, therefore, the outcome anticipated by Jones will be contingent upon the extent to which social work educators in departments of social work training are able to strategically exert influence upon the decisions made by the governing bodies of their academic institutions.

When they are viewed in terms of their historical context, most of the problems referred to in the preceding pages are contemporary re-activations of social work's 'perennial' theory-practice problematic (see chapters two and four). Indeed, these recent developments and the intense policy conflicts that preceded them have to be viewed in broad perspective if they are to be understood in anything other than a very restricted and incomplete way. Reference was made in the second chapter to professional social work's 'credibility-gap', which refers to an historically institutionalized professional misrepresentation concerning the cognitive foundations of social work practice. In that chapter the point was made that since the beginning of the present century successive generations of professionalizing leaders and academic-professionals have attempted to portray social work practice 'as if' it were or else was on the point of becoming an activity involving the practical application of formal academic social science knowledge: the empirical reality, however, is that most social workers do not base their practice on a use of academic disciplinary knowledge. Nor at any time in the history of British social work, including the present, has movement towards practitioner 'use' of academic knowledge showed the slightest sign of being imminent. Contemporary social work's distance from a professionally conjectured academic knowledge base cannot legitimately be 'explained' as a temporary or early stage in the development of a 'new' profession. Social work is not new nor are professionalizing aspirations. The Charity Organization Society (COS) attempted to formulate and then disseminate a portrayal of 'professional' social work as an activity that involved the practical application of formal academic knowledge. The reality was very different; the COS's '... claims to be practitioners of "scientific charity" rested on a combination of general ethical principles and a record of practical experiences derived from agency work of various kinds' (Pinker, 1989, p.87). This is also, by and large, an empirically accurate description of modern social work practice. Different types of social work cognitions are drawn upon by practitioners in different historical periods, but their common denominator is that, with very few exceptions, none of them are drawn from academic disciplinary discourses. In chapter four, reference was made to the 'process' orientation in modern social work education and practice (i.e. the experiential construction of cognitive and emotional social work 'insights' in small group situations) and it was observed that this orientation contradicts any claims by professional(izing) leaders or professional social work educators that an identifiable, transmissible written 'core' of practised academic-professional knowledge exists in social work. It was also observed in chapter four that a large number of empirical studies indicate that social work practitioners rely mainly upon commonsense reasoning and 'practice wisdoms' that are acquired 'on-the-job' and disseminated across the social work community largely by means of social work's pervasive 'oral' culture. In sum, there is no reliable historical or recent evidence to suggest that social workers in general have ever, in their practice, drawn upon formal academic disciplinary knowledge. At every stage in the history of social work, including the present, most of the available evidence shows that social workers do not and never have employed (nor see any useful role for) academic social science knowledge (for example, Bosanquet, 1900; Eliot, 1924; Karpf, 1931; Kadushin, 1959; Gordon, 1963; Bartlett, 1970; Stevenson, 1970; Stevenson and Parsloe, 1978, pp.133-5; Carew, 1979; and Pratt and Grimshaw, 1985).

Professional(izing) social work's amaranthine problem of credibility, in the sense just described, is from a professionalizing standpoint a perennial, historically perpetuated 'skeleton-in-the-cupboard' that is best kept permanently hidden. Otherwise, the 'external' public and political credibility of claims that social work is a 'profession' that should 'therefore' have a training system housed in those higher education institutions where academic disciplines are taught, is greatly reduced. Part of the current crisis in professional social work education is that this perennial problem of professionalizing 'credibility' is becoming more difficult to secrete within the social work community: it is becoming more externally visible to, among others, the governing bodies of academic institutions. For some time, the tendency of professional social work to portray itself as having a meaningful connection to academic social sciences as a means of securing a spurious 'academic' legitimacy for claims to 'professional' status (Boreham, 1983) has attracted criticisms; these are re-worked in Jones's (1983) observations regarding professional social work's 'looting' (ibid., p.89) of academic social science disciplines. Academic criticisms of this kind, however, have been overtaken by other recent developments. In the present period it is not only practitioners and, as described earlier in the chapter, social work employers whose 'rejection' of the role of academic disciplinary knowledge in social work training and practice has contributed to a climate in which the legitimacy of locating social work training in higher education institutions is being challenged: social work students have also played a part in this process. This was noted briefly in chapter three with reference to empirical data. Social work students' rejection of academic knowledge (Davies, 1989) is not a recent phenomenon (for instance, see Bosanquet, 1900; and Eliot, 1924) although it has been recently amplified. Some recent studies indicate that students either regard social work teaching staff as 'social workers' rather than as 'academics' (Barbour, 1985, pp.505-6) or else regard them as having both these roles (Coulshed, 1986, p.122). With regard to the 'process-versus-content' controversy (Simon, 1967, p.10; Harris, et al., 1985) examined in chapter four, a number of studies (for example, Watson and Lee, 1982; Barbour, 1984; Waterhouse, 1987, p.7) indicate that many social work students are more committed to exploring 'personal development' and 'process' issues than the intellectual contents of what Coulshed (1986) refers to as '... the academic portion of training ...' (ibid., p.125). Other recent data indicate that many social work students want much less emphasis than is currently given to academic learning, greater social work employer control over social work curricula, and more time spent outside the academic institution with the bulk of students' time spent on practical work placements (CCETSW, 1988, p.20). As was observed in chapter two, there are no valid grounds for criticizing individual academic teachers nor individual students for the perennial-but-also-contemporary hiatus between academic knowledge and the socially constructed reality of social work practice: if throughout the history of social work each generation of social work students in higher education academic institutions habitually feel that they are in the 'wrong place' for learning the realities of practice, this is because they are involved in a professionally constructed and historically reproduced problem of 'credibility' that is not primarily of their making. It would appear to be the case that this enduring problem can be resolved in either one of two ways: the first involves reshaping training to fit the socially constructed and historically institutionalized reality of social work practice, the second involves re-shaping practice to fit an academic-professional model of education. That is, either the training system might be re-located out of higher education to an agency in-service training model based on supervised practical apprenticeship perhaps supplemented by short occupational induction courses. if necessary with some training administration back-up from local colleges of further education; on the face of it, this would be a rational policy response to the socially constructed reality of practice as it actually is, rather than as professional social work teachers and professional leaders would wish it to be. Or, in order to reshape practice so as to get it to logically 'fit' the academic-professional education model, practitioners (and students) should be exhorted to base their practice on academic disciplinary knowledge: the problem with this last strategy is that it has been tried without success for almost a hundred years.

The tendency of academic-professional and professionalizing leaders to criticize students and practitioners for their 'anti-intellectualism' merely serves to draw attention to and make more visible the timeless problem of implausibility surrounding social work academic-professionalism. Practitioners and students are in some sense not 'responsible' for this apparently imperishable problem of academic-professional credibility: they are involved in its reproduction but it was not they who created it. Nor are they necessarily actors who can do anything about it: to exhort them to do so is likely to be ineffective, unless it is presumed they have the power, not to mention the motivation, to dramatically transform an institutionalized cognitive reality of social work practice that has existed for the best part of a century. The strategy of academic-professional criticism and exhortation directed against fieldworkers and students was tried by Bosanquet (1900) without any obvious success; frequent repetition of it (Urwick, 1904; Eliot, 1924; Bartlett, 1970; Stevenson, 1981, p.22; Satyamurti, 1983, p.36; Harris, 1988, p.23; Jordan, 1988, p.33) merely runs the risk of drawing 'external' attention to, in the terms used earlier, a permanent 'internal' skeleton-in-the-cupboard that, from a professionalizing standpoint, is best kept permanently secreted within the social work community. The professionally disturbing empirical truth of this matter does seem to be that the socially constructed reality of social work practices does not 'require' formal academic disciplinary knowledge, and never has. Nor are there any clear signs that it is likely to. Harris's (1988) academic-professional criticism of the new 'practical' training policies formulated by the CCETSW for the 1990's, is that '... the continued role of higher education in social work courses is dependent on the retention of what we now term "education" as well as "training": else it would be perverse for most of the learning not to be done "on the job"' (ibid., p.23, emphases added). This statement is from Harris's paper to a major social work conference at which employers were represented. If in the statement just quoted it was Harris's intention to fire a warning shot across the bows of social work employers, its strategic effectiveness is open to question. It is not employers but academic-professional and professionalizing actors, together with the CCETSW, who have contingently acquired the stronger motives for retaining social work in higher education. Employers themselves, given their past experience of 'academic' and 'professional' education, have doubts as to whether social work training should be located in higher education academic institutions (Nelson, 1989) and, in particular, have argued that '... the universities are inappropriate places for ... (social work) ... education' (Wright, 1977, p.9).

Sometimes, social work's ubiquitous problem of academic-professional 'credibility' is exacerbated by unexpected critics. An influential 'professional' social work writer, Irvine (1978) observes that (ibid., p.93)

> Knowledge as represented by academic qualifications is undoubtedly useful for impressing those whose recognition confers status, power and autonomy, but if this were all it could justly be dismissed as no more than a part of the "trappings of professionalism" ... I have expressed some doubt concerning ... (its) ... value.

Irvine (1978) goes on to say that '... a good deal of the academic baggage of social workers is more useful for gaining official recognition and status than it is relevant to their actual practice' (ibid., p.100, emphasis added). The context of these criticisms is that they were made during social work's still relatively professionally 'safe' period when, unlike the present, few questions were being asked about the viability of social work training in the higher eduction sector. It is not conceivable that a professional leader such as Irvine, in making her criticism, seriously intended to argue that 'therefore' social work training should be removed from those academic institutions that teach the academic knowledge which she claims has little relevance to 'actual practice' and which she says is 'appropriated' by professional social work for 'status' reasons. For the reason that the conditions-of-action in which social work actors operate are not static, professional actors' constructs that may in their context seem relatively harmless may in another context or another period amount to the scoring of an own goal. This is true of some earlier views expressed by other professional leaders, such as Parsloe (1984) who condemned '... what I believe to be a misguided urge on the part of some social workers and social work educators to claim for social work a professional status akin to that achieved by the traditional professions' (ibid., p.109).

Implicit in the observations just made is a more general and curious social work anomaly. This is the tendency of some professional and academic-professional social work actors to undermine their own professionalizing objectives by arguing on the one hand for the location of training in higher education, and on the other, specifying that social work practice is based on types of knowledge that do not require an academic location and which, indeed, are more effectively acquired elsewhere. Very little sociological analysis of this anomaly has been undertaken. Systematic analysis of its social construction and reproduction in social work discourses would require the use of both historical and contemporary ethnographic data that might illuminate the phenomenological bases underpinning social work actors' use of such terms as 'professional knowledge', 'social work knowledge', and 'academic knowledge': to this list might be added the term 'relevant knowledge' (Armstrong, 1980, pp.17-18). A noticeable feature of this

146

curious anomaly (or which is, at least, curious when analysed in terms that are external to the discourses involved in its production) is that it is constituted through more than one type of social work discourse. Specifically, the types of social work knowledge 'substituted' in place of academic knowledge are variable. For example, unlike the esoteric 'insights' and 'understandings' associated with the psychotherapeutically based 'process' orientation discussed in chapter four, Davies's (1981a, 1985) rejections and marginalizations of academic social science knowledge involve replacing this academic knowledge with 'practice wisdoms'. or what Davies (1985, pp.223-4) calls 'practice knowhow' together with other practical and fairly 'hardheaded' types of knowledge and information (ibid., pp.225-32) of a kind that logically require an 'apprenticeship' model of on-the-job training, perhaps supplemented by short in-house induction courses. Yet Davies (1981c) in various statements that suggest he is aware that others will draw this same conclusion concerning the question of where (given his view of practice) training should be based, also argues that social work education should not be 'removed' from the universities. Davies (1981c) implies the fact that university departments of social work conduct research into social work activities is of itself a reason for basing social work training in universities (ibid., pp.282-3) and he says '... for this reason, if for no other, any suggestion that social work education should be shifted out of the universities should be opposed' (ibid., p.283). Davies's particular concern is with the universities, rather than other academic institutions. However if, as Davies also argues, academic social sciences such as psychology, sociology, and social administration (see chapter three) have no significantly useful role in social work training or in social work practice, this removes the basis of his argument for a university location for social work training. Outside of the social sciences, there is no other university academic discipline that social work might conceivably draw upon: as a basis for assessing ('diagnosing') clients situations or for constructing theories about 'how to do' social work, university disciplines such as engineering or geography or physics are obviously out of the question. Further, to say that university departments might conduct research into social work activities is no logical reason for saying that social work training should 'therefore' be located in those departments; the logic deteriorates further if it is also argued that the types of very practical occupational information required for effective social work practice do not include the academic social science knowledge taught at universities. It does not make sense to suggest that researchers must necessarily also be trainers of their research respondents. Trapeze artistes, jazz musicians, and prime ministers have all at various times come under academic social science's research microscope, but no-one has yet seriously suggested that these research subjects should 'therefore' enrol at a university for an undergraduate training course in social sciences: if it is also insisted they would anyway find these academic disciplines irrelevant to their occupational roles the argument that they 'should' enrol for such a course collapses twice rather than once.

Another version of this curious anomaly in 'professional' social work discourses has already been mentioned. This concerns the arguments of psychotherapeutically oriented advocates of 'process' learning and practice. In this social work discourse, which is fairly widespread among academic-professionals and also among practitioners, claims are made that social work is an intellectually 'complex' 'profession' and that professional education should 'therefore' be based in higher education. However, in the next breath academic disciplinary knowledge is supplanted by a fusion of solipsistic cognitive 'insights' and emotionally grounded 'understandings'. For instance, Gammack (1982) states that '... life is a profound and manifold process' (ibid., p.20). This is probably true, but he goes on to say that 'competent social work interaction' (ibid., p.19) involves casework relationships in which social work 'insights' (i.e. social work knowledge) are formulated experientially during '... the electricity of the face-to-face moment' (ibid. p.8). The governing bodies of academic institutions currently considering their academic role in social work training are likely to look askance at such statements, and at such revelations as '... social work is really an individual's collection of subjective experiences and meanings which, depending on the sensitivity and experience of the individual, will determine ... actions with clients' (Kakabadse, 1982, p.147). In his version of academic-professionalism, Gardiner (1987a) claims social work is a 'profession' and is worried about whether social work training will 'survive' in higher education academic institutions (ibid., p.55). Yet in a statement that seems remarkably impervious to the contradiction in his argument, he also declares that (Gardiner, 1987b, pp.49-50, emphases added)

> It is ... not surprising that major studies fail to demonstrate social workers using theory ... It is practice wisdom and grounded theory rooted in one's own experience that are the basis of competent professional practice ... anything that can be taught to another is relatively inconsequential ... truth that has been personally appropriated and assimilated in experience can not be directly communicated to another ...

This cancels out Gardiner's claim that social work is a 'profession' and that its training system should 'therefore' be housed in higher education. The statement's specification that social work knowledge of the professionally 'competent' kind is privately fashioned out of experiential solipsisms and idiographic (not to mention unteachable and non-communicable) 'insights' confutes any arguments that an identifiable written, transmissible 'core' of practised non-solipsistic academic-professional knowledge exists in social work: and removes all possibility of arguing that 'competent' professional practice has anything to gain from the nomothetic ('generalized') and therefore, in Gardiner's terms, 'inconsequential' cognitive contents of academic social science knowledge such as psychology, sociology, or social administration. It is also worth noting that Gardiner's statement says that 'effective' or 'competent' professional social work knowledge is 'immune' from research inspection. This suggests that there is no real point in attempting research into the cognitive foundations of professional practice; whereas Davies, it was noted earlier, argues that such research is precisely a reason for locating social work training in universities.

There are more twists in the curious tale of this anomaly than there is space to examine here, though one of them is worth mentioning briefly for the reason that it highlights the existence of 'theory-practice' disputes within social work education rather than, in the ways described earlier in the chapter, in the relationship between social work educators and employers and practitioners. This relates to the tendency of some social scientists involved in social work education to, on the one hand, be relatively unconcerned as to whether social work is or is not regarded as a 'profession', but on the other, to advocate an 'academic' approach in social work education that, whether this is intended or not, is an approach that is functional for professionalizing actors to the extent that it actually or at least potentially contributes to the legitimization of the academic-professional motif. Paradoxically, social scientists' attempts to sustain 'academic' discourse in social work education are very often resisted by professional social work teachers: this particular internal tension within social work education is, it is worth noting, another of those 'perennial' complications that span a century of social work history (see for instance Bosanquet, 1890; Cheetham, 1971; Jones, 1983, p.109).

The problem of academic-professional 'credibility' referred to earlier currently poses particular strategic difficulties for academic-professionals and professionalizing actors. These difficulties are centred around the amplification of this problem of credibility as a consequence of social work's protracted internal policy struggles in the 1980's and, as an outcome of these struggles, the previously described movement towards a very 'practical' training scenario for the 1990's. Academic-professionals involved in the new local committee infrastructure established by the CCETSW, are constrained by opposed demands. On the one hand, academic-professionals have to convince employers ('joint programme providers') of the practicality of their courses (see CCETSW, 1987a, 1987b, 1989a, 1989b, and 1990). On the other, they have to convince the governing bodies of their academic institutions that the new training scenario does not remove the academic rationale for those institutions' continued involvement in social work training (see CVCP, 1986; Pinker, 1989, p.101). In this problematic situation, a number of strategies are available to academic-professionals. One of these is to give renewed emphasis to the concept of theory-practice 'integration'. This concept is a way of simultaneously presenting ones' 'practical' credentials to the world of practice and ones' 'academic' credentials to the academic community. The practice community is promised that, although the published course prospectus must be seen to list at least a few named academic disciplines and a modicum of academic disciplinary knowledge will continue to be taught on courses, this will, however, be very closely 'integrated' into teaching on very basic 'everyday' practical social work issues: at the same time, the academic community is informed that although it may 'appear' to be the case that very little academic social science knowledge is being taught, this apparent diminution of academic content in social work training is only because such knowledge is rendered near-invisible by virtue of its being artfully 'integrated' into discussions of highly 'complex' 'professional' social work materials. In any field of activity, not only in social work, merging what Collin's (1975) calls 'intellectual talk' and 'practical talk' (ibid., pp.115-31) into a unified cognitive-practico discourse is inherently difficult. In social work education, for all the reasons examined earlier, this form of discourse is comparatively rare. By and large, the concept of theory-practice 'integration' has become, in social work education and in social work practice, an ideological device: the concept is a way of drawing upon commonsense reasoning, 'practice-wisdoms', and experientially acquired 'insights', and re-designating these as a form of 'academic-professional' knowledge. Kahn (1954) observes that when professional social work practitioners 'account' in written reports for their activities in formal academic-professional language this often involves a use of jargon for professionally 'dressing-up' essentially commonsensical modes of reasoning: he suggests professional social workers use technical terms to describe social work assessments (i.e. assessments of clients' situations) that, in reality, have been arrived at through the combined use of commonsense reasoning and 'practice-wisdoms' acquired during 'on-the-job' practical experience. That an analogous though not identical process occurs in social work education when the concept 'integration' is invoked, is illustrated in a study which examined the teaching of law on social work courses (Ball et al., 1988). Harris (1988), one of the researchers involved, comments that the study found that in 'applying' the academic discipline of law to practical social work teaching, the concept of 'integration' was employed by social work educators in a way that (ibid., p.23, first emphasis added)

> ... was all too often a coded way of not doing very much law. In particular we found a marked tendency for some courses to see "integration" as an alternative to learning substantive knowledge rather than as the next stage in the process i.e. learning to what use to put that which one had learned.

Compared with social science knowledge, law has a relatively 'firmer' epistemological knowledge-mandate and a technically relatively more readily identifiable and specifiable situational context(s) of usage and practical application. If the displacement of cognitive (or 'academic') content identified by Harris occurs in the case of law, such displacement, bearing in mind the various other factors identified in the preceding pages, almost certainly occurs on a grand scale if and when social work teachers 'integrate' academic social science knowledge into practice discourses. Nonetheless, in the current climate of a movement towards a more 'vocationalist' type of social work training it is likely that academic-professionals will in the future make greater strategic use of the concept theory-practice 'integration'.

It is primarily because the relationship of academic knowledge to social work practice has always been ethereal that social work education has, in every historical period, led a relatively separate, marginalized existence within the academic community. This was true of the Charity Organization Society's social work course at London University (Mowat, 1961, p.112 and p.171) and to a large extent remains the position. Referring to the work of Donnison et al. (1975) and their description of social work training at the London School of Economics in the 1950's, Pinker (1989) observes that the social work courses '... were left entirely to the staff concerned with them; it was they who provided most of the teaching and arranged for the contributions made by other lecturers, most of whom were drawn from outside the School' (ibid., p.104). Social work staff were not integrated into the wider academic institution, spent much time engaged in continuous liaison with 'the field', and did relatively little academic research; the impression that social work's 'centre of gravity' lay outside academic life meant that social work training '... led a precarious existence within the School' (Donnison et al., 1975, p.257, cited in Pinker, 1989, p.94). The indications are that the future location of social work training in higher education institutions may become more rather than less precarious as a consequence of the CCETSW's proposals for the future of social work training '... into the next century' (CCETSW, 1990, p.21).

Academic responses to the training-versus-education controversy

It was observed earlier that for social work academic-professionals and other professionalizing actors, academic institutions of higher education are 'obligatory passage points' (Callon et al., 1986) or what Clegg (1989) terms 'necessary nodal points' (ibid.. p.185). If in the future the governing bodies of these academic institutions express doubts about their continued involvement in the new practical training scenario planned by the CCETSW (1990) it is likely that social work educators will evolve various strategies intended to persuade academic institutions that the new training scenario involves no 'threat' to academic standards or academic values. One such possible strategy, described earlier, is to give renewed emphasis to the concept of an 'integration' between academic knowledge and social work practical issues. Another involves the construction of a formulation that 'education' and 'training' are not incompatible. In a formal, uncontextualized use of these terms, the majority of academics and academic decision-makers, including those not involved in social work, probably concur that education and (rather than 'versus') training is an entirely acceptable statement of the role of academic institutions: indeed, this is regularly argued on those occasions when actors consider it may be strategically advantageous to claim that no 'real' conflict exists with regard to this formulation. However the underlying reality of this socially constructed formulation in social work is that different actors often have different and fundamentally opposed objectives in mind when they invoke it, and imbue the two terms within it ('education' and 'training') with entirely different meanings and with very different purposes in mind: were this not so, the major internal social work conflicts described earlier in the chapter would not have occurred (unless they were simply a big 'misunderstanding'!) nor either would the CCETSW's new training scenario have emerged in response to those protracted conflicts of meaning and of purpose. In the remainder of the chapter, greater emphasis will be given to the position of the universities with regard to the unabated controversy over social work education-versus-training. There are two reasons for this. Firstly, as observed earlier, professionalizing actors seem to focus their concerns upon the continued involvement of universities in social work training; and secondly, when compared with other academic institutions, it is the universities who have expressed the strongest reservations about the CCETSW's policy intentions for social work training.

In rejecting the CCETSW's (1986) proposal for a QDSW qualification, the government observed that 'There must be substantial doubt whether such a course would be acceptable to institutions, particularly the universities' (Department of Education and Science, 1987). The Committee of Vice-Chancellors and Principles stated that '... we have to express universities' criticisms and grave concern about ... (the QDSW scheme) ... and its implications ...' (CVCP, 1986, p.1). The CVCP criticized the QDSW's 'technical-training' ethos (ibid., p.4); the 'localism' inherent in the proposed local administrative committee structure which contrasted with universities' local but also national and international frames of reference (ibid., p.3); and the likelihood that an increased administrative work-load would be placed on social work educators, with a consequent reduction in the time available for them to carry out academic research (ibid., p.3, para.12). The CVCP (1986) endorsed the idea of collaboration with external bodies, but demanded clarification of the role of social work employers and other groups (ibid., p.2)

... it is unclear who will have the final say about ... (the QDSW's)

... content and about the award of a qualification for students in higher education ... It is clear that unless the full control of the educational objectives remains with the educational institution, the universities would not be ready to confer academic ... (qualifications) ... on the students.

The ... (QDSW proposal) ... implies university social work courses would have to relate to the CCETSW, to regional planning bodies, to local co-ordinating groups, a curriculum group, and the proposed independent assessment body; and it is not clear how these various groupings will be composed, what powers they will have, and whether they will be advisory or controlling. It would not be acceptable to a university to rely for its decisions about its degrees or diploma awards on the judgement of a panel whose membership it did not control; in particular, university statutes would not allow external examiners to be appointed by an outside body.

The new Dip.SW schemes proposed for the 1990's are designed to implement most of the 'QDSW' principles objected to by the CVCP (see CCETSW, 1989a, 1989b, 1990). This raises a potential question mark about the future of social work training in the universities.

Financial resource issues are relevant factors in so far as staff-student ratios are lower in social work training than in most other university departments (Pinker, 1984, p.12), in recognition of the higher administrative and external liaison work-loads of social work teachers. The cost-intensive nature of social work education is recognized in the recent decision of the University Funding Council (UFC) to provide a higher fee allowance for social work students than for students in other disciplines such as social science. In the current university financial climate, this single decision may have the crucial effect of persuading many universities to retain social work training. There are, though, two complicating factors. One is that other aspects of the UFC's funding criteria are weighted in favour of university departments with high research profiles: this will disadvantage social work departments, which in research terms are generally much less productive than other academic departments (Donnison et al., 1975, p.257; CVCP, 1986, p.3; Pinker, 1989, p.101). The implication for social work courses of the financial weighting in favour of research-led university departments has been criticized (CCETSW Letter to UGC, 1986, p.1) but remains as an issue of concern to the CCETSW (News Item, Community Care, 1989a, p.5). Another complicating resource factor is that the increased administrative workload placed upon social work teachers by the Dip.SW committee infrastructure may require a further lowering of staff-student ratios, and this may erode any financial gains arising from the UFC's increased per capita funding for social work students.

Universities' concern about low research productivity in social work departments pre-dates the QDSW and Dip.SW proposals. If the additional administrative work generated by these proposals has the effect of lowering an already low research output in social work departments, some observers have suggested that for this reason a number of universities may withdraw from social work training. Pinker (1989) argues that the CCETSW's '... insistent inroads into the work schedules of social work departments have constituted the biggest single impediment to social work's chance of becoming ... research-led ...' (ibid., p.101). This in Pinker's view is one of the reasons '... why social work may not survive as a university subject' (ibid.). Harris (1988) protested that the demands made by the CCETSW have reached the point where some social work educators find it '... remarkably difficult sometimes to find the time actually to read a book' (ibid., p.24). Administrative and external liaison pressures of work are undoubtedly the main factor in social work educator's relatively low research output compared with that of most other university academics (Halsey, 1984, pp.82-83). However this is also related to questions about whether social work educators should be regarded as 'social workers' or as 'academics' (Coulshed, 1986, p.122) and there are some attitudinal, normative issues involved: some social work teachers regard 'servicing the field' as their first priority, and as one which conflicts with academic research as a second priority. Richards's (1985) study refers to this normative orientation (ibid., p.27, emphasis added)

> Research and publications are widely accepted tasks for academics and several respondents mentioned being pressured to be actively involved in research ... This meant that research was likely to be geared more to what would 'count' academically than to meet a perceived need from the field.

The CCETSW itself regards university academic research criteria as conflicting with 'servicing the field' (CCETSW Letter to UGC, 1986, p.1) and if, as seems likely, the administrative and liaison work-load of social work teachers under the Dip.SW arrangements further marginalizes academic research activity, some universities may decide to reject this continuation of a social work training tradition that remains '... separate from the academic community' (Pinker, 1989, p.91).

Other university concerns fasten on the 'localism' implied by the CCETSW's committee network. Although this is regarded as a virtue by some social work trainers (Fielding, 1990, p.7), a problem noted some years ago by Pinker (1984) with regard to 'localism' is that '... it seems likely that many of the universities ... would decide to abandon social work education ... They would not want to take part in a network of local apprenticeship schemes' (ibid., p.14). Concerns of this kind were noted during a Commons debate by the chairperson of the Parliamentary Support Group on the Personal Social Services who observed that the CCETSW's policy intentions, if implemented, might herald '... the departure of the universities from ... (social work) ... training' (News Item, Community Care, 1986, p.5). One of the issues raised during the Commons debate was the extent to which the CCETSW might have 'misread' the universities' perceptions, and it was commented '... although the CCETSW believed it had widespread support, there was much evidence of opposition in the universities' (ibid.).

Another factor indirectly related to the issue of 'localism' in the administrative committees involved in the design and control of courses, is the extent to which the universities will accept any further substantial erosion of educational autonomy (CVCP, 1986, p.2). Pinker (1984) argued a measure of autonomy is necessary so that academic institutions can '... on occasion ... challenge rather than reflect current social policy objectives' (ibid., pp.13-14) and so that they can also anticipate new needs other than those currently identified by social work employers (ibid., p.13). In these terms it has been argued that the CCETSW's proposals signify a switch to '... a profoundly conservative educational system because it is highly localized and resistant to change' (Pinker, 1984 in Murray, p.21). Writing at a time when the CCETSW's current policy intentions were at an early stage of formulation, Pinker (1984) suggested that the CCETSW shows 'remarkable indifference to the principle of academic freedom' (ibid., p.13) and some universities may therefore '... withdraw altogether from social work' (ibid.). The universities, it may be noted, are currently becoming more 'outward looking' in terms of actively encouraging the development of consultancy, research, and other collaborative programmes with external public sector bodies in health, social services, housing, education and other fields. However these developments are of the kind that do not involve what some universities may perceive to be problems of unacceptable external controls, administrative workload and resource-intensiveness, the marginalization of academic knowledge and of academic values, and the problems posed for research, that might follow from the CCETSW's current training policies. Indeed, the recent expansion of universities' activities into these external involvements outside the social work training field may itself be a factor in some universities' decisions to withdraw from the basic (Dip.SW) social work training schemes. Actors formulate decisions in terms of their perceptions of the range of alternative options open to them, and as Blau (1964) comments 'The partner with fewer alternative opportunities tends to be the more dependent on and committed to the exchange-relation than the other' (ibid., p.99). For academic-professionals and other professionalizing social work actors the universities (and other higher education institutions) are an 'obligatory passage point', but the reverse of this is not the case. It remains to be seen whether, for example, some universities will withdraw from basic social work training schemes and, in their place, concentrate on undergraduate and postgraduate degrees in social policy and applied social studies together with a research-led expansion of consultancy, research, and short-programme teaching contracts with external public sector organizations.

Even if these developments occur, it seems likely that most polytechnics will remain in the basic social work training field, and the CCETSW also has room for strategic manoeuvre in developing possible alternative sites, other than universities, within the higher education sector. The CCETSW appears to be aware of the need to avoid storing too many eggs in one basket. It is noticeable that some of the first new local Dip.SW schemes are in Colleges or Institutes of Higher Education (Fielding, 1990). Another strand to the CCETSW's (1990) diversification programme is the Open University. It is perhaps significant that the CCETSW's 'continuum of learning' for the 1990's will increasingly involve modular structures and the accumulation and transfer of 'credits': the possibility of 'distance-learning' packages is currently being explored by the CCETSW in conjunction with the Open University '... to examine possibilities for OU involvement in education and training at all levels' (CCETSW, 1990, p.22). Diversification in this sense is a process of 'enrolling' (Callon and Law, 1983) which involves getting a range of institutions to commit resources to the CCETSW's programmes and thereby themselves acquire a vested interest in the continuation (and perhaps also the expansion) of the programmes to which they have institutionally committed themselves; getting other actors to want what the strategic actor wants them to want (Clegg, 1989, p.204) is a process of enrolment through which other actors' '... positions, desires ... what they will want ... is channelled' (Callon and Latour, 1981, p.289). It is in this way that new networks of interests, in social work as in other fields of activity, are constituted and 'consigned', sometimes by 'chance' or through unexpected or fortuitous shifts in the relevant conditions of action; or sometimes intentionally and strategically.

There are, however, some other uncertainties. One is the possibility that at some time within the present decade the Home Office will withdraw the training of probation officers from the new Dip.SW schemes (Green Paper, 1990, pp.33-35). Despite the CCETSW's anxieties on this score (CCETSW, 1990, pp.35-36) it is difficult to predict whether this will happen: if it does, there are some grounds for the fear expressed by the British Association of Social Workers that the 'loss' of probation training will further jeopardize the prospects of basic 'professional' social work training remaining in higher education institutions (Gaffaney, 1990, p.1).

Another uncertainty surrounding social work training is a recent directive from the European Commission which specifies that 'professional' status within EC member states will in future only apply when two conditions are satisfied. Firstly, the occupation or profession in question must be regulated by its member state or by a professional council (such as, in the case of medicine, the General Medical Council). And secondly, basic qualifying training must be in institutions of higher education and for a minimum duration of three years (Mitchell, 1989). Currently, social work in Britain does not comply with either of these criteria. Regarding the need for a regulatory council, the British Association of Social Workers in response to the EC directive predictably urged that a Council be set up as a matter of urgency (Macmillan and Morris, 1989, p.3). This will involve some logistical and political problems (Cohen, 1990; Parker, 1990) but it is likely that, particularly in view of the EC directive, professionalizing lobby groups will continue to press strongly for a Council and it is probable that this will be in place by the mid-1990's. On the question of three-year training in the higher education sector, the BASW called for urgent government action in the light of the EC directive (Gaffaney, 1989, p.2; Cohen, 1990, p.22). Under existing arrangements, the CSS does not 'qualify' because it is taught in the further eduction sector; nor does the CQSW which, though located in the higher education sector, is, in most cases, of only two-years duration. The proposed Dip.SW, though intended to be housed in higher education institutions, is also of two-years duration. If the Dip.SW fails to qualify as a 'professional' qualification in EC terms, this will in turn diminish the prospect of its being registered as a 'professional' qualification under the British NCVQ framework and this, in Harris's (1989) view, will '... inevitably threaten the continuation of social work in the universities' (ibid., p.18). There are, though, some options open to the CCETSW and to professionalizing actors in finding ways of complying with the EC's 'three-year' directive. One is to encourage the development of four-year undergraduate degrees in social science combined with social work, leading to the award of a degree 'plus' the Dip.SW. Another is to switch most of the two-year Dip.SW courses to a postgraduate basis; the three-years spent in higher education for a degree, plus two-years social work training, will in total exceed three years in higher education and thereby 'qualify' under the EC directive. Moreover, this would be attractive to employers and others who wish to remove academic social science from training. Students on the first new Dip.SW scheme approved by the CCETSW '... will be social science graduates, to allow the programme to focus on practice issues' (News Item, Community Care, 1989b, p.3). In announcing this new course, the Director of Social Services for Kent stated it will be '... a pointer for all future developments in social work education' (Warner, 1989, p.3). Any movement, however, to exclusively graduate and postgraduate training will be resisted as 'elitist' by some critics, and will not be unproblematic. Another option is for the CCETSW to press the government to make the Dip.SW a three-year course. If this fails, it is predictable that the CCETSW will respond to the EC directive on 'professional' qualifications by means of devising ways of 'topping-up' the Dip.SW to three-years. This might involve some kind of one-year pre-Dip.SW preparatory course, or else a post-Dip.SW provision to the equivalent of one-years' training. The latter might be achieved through a post-qualifying 'probationary year'; or through use of the CCETSW's (1990) third-tier ('advanced awards') in its new training 'continuum'; or through distance-learning modules provided by the Open University; or through some combination of these methods.

The problems currently facing 'professional' social work education in Britain are only partly related to recent difficulties posed by, for instance, the EC directive. These recent difficulties have merely intensified existing longer-standing uncertainties and controversies surrounding the question of whether basic, 'professional' social work training 'really' belongs in the higher education sector. Throughout social work's major internal policy-struggles during the 1980's various critics of the role of academic knowledge in social work training argued that social work practice is based on those kinds of cognitions (experiential 'insights') and/or types of practical organizational information and very practical skills which, though this was not the intention (far from it!) of these critics, logically negate any 'professional' or 'academic-professional' arguments that social work training should be based in higher education. In his analysis of the possibility that universities will at some stage in the 1990's withdraw from basic, qualifying social work training, Harris (1989) observes that this (ibid., p.18)

> ... would actually come to create a self-fulfilling prophecy: a sub-professional activity with sub-professional training, probably of an apprenticeship kind. And if that happened, many of the most vociferous anti-intellectuals in the profession would quickly discover they had got more - or to be more precise, less - than they had bargained for.

The social work 'anti-intellectuals' referred to by Harris may indeed have scored an own goal. It is not always possible in all circumstances to 'have it both ways' i.e. to define social work practice and training in a way that negates claims to a location in higher education while simultaneously arguing for a location in higher education. Such self-contradictory arguments merely serve to expose their proponents to the criticism that their concerns involve little more than an attempt to 'enrol' academic disciplines and institutions as a way of conferring a spurious 'academic' legitimacy upon claims to 'professional' status. However, it should not be assumed that professionals and academic-professionals in social work will discontinue the struggle for a 'professional' status that has eluded social work throughout its history. The professionalizing motif was formulated by the Charity Organization Society more than a century ago. It has been disseminated across each social work generation and it remains strong: its political negotiation takes place in contingent, shifting conditions-of-action and there are good sociological reasons for saying that it is not possible to reliably predict the future outcomes of professional actors' struggles to keep this motif alive.

8 Conclusion

Social work criticisms of sociology are wide ranging. Some Marxist social work theorists have suggested sociology is a 'bourgeois' academic discipline that supports a conservative and traditional social work profession (Leonard, 1982, pp.vii-viii). On the other hand, sociology has been portrayed as a radical, left-wing attack upon traditional professional social work values and practices (Davies, 1981a, p.195). Sociology as a discipline tends to be seen as 'subversive' by professionals in general, rather than only by social work professionals. Heraud (1979) notes that 'The sociologist as a kind of nagging <u>critic of "the establishment" in the form of established institutions and professions</u> is a not unfamiliar, if much unloved, figure in the eyes of many professionals' (ibid., p.11, emphasis added). Above all, sociology is the whipping post of right-wing academics and politicians. A former minister in the Thatcher government, Edwina Currie, did not mince words in an interview that touched upon the role of sociology in welfare training: she stated that 'Sociology has always been a left-wing subject, and as a result ... (a) ... lot of rubbish' (Currie, 1989, p.13). A question presents itself: should sociology accommodate the views of any of these critics, and if so, which?

The short answer to this question is that it is essential to avoid uncritical sociological endorsement or automatic acceptance of the political views propounded by, to take the examples above, either Leonard (1982), or Davies (1981a), or Currie (1989). There are no defendable grounds for supposing that any academic discipline or any form of intellectual inquiry should proceed on the basis of merely replacing one ideology by another: a different way of putting this is to say that sociology should '... not take the point of view <u>of any group as valid in its own right</u> ' (Rex, 1974, p.9, emphasis added). In particular, for all the reasons discussed in chapter three, non-reductionist sociology is inherently suspicious of those who claim to be the rightful spokespersons 'for' taxonomic collectivities. Viewed in these terms, it would be surprising if sociology were to enjoy universal popularity. Should sociology ever attempt to court such popularity - an impossible aspiration anyway, in the absence of a universal social and political consensus among actors - it will cease to be a critically investigative discourse. It should also be observed that, although not the main concern in this book, the results of sociological investigation very often have practical social policy implications. Sociologists do not, of course, have any legitimate rights to impose moral-political judgements upon others; but sociology can enhance the critical awareness that should inform the making of political judgements. Nor is it the case that sociologists themselves should never become directly politically involved in social policy issues. More than one role is possible in sociology. While avoiding epistemologically dubious claims that analytic-descriptive analyses are presuppositionless (see chapter one) or always entirely devoid of prescriptive contents, it is nevertheless necessary to avoid the simplistic notion, propagated in some social work discourses, that the validity of all social knowledge and empirical understanding should be assessed in terms of values. That is, it is necessary to as far as possible preserve and make explicit a distinction between descriptive and prescriptive forms of analysis. Provided this is done, there is no reason why sociologists should not become directly involved in social policy roles and engage with others in the never easy task of analysing and acting upon the complex and, more often than not, shifting relationships between knowledge, values, and action.

Enough has been said in this and previous chapters to indicate why it is that the form of critical sociology advocated here is unlikely to attract support from all social work academics, professional leaders, and practitioners. An underlying theme in most of the chapters is that there are substantial sociological grounds for concluding that social work in Britain has become insular and highly resistant to change: it is unwilling or unable to understand itself and its relationship to the rest of society other than in terms of its own narrow, self-limiting frames of reference. This is reflected both in the bland ineffectualness of traditional professionalism and in the simplistic latent authoritarianism of radical social work. The evidence examined in the previous chapters suggests that social work has become increasingly remote not merely from modern social science and social policy discourses but also from the discourses of citizens and those whose needs it is supposed to serve. Duke (1990) observes that perestroika means reconstruction, democratization, and decentralization (ibid., p.146): glasnost refers to a principle of openness to new ideas and to alternative viewpoints in all aspects of social organization (ibid.). Social work is cut-off from these impulses, and from the restlessness associated with modernist consciousness and with the growing movement towards rejection of conventional hierarchical, professionally-dominated 'solutions' to the problems of welfare (Rojek et al., 1988, p.162). Rojek et al. advocate '... a subversive approach that calls into question received ideas of language, truth, reality, history, interpretation, and forms of critical understanding' (ibid., p.143). This requires critical re-appraisal of conventional wisdoms ('received ideas') among which are included '... ideas like acceptance, trust, respect, resistance, and defence mechanism in traditional social work; and ideas like collectivism, consciousness-raising, alienation, commitment, and liberation in radical social work' (ibid., p.162).

Whether such re-appraisal will occur within social work is open to question. There are, perhaps, too many vested interests involved, too many habitualized ways of thinking, and too many ideological defences. A familiar social work defence against radical critique is to sidestep the substantive contents of critique and leave these virtually unaddressed: instead, radical critics of the social work status quo are quickly told to come up with an alternative blueprint! If one is produced it is then promptly shot down! Moreover, reflexive (critically self-aware) modern welfare radicalism has a generalized directionality that involves, as in Rojek's (1989) and Rojek et al.'s (1988) form of radicalism, a search for decentralized, democratized organizational methods for shifting power to local citizens and service-users, while also specifying that no detailed blueprint can or should be imposed but should emerge out of democratic dialogue in which citizens and client groups are accorded, through explicit practical mechanisms created for this purpose, a direct say in the design and delivery of services (Rojek, 1989, p.180). The point of radical welfare critique, in the reflexive sense of this term, is to encourage social work actors to engage with others in addressing the contents of critique systematically, to work step-by-step through these contents so as to critically assess their adequacy and their possible implications. Often, this process is ideologically side-stepped by social work actors as part of their unwillingness to engage in close, critical analysis of the cognitive, organizational, and practice foundations of the professional status quo of which they are a part. Every social work actor has grumbles and criticisms to make about some aspect of established social work: but these are invariably innocuous criticisms that do not involve a sustained and genuinely radical root-and-branch re-assessment of the basic, underlying assumptions upon which the edifice of professional social work is built.

Anti-reductionist sociology, in terms of its implications for conventional social work actors, is inherently subversive: it challenges the vested professional and bureaucratic 'establishment' interests formulated by traditional and radical professionals. This arises from rejection of those ideological defences of established social work that rely upon theories of structural predetermination or inevitability. Reductionist structural theories have, until now at least, provided 'radical' social work theorists with convenient formulae for preserving the principle of organizational hierarchy and other features of bureau-professional service-delivery. Radical careerism (Hearn, 1982a) and radical-professionals' opposition to proposals that might give real effect to the idea of 'client-power', are two expressions of a contemporary radical social work genre that has appropriated reductionist theories for ideological purposes in defence of existing social work arrangements. Sloganized references to mysterious structural 'forces', 'needs', or 'contradictions', to 'the interests of capitalism', of 'patriarchy', and the like, have in various ways contributed towards the social reproduction of the assumptions and principles of hierarchical professional organization associated with established social work.

Nor, when we turn to another widely deployed professional ideological defence of conventional social work, can the components of modern social work (its organizational conventions, its forms of thought, its training system, its 'everyday' practices, etc.) be legitimately 'explained' as 'effects' of the action of governments. There are many loci of power in society, none of which have a structurally 'fixed' capacity to control events across a wide range of sites of action that are dispersed across social space and time: social work is contingently and strategically produced and reproduced (or changed) through interactions among a variety of individual actors and social actors (see chapter three). Traditional and radical professionalizing social work lobby groups typically argue that they had no hand in the creation of modern 'bureau-professional' social work; have no particular vested interests in its future continuation; and in any case have no power to alter it. Very often, the shape of established bureau-professional social work is 'explained' as an irremovable 'consequence' of Thatcherism! This remarkable argument ignores the active role of social work educators and other professionalizing social work lobby groups in the 1960's (Seed, 1973, pp.70-80) who initiated the first steps towards the construction of a bureau-professional organizational form that, long before Thatcherism came into the picture, was given expression in the Seebohm Report (1968) and then professionally defended and reproduced through the highly proactive role of professionalizing social work lobbies throughout the 1970's (Whittington and Bellaby, 1979). It is, too, an argument that is seemingly oblivious to empirical evidence, discussed in chapter five, that bureau-professionalism is faced by a legitimation crisis that began in the mid-1970's, this crisis taking the form of citizen and service-user rejections of the dominant mode of social services organization and service-delivery. Later, the Thatcher government ideologically appropriated this 'crisis' for its own electoral purposes but did not 'create' the crisis, and indeed, became not a supporter but one of the arch critics of social work bureau-professionalism. Arguments of the kind just referred to are a measure of professional social work's inward-looking preoccupations. Professional ideologists who argue that established social work is an immutable expression of someone else's 'interests' appear to be remarkably insulated from the realities of contemporary British welfare politics and the deepening criticism of statism and welfare professionalism by citizens and service-users as well as by the organized political left, centre, and the right (Lee and Raban, 1988, p.223).

Professionals' ideological defence of established social work is a form of defence that involves a self-portrayal of social work actors as individually and collectively reactive, hapless, and powerless 'agents' of governments, or of mysterious structural 'forces' of one kind or another. This defence is conveniently breached for some professional purposes. A case in point is professional actors' energetic role in the expansion of 'statutory' social work in the 1980's. For example, in their social construction of 'child-abuse', particularly sexual abuse, professional social work actors have been proactive to the point of evangelical fervour in proclaiming, largely on the basis of anecdotal or in some other way unreliable evidence, that a massive hidden problem exists and in opportunistically shaping child care policies in ways that involve the expansion of professional social work. In the field of social policy studies, the need to develop methodological tools that avoid reductionist interpretations of social policy material, has been recognized for some time. This is reflected in Ham and Hill's (1984, p.186) observation that

... any theory of policy formulation must take account of the role played by professionals, bureaucrats .... Not least, the interests of these groupings in the maintenance and growth of large-scale bureaucracies ... It is for this reason that we reject explanations expressed in terms of structural determinism.

A similar point is made by Clapham (1986) whose study of local government organization led him to conclude that '... at least some power ... is based on professional self-interest ...' (ibid., p.40). The idea that organizational and professional processes reflect 'objective' structural 'interests' (the interests of 'classes', of 'capitalism', of 'patriarchy', etc.) is rejected by Clapham (ibid.) who observes that in the analysis of organizational processes and their social reproduction '... it is dangerous to underestimate the power of the organizational interests involved' (ibid., p.41). Anti-reductionist sociology builds upon and extends these forms of understanding concerning the social construction and reproduction of established institutions and professions, established forms of thought, and conventional modes of practice. In a very fundamental sense, modern anti-reductionist sociology is in the process of becoming the 'radical' or 'critical' sociology of the 1990's; the 'new' sociology of social work is part of this larger development.

Bibliography

Abercrombie, N., Hill, S. and Turner, B.S. (1980), The Dominant Ideology Thesis, Allen and Unwin, London.

Acker, J. (1989), 'The problem with patriarchy', Sociology, Vol.23, No.2, pp.235-40.

Adams, B. (1989), 'Feminist social theory needs time', The Sociological Review, Vol.37, No.3, pp.458-73.

ADSS (1986), Association of Directors of Social Services, 'Editorial Comment', Social Services Insight, 22 February - 1 March 1986, p.2.

Aiken, M. and Hage, J. (1966), 'Organizational alienation: a comparative analysis', American Sociological Review, Vol.31, No.4, pp.497-507.

Alden, P. (1905), The Unemployed: A National Question, P.S. King, London.

Anderson, T. and Workow, S. (1961), 'Organizational size and functional complexity: a study of administration in hospitals', American Sociological Review, Vol.26, No.1, pp.23-28.

Arlene, D.K. (1969), 'The captive professional', Journal Of Health And Social Behaviour, Vol.10, No.4, pp.225-64.

Armstrong, P. (1980), Servicing The Professions: Spurious Legitimacy In The Development Of Vocational Training, Paper presented at British Sociological Assocation Annual Conference 1980, Lancaster.

Atkinson, P. (1983), 'The reproduction of the professional community', in Dingwall, R. and Lewis, P. (eds), The Sociology Of The Professions, Macmillan, London and Basingstoke, pp.224-41.

Atkinson, P. and Delamont, S. (1990), 'Professions and powerlessness', The Sociological Review, Vol.38, No.1, pp.90-110.

ATSWE (1983), ATSWE Response To NISW The Barclay Report. Association of Teachers in Social Work Education, University of Leicester, Leicester.

ATSWE (1984), Association of Teachers in Social Work Education, 'Editorial Comment', Issues In Social Work Education, Vol.4, No.1, p.2.

ATSWE (1986), Association of Teachers in Social Work Education, 'Editorial Comment', Issues In Social Work Education, Vol.6, No.2, pp.85-87.

Austin, L. (1950), 'Trends in differential treatment in social casework', in Kasius, C. (ed.), Principles And Techniques In Social Casework, Family Service Association of America, New York, pp.324-38.

Bachrach, P. and Baratz, M.S. (1962), 'Two faces of power', American Political Science Review, Vol.56, pp.947-52.

Baert, P.J.N. (1989), Unintended Consequences, (Un)awareness And (Re)production, Paper presented at British Sociological Association Annual Conference 1989, Plymouth.

Bailey, C. and McGrath, M. (1984), 'Patchwork: the extrapolation of principles', Community Care. 31 May 1984, pp.18-19.

Bailey, R. (1982) 'Theory and practice in social work - a kaleidoscope', in Bailey, R. and Lee, P. (eds), Theory And Practice In Social Work, Blackwell, Oxford, pp.1-14.

Bailey, R. (1984), 'A question of priorities' Issues In Social Work Education, Vol.4, No.1, pp.58-60.

Bailey, R. and Brake, M. (eds) (1975), Radical Social Work, Edward Arnold, London.

Baker, R. (1983), 'Is there a future for integrated practice? Obstacles to its development in practice and education', Issues In Social Work Education, Vol.3, No.1, pp.3-16.

Ball, C., Harris, R.J., Roberts, G. and Vernon, S. (1988), The Law Report: Teaching And Assessment Of Law In Social Work Education, Paper 4.1, Central Council for Education and Training in Social Work, London.

Bamford, T. (1984), Chair of British Association of Social Workers, quoted in Murray, N. 'Two into one won't go: or will it?', Community Care, 10 May, 1984, p.21.

Bamford, T. (1990), The Future Of Social Work, Macmillan, London and Basingstoke.

Bandura, A. (1969), Principles Of Behaviour Modification, Holt, Rinehart and Winston, New York.

Banting, K. (1986), 'The social policy process', in Bulmer, M., Banting, K., Blume, S., Carley, M. and Weiss, C., Social Science And Social Policy, Allen and Unwin, London, pp.41-59.

Barbalet, J.M. (1985), 'Power and resistance', British Journal Of Sociology, Vol.xxxvi, No.4, pp.531-48.

Barbour, R.S. (1984), 'Social work education: tackling the theory-practice dilemma', British Journal Of Social Work, Vol.14, No.6, pp.557-78.

Barbour, R.S. (1985), 'Dealing with the transituational demands of professional socialization', The Sociological Review, Vol.33, No.3, pp.495-531.

Barclay Report (1982), National Institute of Social Work Training Barclay Working Party Report, Social Workers: Their Role And Tasks, Bedford Square Press, London.

Barker, M. (1981), 'Organization Theory', in Hardiker, P. and Barker, M. (eds), Theories Of Practice In Social Work, Academic Press, London.

Barnes, B. (1974), Scientific Knowledge And Sociological Theory, Routledge, London.

Barnes, B. (1985), About Science, Blackwell, Oxford.

Barnes, B. (1986), 'On authority and its relationship to power', in Law, J. (ed.), Power, Action And Belief: Towards A New Sociology Of Knowledge?, Routledge, London, pp.180-95.

Barrett, S. and Hill, M.J. (1981), Report To The SSRC Central-Local Government Relations Panel On the 'Core' Or Theoretical Component Of The Research On Implementation, Social Science Research Council, London.

Bartlett, H. (1970), The Common Base Of Social Work Practice, National Association of Social Workers, Washington.

BASW (1977), British Association of Social Workers, The Social Work Task: BASW Working Party Report, British Association of Social Workers, Birmingham.

Becker, H. (1962), 'The nature of a profession', in Sixty-First Year Book of The National Society for the Study of Education Part III, Education For The Professions, University of Chicago Press, Chicago, pp.27-46.

Benn, T., M.P. (1983), quoted in Murray, N. 'Decentralization is here to stay', Community Care, 17 April, 1983, p.12.

Bennett, B. (1980), 'The sub-office: a team approach to local authority fieldwork practice', in Brake, M. and Bailey, R. (eds), Radical Social Work And Practice, Edward Arnold, London, pp.155-81.

Benson, J.K. (1973), 'The analysis of bureaucratic-professional conflict: functional versus dialectical approaches', The Sociological Quarterly, No.14, pp.40-53.

Benton, T. (1981), '"Objective" interests and the sociology of power', Sociology, Vol.15, No.2, pp.161-84.

Beresford, P. (1983), 'Patch: power to the people', Community Care, 23 November 1983, pp.18-21.

Beresford, P. and Croft, S. (1984a), 'Welfare Pluralism: the new face of Fabianism', Critical Social Policy, Issue 9, pp.19-39.

Beresford, P. and Croft, S. (1984b), 'A solution or just another problem?', Community Care, 26 January 1984, p.21.

Beresford, P. and Lyons, K. (1986), 'Patch: training focus', Social Services Insight, 17 May - 24 May 1986, pp.18-19.

Berger, P. and Luckmann, T. (1972), The Social Construction Of Reality, Penguin, London.

Berlant, J.L. (1975), Profession And Monopoly: A Study Of Medicine In The United States And Great Britain, University of California Press, Berkeley.

Bernardes, J. (1985), 'Family ideology: identification and exploration', The Sociological Review, Vol.33, No.2, pp.275-97.

Betts, K. (1986), 'The conditons of action, power, and the problem of interests', The Sociological Review, Vol.34, No.1, pp.39-64.

Beuret, K. and Stoker, G. (1986), 'The Labour Party and Neighbourhood decentralization: flirtation or commitment?', Critical Social Policy, Issue 17, pp.4-22.

Bhaskar, R. (1978), A Realist Theory Of Science, Harvester Press, Brighton.

Billingsley, A. (1964), 'Bureaucratic and professional orientation patterns in social casework', Social Services Review, Vol.38, No.4, pp.400-407.

Billis, D., Bromley, G., Hey, A. and Rowbottom, R. (1980), Organizing Social Services Departments: Further Studies By The Brunel Social Services Unit, Heinemann, London.

Blau, P. (1964), Exchange And Power In Social Life, John Wiley, London.

Bleicher, J. (1980), Contemporary Hermeneutics: Hermeneutics As Method, Philosophy And Critique, Routledge, London.

Bolger, S., Corrigan, P., Docking, J. and Frost, N. (1981), Towards Socialist Welfare Work, Macmillan, London and Basingstoke.

Bolt, J. (1984), 'Rejecting colonial care', Community Care, 4 October 1984, pp.21-22.

Bordieu, P. and Passeron, J.C. (1977), Reproduction In Education And Society, Sage, London.

Bosanquet, B. (1890), quoted in Muirhead, J.H. (ed.), Bernard Bosanquet And His Friends, (1935), Allen and Unwin, London, pp.73-74.

Bosanquet, B. (1909), cited in Timms, N. (1983), Social Work Values: An Enquiry, Routledge, London, p.71.

Bosanquet, H. (1900), 'Methods of Training' COS Occasional Papers (Third Series) No.3 quoted in Smith, M.J. (1965), Professional Education For Social Work In Britain: An Historical Account, Allen and Unwin, London, p.87.

Bosanquet, H. (1914), Social Work In London 1869-1912 (1973 Harvester Press, Brighton).

Bouchier, D. (1977), 'Radical ideologies and the sociology of knowledge: a model for comparative analysis', Sociology, Vol.11, No.1, pp.25-46.

Brandon, J. and Davies, M. (1979), 'The limits of competence in social work: the assessment of marginal students in social work education', British Journal Of Social Work, Vol.9, No.3, pp.295-347.

Braverman, H. (1974) 'Labour and monopoly capitalism: the degradation of work in the twentieth century', Monthly Review Press, New York, pp.85-123.

Brenton, M. (1985), The Voluntary Sector In British Social Services, Longman, London.

Brown, K.M. (1985), 'Turning a blind eye: racial oppression and the unintended consequences of white "non-racism"', The Sociological Review, Vol.33, No.4, pp.670-90.

Brown, M. (1974), (Review), Social Service Quarterly, Summer, p.185.

Brown, W. (1960), Exploration In Management, Heinnemann, London.

Bruce, S. and Wallis, R. (1983), 'Rescuing motives', British Journal Of Sociology, Vol.34, No.1, pp.61-71.

Bucher, R. and Strauss, A. (1960), 'Professions in process', American Journal Of Sociology, No.66, pp.325-34.

Bulmer, M. (1985) 'The rejuvenation of community studies'? Neighbours, networks and policy', The Sociological Review, Vol.33, No.3, pp.430-48.

Bulmer, M. (1986), Neighbours: The Work Of Philip Abrams, Cambridge University Press, Cambridge.

Bulmer, M., Banting, K.G., Blume, S., Carley, M. and Weiss, C. (1986), Social Science And Social Policy, Allen and Unwin, London.

Burns, T.R. (1986) 'Actors, transactions and social structure', in Himmelstrand, U. (ed.), The Social Reproduction Of Organization And Culture, Sage, London.

Burns, T. and Stalker, G. (1961), The Management Of Innovation, Tavistock, London.

Butcher, H., Collis, P., Glen, A. and Sills, P. (1980), Community Groups In Action: Case Studies And Analysis, Routledge, London.

Butler, D. and Kavannagh, D. (1984), The British General Election Of 1983, Macmillan, London and Basingstoke.

Butler-Sloss Report (1988), Report Of The Inquiry Into Child Abuse In Cleveland 1987, Cmnd.412, Stationery Office, London.

Butrym, Z. (1973), Conference Paper, quoted in Wilson, D., 'The social work dilemma', Social Work Today, 8 February 1973, p.vi.

Butrym, Z. (1976), The Nature Of Social Work, Macmillan, London.

Butrym, Z.T., Stevenson, O. and Harris, R.J. (1981) 'The roles and tasks of social workers', Issues In Social Work Eduction, Vol.1, No.1, pp.3-26.

Cain, M. (1986), 'Realism, feminism, methodology and law', International Journal Of The Sociology Of Law, Vol.14, pp.255-67.

Callon, M. (1986), 'Some elements of a sociology of translation: domestication of the scallops and the fishermen of St. Brieuc Bay', in Law. J. (ed.), Power, Action And Belief: A New Sociology Of Knowledge?', Routledge, London, pp.196-233.

Callon, M. and Latour, B. (1981), 'Unscrewing the big Leviathan: how actors macro-structure reality and how sociologists help them to do so', in Knorr-Cetina, K. and Cicourel, A.V. (eds.), Advances In Social Theory and Methodology: Towards An Integration Of Micro- And Macro-Sociologies, Routledge, London, pp.277-303.

Callon, M. and Law, J. (1982), 'On interests and their transformation: enrolment and counter-enrolment', Social Studies Of Science, No.12, pp.615-25.

Callon, M., Courtial, J.P., Turner, W.A. and Bauin, S. (1983), 'From translations to problematic networks; an introduction to co-word analysis', Social Science Information, No.22, pp.199-235.

Callon, M., Law, J. and Rip. A. (eds) (1986), Mapping Out The Dynamics Of Science And Technology: Sociology Of Science In The Real World, Macmillan, London and Basingstoke.

Carchedi, G. (1975), 'On the economic identification of the new middle class', Economy And Society, Vol.4, No.1.

Carew, R. (1979) 'The place of knowledge in social work', British Journal Of Social Work, Vol.9, No.3, pp.349-64.

Caring For People (1989), Caring For People: Community Care In The Next Decade and Beyond, HMSO, London.

Carter, D. (1985), 'Another blind leap into the dark', Community Care, 20 June 1985, pp.27-29.

CCETSW (1972), Central Council for Education and Training in Social Work, The Teaching Of Sociology In Social Work Courses: Discussion Document No.5, CCETSW, Lonodn.

CCETSW (1975), Central Council for Education and Training in Social Work, Paper 9.1. The Certificate In Social Service: A New Form Of Training, CCETSW, London.

CCETSW (1982), Central Council for Education and Training in Social Work, Paper 20.1: Review Of Qualifying Training-Report Of Council Working Group, CCETSW, London.

CCETSW (1985), Central Council for Education and Training in Social Work, Paper 20.3: Policies For Qualifying Training In Social Work - The Council's Proposals, CCETSW, London.

CCETSW Letter to UGC (1986), Director of CCETSW Letter to Chair of University Grants Committee, 13 November 1986.

CCETSW (1986), Central Council for Education and Training in Social Work, Paper 20.6: Three Years and Different Routes - Council's Expectations And Intentions For Social Work Training, CCETSW, London.

CCETSW (1987a). Central Council for Education and Training in Social Work, Paper 26.1: Accreditation Of Agencies And Practice Teachers In Social Work Education, CCETSW, London.

CCETSW (1987b), Central Council for Education and Training in Social Work, Paper 20.8: The Qualifying Diploma In Social Work - A Policy Statement. CCETSW, London.

CCETSW (1988), Central Council for Education and Training in Social Work, CCETSW Reporting, No.9 (June), CCETSW, London.

CCETSW (1989a), Central Council for Education and Training in Social Work, Guidance Notes On The Monitoring Of Dip S.W. Programmes And Its Application To Current CSS Schemes And CQSW Courses, CCETSW, London.

CCETSW (1989b), Central Council for Education and Training in Social Work, Paper 30: Dip.S.W. - Requirements And Regulations For The Diploma In Social Work, CCETSW, London.

CCETSW (1990), Central Council for Education and Training in Social Work, CCETSW 1988/9, CCETSW, London.

Cecil, R., Offer, J. and St.Leger, F. (1987), Informal Welfare, Gower, Aldershot.

Charles, N. (1990), 'Women and class: a problematic relationship?', The Sociological Review, Vol.38, No.1, pp.43-89.

Cheetham, J. (1971), 'Social work education and the departments of social work', Social Work Today, Vol.1, No.12, pp.5-10.

Child, A. (1941), 'The problem of imputation in the sociology of knowledge', Ethics, Vol.51, No.2, pp.200-19.

Child, A. (1942), 'The existential determination of thought', Ethics, Vol.52, No.2, pp.153-85.

Clapham, D. (1986), 'Management of the local state: the example of corporate planning', Critical Social Policy, Issue 14, pp.27-42.

Clark, C.L. and Asquith, S. (1985), Social Work And Social Philosophy, Routledge, London.

Clarke, J. (1979), 'Critical sociology and radical social work: problems of theory and practice', in Parry, N., Rustin, M. and Satyamurti, C. (eds), Social Work, Welfare And The State, Edward Arnold, London, pp.123-39.

Clegg, S.R. (1989), Frameworks Of Power, Sage, london.

Cockburn, C. (1977), Management Of Cities And People, Pluto Press, London.

Cogan, M. (1953), 'Towards a definition of profession', Harvard Educational Review, Vol.xxiii , pp.33-50.

Cohen, P. (1990), 'Anyone for a general council?', Community Care, 3 May 1990, pp.22-24.

Cohen, S. (1980), Folk Devils And Moral Panics (2nd. ed.), Martin Robertson, Oxford.

Collins, R. (1975), Conflict Sociology: Towards An Explanatory Science, Academic Press, New York, San Francisco and London.

Collins, S. and Stein, M. (1989), 'Users fight back: collectives in social work', in Rojek, C., Peacock, G. and Collins, S. (eds.), The Haunt of Misery: Critical Essays In Social Work And Helping, Routledge, London, pp.84-108.

Connell, R.W. (1987), Gender And Power, Polity Press, Cambridge.

Cooley, C. (1902), Human Nature And The Social Order, Charles Scribner, New York.

Cooper, J. (1986), 'The making of a social worker', Community Care, 17 April 1986, pp.18-20.

Cooper, M. (1975), Neighbourhood Work In A Social Services Department: An Experiment Linking Community Work And Casework, City of Wakefield Social Services Department, Wakefield.

Cooper, M. and Denne, J. (1983), 'Patch: a problem of co-ordination', Community Care, 31 March 1983, pp.16-18.

Cootes, R.J. (1966), The Making Of The Welfare State, Longman, London.

Corrigan, P. and Leonard, P. (1979), Social Work Practice Under Capitalism: A Marxist Approach, Macmillan, London and Basingstoke.

COS Review Vol.10 (1881), Charity Organization Society Review Vol.10, p.50. quoted in Jones, C. (1983) State Social Work And The Working Class, Macmillan, London and Basingstoke, p.76.

COS Report (1892), COS Report 1892 quoted in Leonard, P. (1966), Sociology In Social Work, Routledge, London, p.6.

Coulshed, V. (1986), 'What do social work students give to training? A survey', Issues In Social Work Education, Vol.6, No.2, pp.119-27.

Cox, R.E. (1982), The educational expectations of social work students', British Journal Of Social Work, Vol.12, No.4, pp.381-94.

Croft, S. and Beresford, P. (1989), 'User-involvement, citizenship and social policy', Critical Social Policy, Issue 26, pp.5-18.

Crompton, R. (1989), 'Class theory and gender', British Journal Of Sociology, Vol.40, No.4, pp.565-87.

Crosland, A. (1956), The Future Of Socialism, Jonathan Cape, London.

Crouch, C. (1982), Trade Unions, Fontana, Glasgow.

Crow, G. (1989), 'The use of the concept "strategy" in recent sociological literature', Sociology, Vol.23, No.1, pp.1-24.

Curnock, K. and Hardiker, P. (1979), Towards Practice Theory: Skills And Methods In Social Assessments, Routledge, London.

Currie, E. MP (1989), quoted in Lunn, T. 'The politician as author', Community Care, 9 November 1989, p.13.

CVCP (1986), Committee of Vice-Chancellors And Principals, Response To CCETSW Paper 20.6, CVCP VC/86/125, 4 November 1986, London.

Cypher, J. (1983), 'Introduction: getting the debate started' in Social Work Today Publications, The Concise Barclay: A Digest And Commentary, Social Work Today, Birmingham, pp.3-4.

Dahl, R. (1958), 'A critique of the ruling elite model', American Political Science Review Vol.52, pp.463-69.

Davies, C. (1983), 'Professionals in bureaucracies', in Dingwall, R. and Lewis, P. (eds), The Sociology Of The Professions, Macmillan, London and Basingstoke, pp.177-94.

Davies, M (1981a), The Essential Social Worker: A Guide To Positive Practice, Heinnemann, London.

Davies, M. (1981b), 'What we have to learn about social work education', Community Care, 15 January 1981, pp.18-20.

Davies, M. (1981c), 'Social work, the state, and the university', British Journal Of Social Work, Vol.11, No.3, pp.275-88.

Davies, M. (1982), 'A comment on "heart or head"', Issues In Social Work Education, Vol.2, No.1, pp.57-59.

Davies, M. (1983), 'Questions to be asked', in Philpott, T. (ed.) A New Direction For Social Work? The Barclay Report And Its Implications, Community Care/IPC Business Press, London.

Davies, M. (1985), The Essential Social Worker: A Guide To Positive Practice, (2nd. ed.), Gower, Aldershot.

Davies, M. (1989), A Consumer Evaluation Of Probation Training: A Research Report Prepared By Professor Martin Davies For The Home Office, University of East Anglia, Norwich.

Davies, M. (ed.) (1991), The Sociology of Social Work, Routledge, London.

Deacon, B. (1981), 'Social administration, social policy and socialism', Critical Social Policy, Vol.1, No.1, pp.43-46.

Deacon, B. (1986), 'Strategies for welfare: east and west Europe', Critical Social Policy, Issue 14, pp.4-26.

Deacon, R. and Bartley, M. (1975), 'Becoming a social worker', in Jones, H. (ed.), Towards A New Social Work, Routledge, London, pp.69-86.

Department of Eduction and Science (1987), Letter 28 May 1987 from Parliamentary Secretary of State to British Association of Social Workers.

Dingwall, R. (1974), 'Some sociological aspects of nursing research', The Sociological Review, Vol.22, No.1, pp.45-55.

Dingwall, R. (1976), 'Accomplishing profession', The Sociological Review, Vol.24, No.2, pp.331-49.
Dingwall, R. (1977), The Social Organization Of Health Visitor Training, Croom Helm, London.
Doal, M. (1990), 'Putting heart into the curriculum', Community Care, 18 January 1990, pp.20-22.
Dominelli, L. (1988), Anti-Racist Social Work, Macmillan, London and Basingstoke.
Dominelli, L. and McLeod, E. (1989), Feminist Social Work, Macmillan, London and Basingstoke.
Donnison, D., Chapman, V., Meacher, M., Sears, A. and Urwin, K. (1975), Social Policy And Administration Revisited, Allen and Unwin, London.
Duke, V. (1990). 'Perestroika in progress?', The British Journal Of Sociology, Vol.41, No.2, pp.145-56.
Duster, T. (1981), 'Intermediate steps between micro- and macro-integration: the case of screening for inherited disorders', in Knorr-Cetina, K. and Cicourel, A.V. (eds), Advances In Social Theory And Methodology: Towards An Integration Of Micro- And Macro-Sociologies, Routledge, London.
Editorial ATSWE, (1984), Association of Teachers in Social Work Education, 'Editorial', Issues In Social Work Education, Vol.4, No.1, pp.1-3.
Editorial Social Work Today (1971), 'Editorial', Social Work Today, 8 April 1971, p.2.
Ehrenreich, B. and Ehrenreich, J. (1979), 'The professional-managerial class', in Walker, P. (ed.), Between Labour And Capital, Harvester Press, Sussex.
Elger, A.J. (1975), 'Industrial organizations: a processual perspective', in McKinlay, J.B. (ed.), Processing People: Cases In Organizational Behaviour, Rinehart and Winston, London.
Elias, N. (1978), What Is Sociology?, Hutchinson, London.
Eliot, T. (1924), 'Sociology as a pre-vocational subject: the verdict of sixty social workers', American Journal Of Sociology, Vol.29, No.1, p.2.
Elliot, P. (1973), 'Professional ideology and social situation', The Sociological Review, Vol.21, No.2, pp.211-28.
Elmore, R. (1978), 'Organizational models of social program implementation', Public Policy, Vol.26, No.2.
Elster, J. (1985), Making Sense Of Marx, Cambridge University Press, Cambridge.
Epstein, I. (1970), 'Professional role orientation and conflict strategies', Social Work, Vol.15, No.4, pp.87-92.
Esland, G. (1980), 'Professions and professionalism', in Esland, G. and Salaman, G. (eds), The Politics Of Work And Occupations, Open University Press, Milton Keynes, pp.213-50.
Etzioni, A. (1965), The Semi-Professions And Their Organization: Teachers, Nurses, Social Workers, Free Press, New York.
Eysenck, H.J. (1953), Uses And Abuses Of Psychology, Penguin, Harmondsworth.
Farrer, M. (1988), 'The politics of black youth workers in Leeds', Critical Social Policy, Issue 23, pp.94-117.
Fay, B. (1977), Social Theory And Political Practice, Allen and Unwin, London.
Fay, B. (1987), Critical Social Science: Liberation And Its Limits, Polity Press, Cambridge.
Fielding, N. (1990), 'Appetizing first course', Community Care, 8 February 1990, p.7.

Finch, J. (1984), 'Community care: developing non-sexist alternatives,' Critical Social Policy, Issue 9, pp.6-18.

Finch, J. and Groves, D. (eds) (1983), A Labour Of Love: Women, Work and Caring, Routledge, London.

Flax, J. (1987), 'Postmodernism and gender relations in feminist theory', Signs, No.12, pp.621-43.

Fleck, L. (1979), Genesis And Development Of A Scientific Fact, University of Chicago Press, Chicago.

Flexner, A. (1915), 'Is social work a profession?' Studies In Social Work, No.4, New York School of Philanthropy, New York.

Frankenberg, R. (1966), Communities In Britain, Penguin, Harmondsworth.

Frazer, E. (1988), 'Teenage girls talking about class', Sociology, Vol.22, No.3, pp.343-58.

Free, L. and Cantrill, A. (1967), The Political Beliefs Of Americans, Rutgers University Press.

Freidson, E. (1970), Profession Of Medicine: A Study In The Sociology Of Dominance, Aldene Publishing Company, New York.

Freidson, E. (1973). 'Professions and the occupational principle', in Freidson, E. (ed.), The Professions And Their Prospects, Sage, New York.

Freidson, E. (1983), 'The theory of professions', in Dingwall, R., and Lewis, P. (eds), The Sociology Of Profession, Macmillan, London and Basingstoke.

Frey, F.W. (1971), 'Comment: "On issues and non-issues in the study of power"', American Political Science Review, Vol.65, pp.1081-1101.

Gaffaney, P. (1989), 'UK training fails to convince Europeans', Community Care, 2 November 1989, p.2.

Gaffaney, P. (1990), 'CCETSW could well resist probation training plans', Community Care, 15 February 1990, p.1..

Gammack, G, (1982), 'Social work as uncommon sense', British Journal of Social Work, Vol.12, No.1, pp.3-21.

Gardiner, D. (1987a), 'Towards internal monitoring and evaluation of social work courses', Issues In Social Work Education, Vol.7, No.1, pp.53-55.

Gardiner, D. (1987b), 'Debate', Issues In Social Work Education, Vol.7, No.1, pp.47-52.

Garfield, S. and Bergin, A. (eds) (1987), Handbook Of Psychotherapy And Behaviour Change, 2nd. ed., Wiley and Company, New York, Chapter 7.

Gellner, E. (1974), Legitimation Of Belief, Cambridge University Press, Cambridge.

George, V. and Wilding, P. (1985), Ideology And Social Welfare (Revised ed.), Routledge, London.

Germaine, L.B. (1983), 'A comment on "Central issues in developing a scheme for specialization in social work education" by Gross, Murphy and Steiner', Issues In Social Work Education, Vol.3, No.1, pp.49-53.

Gibson, R. (1984), Structuralism And Education, Hodder and Stoughton, London.

Gibson, T. (1979), People Power: Community And Work Groups In Action, Penguin, Harmondsworth.

Giddens, A. (1982), Profiles And Critiques In Social Theory, Macmillan, London and Basingstoke.

Giddens, A. (1988), Social Theory And Modern Sociology. Blackwell, Oxford.

Giddens, A. (1989). Sociology, Blackwell. Oxford.

Gilbert, G.N. and Specht. H. (1977), 'The incomplete profession', in Specht. H. and Vickery, A. (eds), Integrating Social Work Methods, Allen and Unwin, London.

Gladstone, F. (1984), cited in Beresford, P. and Croft, S. (1984) 'Welfare pluralism: the new face of Fabianism', Critical Social Policy, Issue 9, p.27.

Glucksmann, M. (1974), 'The structuralism of Levi-Strauss and Althusser', in Rex, J. (ed.), Approaches To Sociology, Routledge, London, pp.230-45.

Goode, W. (1957), 'Community within a community: the professions', American Sociological Review, Vol.xx, pp.194-200.

Gordon, W. (1963), 'Preliminary report on social work methods', NASW Commission On Practice, National Association of Social Workers, New York.

Gough, I. (1980), 'Thatcherism and the welfare state', Marxism Today, July 1980, pp.6-9.

Gould, J. (1977), The Attack On Higher Education: Marxism And Radical Penetration, Institute for the Study of Conflict, London.

Gouldner, A. (1965), 'Explorations in applied social science', in Gouldner, A. and Miller, S. (eds), Applied Sociology, Free Press, New York.

Graham, H. (1983), 'Caring: a labour of love', in Finch, J. and Groves, D. (eds), A Labour Of Love: Women, Work And Caring, Routledge, London.

Green Paper (1990), Supervision And Punishment In The Community: A Framework For Action, Cm.966, HMSO, London.

Greenwell, S. and Howard, B. (1986), 'An exercise in collaboration', Issues In Social Work Education, Vol.6, No.2, p.129-36.

Greenwood, E. (1957), 'Attributes of a profession', Social Work, Vol.2., No.3, pp.40-48.

Gregory, D. (1989), 'Presences and absences: time-space relations and structuration theory', in Held, D. and Thompson, J.B. (eds), Social Theory Of Modern Societies: Anthony Giddens And His Critics, Cambridge University Press, Cambridge, pp.185-214.

Gross, G., Murphy, D. and Steiner, D. (1982), 'Central issues in developing a scheme for specialization in social work education', Issues In Social Work Education, Vol.2, No.2, pp.77-94.

Gurnah, A. (1989), 'Translating race equality policies into practice' Critical Social Policy, Issue 27, pp.110-24.

Habermas, J. (1979), Communication And The Evolution Of Society, Beacon, Boston.

Hadley, R., Cooper, M., Dale, P. and Stacey, G. (1987), A Community Social Workers Handbook, Tavistock, London.

Hadley, R. and Hatch, R. (1981), Social Welfare And The Failure Of The State: Centralized Social Services And Participatory Alternatives, Allen and Unwin, London.

Hadley, R. and McGrath, M. (1984), When Social Services Are Local: The Normanton Experience, Allen and Unwin, London.

Hagstrom, W.O. (1965), The Scientific Community, Basic Books, New York.

Haines, J. (1975), Skills And Methods In Social Work, Constable, London.

Haines, J. (1985), 'Alternative frameworks for organizing the social work syllabus', in Harris, R.J., Barker, M.W., Reading, P., Richards, M. and Youll, P. (eds), Educating Social Workers, Association of Teachers in Social Work Education, University of Leicester, pp.124-33.

Hall, R. (1963), 'Bureaucracy and small organizations', Sociology And Social Research', Vol.48, pp.38-46.

Hall, R. (1967), 'Some organizational considerations in the professional-organizational relationship', Administrative Science Quarterly, Vol.12, No.3, pp.461-78.

Hall, R. (1968), 'Professionalization and bureaucratization', American Sociological Review, Vol.33, No.1, pp.92-104.

Halliday, T.C. (1985), 'Knowledge mandates: collective influence by scientific, normative, and syncretic professions', British Journal Of Sociology, Vol.xxxvi, No.3, pp.421-47.

Halsey, A.H. (1984), 'Professionalism, social work, and paper 20.1', Issues In Social Work Eduction, Vol.4, No.2, pp.77-84.

Ham, C. and Hill, M. (1984), The Policy Process In The Modern Capitalist State, Harvester Press, Sussex.

Hanmer, J. and Statham D. (1988), Women And Social Work: Towards A Woman-Centred Practice, Macmillan, London.

Harbert, W. (1984), quoted in Murray, N. (1984), 'Two into one won't go: or will it?', Community Care, 10 May 1984, p.21.

Harbert, W. (1985a), 'Status professionalism', Community Care, 10 October 1985, pp.14-15.

Harbert, W. (1985b), 'Crisis in social work', Community Care, 21 March 1985, pp.14-16.

Hardiker, P. (1977), 'Social work ideologies in the probation service', British Journal Of Social Work, Vol.7, No.2, pp.131-54.

Hardiker, P. (1981), 'Heart or head: the function and role of knowledge in social work', Issues In Social Work Education, Vol.1, No.2, pp.85-111.

Hardiker, P. and Webb, D. (1979), 'Explaining deviant behaviour: the social context of "action" and "infraction" accounts in the probation service', Sociology, Vol.13, No.1, pp.1-17.

Hardiker, P. and Barker, M. (eds) (1981), Theories Of Practice In Social Work, Academic Press, London.

Hardy, J. (1981), Values In Social Policy, Routledge, London.

Harre. R. (1981), 'Philosophical aspects of the macro-micro problem', in Knorr-Cetina, K.C. and Cicourel, A.V. (eds), Advances In Social Theory And Methodology: Towards An Integration Of Micro- And Macro-Sociologies, Routledge, London.

Harris, J. (1989), 'The Webbs, the COS and the Ratan Tata Foundation: Social Policy from the perspective of 1912' in Bulmer, M., Lewis, J. and Piachaud, D. (eds), The Goals Of Social Policy, Unwin Hyman, London, pp.27-63.

Harris, R. (1985), 'End points and starting points', Critical Social Policy, Issue 12, pp.115-22.

Harris, R.J. (1983), 'Social work education and the transfer of learning', Issues In Social Work Education, Vol.3, No.2, 1983, pp.103-17.

Harris, R.J. (1985), 'The transfer of learning in social work education', in Harris, R.J., Barker, M.W., Reading, P., Richards, M. and Youll, P. (eds), Educating Social Workers, Association of Teachers in Social Work Education, University of Leicester, pp.80-90.

Harris, R.J. (1988), 'Education and Training: what is the balance?', in CCETSW Paper 18.1 Partnership In Probation Education And Training: A Conference Report, Central Council for Eduction and Training in Social Work, London, pp.18-29.

Harris, R.J. (1989), 'Second European directive: outside looking in?', Community Care, 7 December 1989, pp.16-18.

Harris, R.J., Barker, M.W., Reading, P., Richards, M. and Youll, P. (eds) (1985), Educating Social Workers, Association of Teachers in Social Work Education, University of Leicester.

Harris, R.J. and Webb, D. (1987), Welfare, Power And Juvenile Justice: The Social Control Of Delinquent Youth, Tavistock, London.

Harrison, A. and Gretton, J. (1985), Health Care UK, Chartered Institute of Public Finance and Accountancy, London.

Harrison, B. (1966), 'Philanthropy and the Victorians', *Victorian Studies*, Vol.ix, June, Indiana University Press, pp.31-42.

Hartley, P. (1982), *Child Abuse, Social Work And The Press: Towards The History Of A Moral Panic*, unpublished MA thesis, University of Warwick.

Hearn, J. (1982a), 'Radical social work: contradictions, limitations, and political possibilities', *Critical Social Policy*, Vol.2, No.1, pp.19-34.

Hearn, J. (1982b), 'The problem(s) of theory and practice in social work and social work education', *Issues In Social Work Education*, Vol.2, No.2, pp.95-118.

Hefferman, W. (1964), 'Political activity and social work executives', *Social Work*, Vol.9, No.2, pp.18-23.

Held, D. and Thompson, J.B. (1989), 'Introduction' in Held, D. and Thompson, J.B. (eds), *Social Theory Of Modern Societies: Anthony Giddens And His Critics*, Cambridge University Press, Cambridge, pp.1-18.

Henkel, M. (1984), 'Cutting the Gordian Knot?', *Issues In Social Work Education*, Vol.4, No.1, pp.17-25.

Heraud, B. (1970), *Sociology And Social Work: Perspectives And Problems*, Pergamon, Oxford.

Heraud, B. (1979), *Sociology In The Professions*, Open Books, London.

Heraud, B. (1981), *Training For Uncertainty: A Sociological Approach To Social Work Education*, Routledge, London.

Hill, O. (1884), *Homes Of The London Poor*, Macmillan, London.

Hindess, B. (1982), 'Power, interests and the outcomes of struggles', *Sociology*, Vol.16, No.4, pp.498-511.

Hindess, B. (1986a), 'Actors and social relations', in Wardell, M.L. and Turner, S.P. (eds), *Sociological Theory In Transition*, Allen and Unwin, pp.113-26.

Hindess, B. (1986b), 'Interests in political analysis', in Law, J. (ed.), *Power, Action And Belief: A New Sociology Of Knowledge?*, Routledge, London, pp.112-31.

Hindess. B. (1986c) (Review) in *The Sociological Review*, Vol.34, No.2, pp.440-42.

Hindess, B. (1987), *Politics And Class Analysis*, Blackwell, Oxford.

Hindess, B. (1988), *Choice, Rationality, And Social Theory*, Unwin Hyman, London.

Hjern, B. and Porter, D.O. (1981), 'Implementation structures: a new unit of administrative analysis', *Organizational Studies*, No.2.

Hoggett, P. and Hambleton, R. (1988), 'Introduction', in Hoggett, P. and Hambleton, R. (eds), *Decentralization And Democracy: Localising Public Services*, Occasional Paper 28, School for Advanced Urban Studies, University of Bristol, Bristol, pp.1-8.

Holman, B. (1989), 'Taking home the wages of socialism', *The Guardian*, 1 May 1989, p.22.

Holzner, B. (1968), *Reality Construction In Society*, Schenkman Publishing Company, New York.

Howe, D. (1983), 'The social work imagination in practice and education', *Issues In Social Work Education*, Vol.3, No.2, pp.77-89.

Howe, D. (1986), 'The segregation of women and their work in the personal social services', *Critical Social Policy*, Issue 15, pp.21-35.

Howe, D. (1987), *An Introduction To Social Work Theory*, Gower, Aldershot.

Howe, D. (1988) (Review), *Issues In Social Work Education*, Vol.8. No.1, pp.65-66.

Hughes, E.C. (1958), *Men And Their Work*, Glencoe, Ill.

Hutchinson-Reis, M. (1989), '"And for those of us who are black?" Black politics in social work', in Langan, M. and Lee, P. (eds) Radical Social Work Today, Unwin Hyman, London, pp.165-77.

Irvine, E. (1969), 'Education for social work: science or humanity?', Social Work, Vol.26, No.4, pp.23-34.

Irvine, E. (1975), 'Forward', in Morris, C. (ed.), Literature And The Social Worker: A Reading List For Practitioners, Teachers, Students, and Voluntary Workers, The Library Association, London, pp.5-6.

Irvine, E. (1978), 'Professional claims and the professional task', Unit 27, Part 2, Course DE206, Social Work, Community Work And Society, Open University Press, Milton Keynes.

Jacobs, S. (1987), 'Scientific community: formulations and critique of a sociological motif', The British Journal Of Sociology, Vol.xxxviii, No.2, pp.266-76.

Jamous, H. and Peloille, B. (1970), 'Changes in the French University-Hospital System', in Jackson, J. (ed.), Professions and Professionalization, Cambridge University Press, Cambridge, pp.111-52.

Jaques, E. (1975), 'Social-analysis and the Glacier project', in Brown, W. and Jaques, E. Glacier Project Papers, Heinemann, London.

Jaques, E. (1977), A General Theory Of Bureaucracy, Heinemann, London.

Jeffreys, M. (1965), An Anatomy Of Social Welfare Services; Michael Joseph, London. p.47 cited in Jones, C. (1983), State Social Work And The Working Class, Macmillan, London and Basingstoke, p.12.

Jehu, D., Hardiker, P., Yelloly, M. and Shaw, M. (1972), Behaviour Modification In Social Work, John Wiley, London.

Jervis, M. (1990), 'Assessing attitudes', Social Work Today, 12 July 1990, pp.22-23.

Johnson, T. (1972), Professions And Power, Macmillan, London.

Jones, C. (1976), 'The foundations of social work education', Working Papers In Sociology No.11, Department of Sociology and Social Administration, University of Durham, Durham.

Jones, C. (1979), 'Social work education 1900-1977', in Parry, N., Rustin, M. and Satyamurti, C. (eds), Social Work, Welfare And The State, Edward Arnold, London, pp.72-88.

Jones, C. (1983), State Social Work And The Working Class, Macmillan, London and Basingstoke.

Jones, C. (1989), 'The end of the road? Issues in social work education', in Carter, P., Jeffs, T. and Smith, M. (eds), Social Work And Social Welfare, Yearbook 1, Open University Press, Milton Keynes, pp.204-16.

Jones, D. (1988), General Secretary of British Association of Social Workers, quoted in The Guardian, 7 July 1988, p.5.

Jones, R. (1982), 'A comment on "Through experience towards theory: a psychodynamic contribution to social work education" by Mary Barker', Issues In Social Work Education, Vol.2, No.2, pp.149-52.

Jordan, B. (1974), Poor Parents: Social Policy And The 'Cycle Of Deprivation', Routledge, London.

Jordan, B. (1982), 'Generic training and specialist skills', in Bailey, R. and Lee, P. (eds), Theory And Practice In Social Work, Blackwell, Oxford, pp.98-111.

Jordan, B. (1988), 'What price partnership? Costs and benefits', in CCETSW, Paper 18.1, Partnership In Probation Education And Training: A Conference Report, Central Council for Education and Training In Social Work, London, pp.30-39.

Jordan, M. (1982), 'Piggy in the middle: social work education - a view from the field' in Bailey, R. and Lee, P. (eds), Theory And Practice In Social Work, Blackwell, Oxford, pp.128-35.

Kadushin, A. (1959), 'The knowledge base of social work', in Kahn, A. (ed.), Issues In American Social Work, Columbia University Press, New York, pp.39-79.

Kahan, B. (1979), Growing Up In Care, Blackwell, Oxford.

Kahn, A.J. (1954), 'The nature of social work', in Kasius, C. (ed.), New Directions In Social Work, Harper and Bros., New York, pp.194-213.

Kakabadse, A. (1982), Culture Of Social Services, Gower, Aldershot.

Kakabadse, A. and Worral, R. (1976), 'Job satisfaction and organizational structure: a comparative study of nine social services departments', British Journal Of Social Work, Vol.8, No.1, pp.51-70.

Karpf, M. (1931), The Scientific Base Of Social Work, Columbia University Press, New York.

Kempe, C.H. (1962), 'The battered child syndrome', Journal Of The American Medical Association, No.181, pp.,17-24.

King, J. (1989), 'Polish up the public image', Community Care, 16 March 1989, pp.16-18.

Klein, M. and Snyder, N. (1965), 'The detached worker: uniformities and variances in work style', Social Work, Vol.10, No.4, pp.60-68.

Knorr-Cetina, K. (1981), 'Introduction: the micro-sociological challenge of macro-sociology: towards a reconstruction of social theory and methodology', in Knorr-Cetina, K. and Cicourel, A.V. (eds), Advances In Social Theory And Methodology: Towards An Integration Of Micro- And Macro-Sociologies, Routledge, London, pp.1-47.

Knorr-Cetina, K. (1982), 'Scientific communities or transepistemic arenas of research? a critique of quasi-economic models of science', Social Studies of Science, No.12.

Kuhn, T.S. (1970), The Structure Of Scientific Revolutions, 2nd. edn., University of Chicago Press, Chicago.

Laclau, E. and Mouffe, C. (1985), Hegemony And Socialist Strategy, Verso, London.

Langan, M. and Lee, P. (eds) (1989a), Radical Social Work Today, Unwin Hyman. London.

Langan, M. and Lee, P. (1989b), 'Whatever happened to radical social work?', in Langan, M. and Lee, P. (eds), Radical Social Work Today, Unwin Hyman, London, pp.1-18.

Larson, M.L. (1977), The Rise Of Professionalism: A Sociological Analysis, University of California Press, Berkeley.

Latour, B. (1986), 'The powers of association', in Law, J. (ed.), Power, Action And Belief: A New Sociology Of Knowledge?, Routledge, London, pp.264-80.

Law, J. (1986a), 'On power and its tactics: a view from the sociology of science', The Sociological Review, Vol.34, No.1, pp.1-38.

Law, J. (1986b), 'Editor's Introduction' in Law, J. (ed.), Power, Action And Belief: A New Sociology Of Knowledge, Routledge, London, pp.1-19.

Lawrence, R. (1983), 'Voluntary action: a stalking horse for the right?', Critical Social Policy, Vol.2, No.3, pp.14-30.

Layder, D. (1986), 'Social reality as figuration: a critique of Norbert Elias's conception of sociological analysis', Sociology, Vol.20, No.3, pp.367-86.

Layder, D. (1987), 'Key issues in structuration theory: some critical remarks', Current Perspectives In Social Theory, 8, pp.25-46.

Lee, A. (1978), Sociology For Whom?, Oxford University Press, New York.

Lee, P. (1982), 'Some contemporary and perennial problems of relating theory to practice in social work', in Bailey, R. and Lee, P. (eds), Theory And Practice In Social Work, Blackwell, Oxford, pp.15-45.

Lee, P. and Raban, C. (1988), Welfare Theory And Social Policy: Reform Or Revolution?, Sage, London.

Lees, R. (1972), Politics And Social Work, Routledge, London.

Leonard, P. (1966), Sociology In Social Work, Routledge, London.

Leonard, P. (1979), 'Introduction' in Gough, I., The Political Economy Of The Welfare State, Macmillan, London and Basingstoke, pp.vii-ix.

Leonard, P. (1984), Personality And Ideology: Towards A Materialist Understanding Of The Individual, Macmillan, London and Basingstoke.

Levitas, R.A. (1976), 'The social location of ideas', The Sociological Review, Vol.24, No.3, pp.545-57.

Levitas, R. (ed.) (1986), The Ideology Of The New Right, Polity Press, Oxford.

Lewins, F. (1989), 'Recasting the concept of ideology: a content approach', The British Journal Of Sociology, Vol.40, No.4, pp.678-93.

Lewis, J. and Meredith, B. (1988), Daughters Who Care: Daughters Caring For Mothers At Home, Routledge, London.

Lidz. V. (1981), 'Transformational theory and the internal environment of action systems', in Knorr-Cetina, K.C. and Cicourel, A.V. (eds.), Advances In Social Theory And Methodology: Towards An Integration Of Micro- And Macro-Sociologies, Routledge, London, pp.205-33.

Litwak, E. (1970), 'An approach to linkage in grass roots community organization', in Cox, F. (ed.), Strategies Of Community Organization: A Book Of Readings, Peacock, Itasca, Illinois, pp.126-38.

Litwak, E. and Meyer, H. (1966), 'A balance theory of co-ordination between bureaucratic organizations and community primary groups', Administrative Science Quarterly, Vol.11, No.1, pp.31-58.

Litwak, E. and Meyer, H. (1967), 'The school and the family: linking organizations and external primary groups', in Lazarsfeld, P. (ed.), The Uses Of Sociology, Basic Books, New York, pp.522-43.

Loch, C.S. (1877), quoted in Timms, N. (1983), Social Work Values: An Enquiry, Routledge, London, p.70.

Loch, C.S. (1906), Introduction To Annual Charities Register And Digest 15th, ed,, Longman, London, quoted in Jones, C. (1983), State Social Work And The Working Class, Macmillan, London and Basingstoke, p.81.

London University Executive Committee On Social Work Education (1903), quoted in Smith, M.J. (1965), Professional Education For Social Work In Britain: An Historical Account, Allen and Unwin, London, p.40.

Lorch, W. and Lawrence, P. (1968), Environmental Factors And Organizational Integration, (Mimeograph), American Sociological Association, Boston, Massachusetts.

Lukes, S. (1974), Power: A Radical View, Macmillan, London.

Macmillan, I. and Morris, P. (1989), 'Council calls', Community Care, 3 April 1989, p.3.

Mann, M. (1970), 'The social cohesion of liberal democracy', American Sociological Review, No.35, pp.423-39.

Mann, M. (1986), The Sources Of Social Power, Vol.1: A History Of Power From The Beginning To A.D.1760, Cambridge University Press, Cambridge.

Mannheim, K. (1972), Ideology And Utopia, trans. Shils, E., Routledge, London.

Marglin, S. (1980), 'The origins and functions of hierarchy in capitalist production', in Nichols, T. (ed.), Capital And Labour, Fontana, London.

Marsland, D. (1984), 'Public opinion and the welfare state: some problems in the interpretation of facts', Sociology, Vol.18, No.1, pp.83-87.

Martin, B. (1981), A Sociology Of Contemporary Cultural Change, Blackwell, Oxford.

Martinez-Brawley, E.E. (1986), 'Community-orientated social work in a rural and remote Hebridean patch', International Social Work, Vol.29, No.4, pp.349-72.

Mayer, J.E. and Timms, N. (1969), 'Clash in perspective between worker and client', Social Casework, No.50, pp.32-39.

McCord, N. (1976), 'The poor law and philanthropy', in Fraser, D. (ed.), The New Poor Law In The Nineteenth Century, Macmillan, London.

McKee, L. (1982), 'Fathers' participation in infant care; a critique' in McKee, L. and O'Brien, M. (eds), The Father Figure, Tavistock, London.

McKinlay, J.B. (1973), 'On the professional regulation of change', in Halmos, P. (ed.), Professionalization And Social Change, Sociological Review Monograph No.20, University of Keele, Keele, pp.61-84.

Measures, P. (1986), 'Professionalism', Community Care, 17 April 1986, pp.16-17.

Meltzer, B., Petras, J.W. and Reynolds, L.T. (1975), Symbolic Interactionism: Genesis, Varieties, And Criticisms, Routledge, London.

Millerson. G. (1964), The Qualifying Associations: A Study In Professionalization, Routledge. London.

Mishra, R. (1986), 'The left and the welfare state: a critical analysis', Critical Social Policy, Issue 15, pp.4-19.

Mitchell, D. (1989), '1992 poses double blow to social work', Community Care, 29 June 1989, p.6.

Moffett, J. (1972), Concepts In Casework Treatment, Routledge, London.

Moore, P. (1976), 'Personally speaking', Community Care, 2 June 1976, p.10.

Morgan, D.H.J. (1989), 'Strategies and sociologists: a comment on Crow', Sociology, Vol.23, No.1, pp.25-29.

Morris, C. (ed.) (1975), Literature And The Social Worker: A Reading List For Practitioners, Teachers, Students And Voluntary Workers, The Library Association, London.

Morris, P. (1975), 'Case Con: the maturing five year old', Community Care, 26 November 1975, pp.18-19.

Mowat, C.L. (1961), The Charity Organization Society 1869-1913: Its Ideas And Work, Methuen, London.

Munday, D. (1972), 'What is happening to social work students?', Social Work Today, 15 June 1972, pp.4-5.

Navarro, V. (1976), Medicine Under Capitalism, Croom Helm, London.

Nelson, A. (1990), 'Equal opportunities: dilemmas, contradictions, white men and class', Critical Social Policy, Issue 28, pp.25-42.

Nelson, S. (1989), 'Last twenty years have failed to train staff', Community Care, 7 September 1989, p.2.

'News Item' Community Care (1986), 'News item: CCETSW plans worry universities', Community Care, 13 March 1986, p.5.

'News Item' Community Care (1989a), Community Care, 21 September 1989, p.5.

'News Item' Community Care (1989b), Community Care, 1989, p.3.

North, M. (1972), The Secular Priests: Psychotherapists In Contemporary Society, Allen and Unwin, London.

Offe, C. (1984), Contradictions Of The Welfare State, (ed.) Keane, J., Hutchinson, London.

Offer, J., St. Leger, F. and Cecil, R. (1988), Aspects Of Informal Care: Some Results From A Study Of A Small Town In Northern Ireland, Department of Health and Social Services Inspectorate, Belfast.

Owen, D. (1965), English Philanthropy 1660-1960, Oxford University Press, Oxford.

Pahl, R.E. (1984), Divisions Of Labour, Blackwell, Oxford.

Pakulski, J. (1986), 'Leaders of the Solidarity movement: a sociological portrait', Sociology, Vol.20, No.1, pp.64-81.

Paley, J. (1984), 'The devolution of knowledge in social work education', Social Work Education, Vol.3, No.2, pp.19-21.

Papadakis, E. (1988), 'Social movements, self-limiting radicalism, and the Green Party in West Germany', Sociology, Vol.22, No.3, pp.433-54.

Parker, R. (1971), 'The future of the personal social services', in Robson, W.A. and Crick, B. (eds), The Future Of The Social Services, Penguin, Harmondsworth, pp.105-15.

Parker, R. (1990), cited in Gaffaney, P. 'Call for a social services council strengthens', Community Care, 15 March 1990, p.1.

Parry, N. and Parry, J. (1979), 'Social work, professionalism, and the state', in Parry, N., Rustin, M. and Satyamurti. C. (eds), Social Work, Welfare And The State, Edward Arnold, London, pp.21-47.

Parry, N., Rustin, M. and Satyamurti, C. (1979), 'Social work today: some problems and proposals', in Parry, N., Rustin, M. and Satyamurti, C. (eds), Social Work, Welfare And The State, Edward Arnold, London, pp.161-76.

Parsloe, P. (1984), 'The review of qualifying training: a comment from Phyllida Parsloe', Issues In Social Work Education, Vol.4, No.2, pp.107-17.

Parsloe, P. (1985), (Review), Issues In Social Work Education, Vol.5, No.2, pp.158-59.

Parsons, T. (1968), 'Professions', in Sills. D. (ed.), International Encyclopaedia Of The Social Sciences, Macmillan and Free Press, London and New York.

Parton, N. (1979), 'The natural history of child abuse: a study in social problem definition', British Journal Of Social Work, Vol.9, No.4, pp.431-53.

Pearson, G. (1975), The Deviant Imagination: Psychiatry, Social Work, And Social Change, Macmillan, London and Basingstoke.

Pearson, G. (1983), 'The Barclay Report and Community Social Work', Critical Social Policy, Vol.2, No.3, pp.78-86.

Pearson, G. (1989), 'Women and men without work: the political economy is personal', in Rojek, C., Peacock, G. and Collins, S. (eds), The Haunt Of Misery: Critical Essays In Social Work And Helping, Routledge, London, pp.11-41.

Perlman, H. (1976), 'Once more, with feeling', in Mullen, E.J. and Dumpson, J.R. (eds), Evaluation Of Social Intervention, Jossey Bass, San Francisco and London, pp.191-209.

Perrucci, R. (1976), 'In the service of man: radical movements in the professions', in Gerstl, J. and Jacobs, G. (eds), Professions For People: The Politics Of Skill, Harvard University Press.

Philp, M. (1979), 'Notes on the form of knowledge in social work', The Sociological Review, Vol.27, No.1, pp.83-111.

Philpott, T. (1990), 'Forward to the future', Community Care, 18 January 1990, p.27.

Pierson, C. (1984), 'New theories of state and civil society: recent developments in post-marxist analysis of the state', Sociology, Vol.18, No.4, pp.563-71.

Pinker, R. (1982), 'A fussiness of thinking', Community Care, 14 October 1982, pp.12-14.

Pinker, R. (1983a), 'Social welfare and the education of social workers', in Bean, P. and MacPherson, S. (eds), Approaches To Welfare, Routledge, London, pp.150-65.

Pinker, R. (1983b), 'Social work is casework', in Philpott, T. (ed.). A New Direction For Social Work? The Barclay Report And Its Implications, Community Care/IPC Business Press, London, pp.68-74.

Pinker, R. (1984), 'The threat to professional standards in social work education: a response to some recent proposals', Issues In Social Work Education, Vol.4, No.1, pp.5-15.

Pinker (1984) in Murray, Pinker quoted in Murray, N. (1984) 'Two into one won't go: or will it?', Community Care, 10 May 1984, p.21.

Pinker, R. (1986), 'Time to stop CCETSW in its tracks', Community Care, 18 September 1986, pp.21-22.

Pinker, R. (1989), 'Social work and social policy in the twentieth century: retrospect and prospect' in Bulmer, M., Lewis, J. and Piachaud, D. (eds), The Goals Of Social Policy, Unwin Hyman, London, pp.84-107.

Polsby, N.W. (1980), Community Power And Political Theory: A Further Look At Problems Of Evidence And Inference, Yale University Press, New Haven.

Portwood, D. and Fielding (1981), 'Privilige in the professions', The Sociological Review, Vol.29, No.4, pp.749-73.

Poulantzas, N. (1975), Classes In Contemporary Capitalism, New Left Books, London.

Pratt, J. and Grimshaw, R. (1985), 'A study of a social work agency: the occupational routines and working practices of the education social work service', The Sociological Review, Vol.33, No.1, pp.106-35.

Priestly, P. (1975), 'New careers: power sharing in social work', in Jones, H. (ed.), Towards A New Social Work, Routledge, London, pp.122-37.

Prins, H. (1975), 'A danger to themselves and others', British Journal Of Social Work, Vol.5, No.3, pp.297-303.

Pritchard, C. and Taylor, R. (1978), Social Work: Reform Or Revolution?, Routledge, London.

Pugh, D. (1969), 'The context of organizational structure', Administration Science Quarterly, Vol.14, No.1, pp.91-113.

Ramazanoglu, C. (1989), 'Improving on sociology: problems in taking a feminist viewpoint', Sociology, Vol.23, No.3, pp.427-42.

Reading, P. (1985), 'Part two: Introduction', in Harris, R.J., Barker, M.W., Reading, P., Richards, M. and Youll, P. (eds), Educating Social Workers, Association of Teachers in Social Work Education, University of Leicester, Leicester, pp.35-36.

Rees, S. and Wallace, A. (1982), Verdicts On Social Work, Edward Arnold, London.

Reid, I. (1989), Social Class Differences In Britain (third ed.), Fontana Press, London.

Rein, M. (1976), Social Science And Public Policy, Penguin, Harmondsworth.

Report of Joint Working Party (1986), Association of Teachers in Social Work Education, Joint University Council Social Work Education Committee, Standing Conference of Heads of CQSW Courses, Preparing For Practice: Towards A Future Educational Strategy In Social Work, June.

Rex, J. (1974), Sociology And The De-Mystification Of The Modern World, Routledge, London.

Richards, K. (1971), 'The new social services departments', Social Work Today, 8 April 1971, pp.3-7.

Richards, M. (1985), 'In defence of social work teachers: a study of their development needs', in Harris, R.J., Barker, M.W., Reading, P., Richards, M. and Youll, P. (eds), Educating Social Workers, Association of Teachers in Social Work Education, University of Leicester, Leicester, pp.25-32.

Ricoeur, P. (1971), 'The meaning of the text: meaningful action considered as a text', Social Research, Vol.38, No.3, pp.531-42.

Riddell, P. (1983), The Thatcher Government, Martin Robertson, London.
Ringer, B.B. and Lawless, E. (1989), Race, Ethnicity And Society, Routledge, London.
Rojek, C. (1989), 'Social work and self-management', in Rojek, C., Peacock, G. and Collins, S. (eds), The Haunt Of Misery: Critical Essays In Social Work And Helping, Routledge, London, pp.173-88.
Rojek, C., Peacock. G. and Collins, S. (1988), Social Work And Received Ideas, Routledge, London.
Rojek, C., Peacock. G. and Collins, S. (eds) (1989), The Haunt Of Misery: Critical Essays In Social Work And Helping, Routledge, London.
Roth, J. (1974), 'Professionalism: the sociologists' decoy', Sociology Of Work And Occupations, Vol.1, No.1, pp.13-27.
Rootes, C.A. (1981), 'The dominant ideology thesis and its critics', Sociology, Vol.15, No.3, pp.436-44.
Sainsbury, E. (1977), The Personal Social Services, Pitman, London.
Sainsbury, E. (1985), 'Diversity in social work practice: an overview of the problem', Issues In Social Work Education, Vol.5, No.1, pp.3-12.
Saks, M. (1983), 'Removing the blinkers? A critique of recent contributions to the sociology of professions', The Sociological Review, Vol.31, No.1, pp.1-21.
Sapir, E. (1966), Culture, Language And Personality, University of California Press, Berkeley and Los Angeles.
Sargent, J. (1985), 'The use of self in teaching social work', in Harris, R.J., Barker, M.W., Reading, P., Richards, M. and Youll, P. (eds), Educating Social Workers, Association of Teachers in Social Work Education, University of Leicester, Leicester, pp.103-7.
Satyamurti, C. (1981), Occupational Survival: The Case Of The Local Authority Social Worker, Blackwell, Oxford.
Satyamurti, C. (1983), 'Discomfort and defence in learning to be a helping professional', Issues In Social Work Education, Vol.3, No.1, pp.27-38.
Saunders, P. (1979), Urban Politics, Penguin, Harmondsworth.
Saunders, P. (1990), Social Class And Stratification, Routledge, London.
Schutz, A. (1964), Collected Papers 11, Martinus Nijhoff, The Hague.
Schwartz, D. (1973), 'The invocation of legal norms: an empirical investigation of Durkheim and Weber', American Sociological Review, No.38, pp.340-54.
Scott, A. (1988), 'Imputing beliefs: a controversy in the sociology of knowledge', The Sociological Review, Vol.36, No.1, pp.331-56.
Scott, R.W. (1965), 'Reactions to supervision in a heteronomous professional organization', Administrative Science Quarterly, Vol.10, pp.65-81.
Seebohm Report (1968), Home Office Report Of The Committee On Local Authority And Allied Personal Services, Cmnd. 3703, HMSO, London.
Seed, P. (1977), The Expansion Of Social Work In Britain, Routledge, London.
Shah, N. (1989), 'It's up to you sisters; black women and radical social work', in Langan, M. and Lee, P. (eds), Radical Social Work Today, Unwin Hyman, London, pp.178-91.
Sharp, R. (1980), Knowledge, Ideology And Politics Of Schooling: Towards A Marxist Analysis Of Education, Routledge, London.
Shaw, I. (1975), 'Making use of research', in Jones, H. (ed.), Towards A New Social Work, Routledge, London, pp.151-66.
Shaw, J. (1974), The Self In Social Work, Routledge, London.
Sheppard, M.G. (1984), 'Notes on the use of social explanation to social work', Issues In Social Work Education, Vol.4, No.1, pp.27-41.

Sherman, M. (1986), 'A great momentum runs out of steam', The Guardian, 17 April 1986, p.9.

Sibeon, R. (1982), 'Theory-practice symbolizations', Issues In Social Work Education, Vol.2, No.2, pp.119-47.

Sibeon, R. (1983) 'The youngest profession? Social work education: contemporary problems and issues', Social Work Today, Vol.14, No.18 (January), pp.14-18.

Sibeon, R. (1989a), Cognitive Indeterminacy And Technical Rationality In Professional Social Work, Paper presented at British Sociological Association Annual Conference 1989, Plymouth.

Sibeon, R. (1989b), 'Comments on the structure and forms of social work knowledge', Social Work And Social Sciences Review, Vol.1, No.1, pp.29-44.

Sibeon, R. (1991), 'The construction of a contemporary sociology of social work', Part One in Davies, M. (ed.), The Sociology Of Social Work, Routledge, London.

Silverman, D. and Torode, B. (1980), The Material World: Some Theories Of Language And Its Limits, Routledge, London.

Simon, B.S. (1967), The Nature And Objectives Of Professional Education, Association of Social Work Teachers Annual Meeting, University of Leicester, February.

Simpkin, M. (1982), (Review), Critical Social Policy, Vol.1, No.3, pp.92-94.

Simpkin, M. (1989), 'Radical social work: lessons for the 1990's', in Carter, P., Jeffs, T. and Smith, M. (eds), Social Work And Social Welfare Yearbook 1, Open University Press, Milton Keynes, pp.159-74.

Skocpol, T. (1979), States And Social Revolutions: A Comparative Analysis Of France, Russia and China, Cambridge University Press, Cambridge.

Small, N. (1987), 'Putting violence towards social workers into context', Critical Social Policy, Issue 19, pp.40-51.

Smart, C. (1979), 'The new female criminal: reality or myth?', British Journal Of Criminology, Vol.19, No.1, pp.20-35.

Smith, G. (1971), 'On everyday theory in social work practice', Social Work Today, Vol.2, No.3, May, pp.25-28.

Smith, G. (1979), Social Work And The Sociology Of Organizations (revised ed.), Routledge, London.

Social Work Today (1983), The Concise Barclay: A Digest and Commentary, Social Work Today Publications, Birmingham.

Spencer, H. (1877), Principles Of Sociology, Williams and Worgate, London.

SSORU (1974), Social Science Organization Research Unit, Brunel Institute Of Organization And Social Studies, Social Services Departments: Developing Patterns Of Work And Organization, Heinemann, London.

Standing Conference Certificate in Social Service (1985), A Revised Model For An Integrated System Of Education And Training For The Personal Social Services, Standing Conference Certificate In Social Service, Ballymena.

Statham D. (1978), Radicals In Social Work, Routledge, London.

Statham D. (1984), (Review), Critical Social Policy, Issue 11, pp.126-27.

Stedman Jones, G. (1971), Outcast London, Clarendon Press, London.

Stevenson, O. (1970), 'The knowledge base for social work', British Journal Of Social Work, Vol.1, No.2, pp.225-37.

Stevenson, O. (1971), 'Knowledge for social work', in Conference Report Bournemouth 1971, The Common Base Of Social Work Practice, Central Training Council in Child Care, London.

Stevenson, O. (1981), Specialization In Social Services Teams, Allen and Unwin, London.

Stevenson, O. and Parsloe, P. (1978), Social Services Teams: The Practitioner's View, Department of Health and Social Services, London.

Stone, M. (1986), 'An approach to decentralization and neighbourhood work: the implications for social work education and training', Issues In Social Work Education, Vol.6, No.1, pp.27-40.

Strauss, A. (1978), Negotiations: Varieties, Contexts, Processes And Social Order, Jossey-Bass, London.

Sullivan, M. (1987), Sociology And Social Welfare, Allen and Unwin. London.

Taylor, D. (1989), 'Citizenship and social power', Critical Social Policy, Issue 26, pp.19-31.

Taylor-Gooby, P. (1983), 'Legitimation deficit, public opinion, and the welfare state', Sociology, Vol.17, No.2, pp.165-84.

Taylor-Gooby, P. (1984), 'The hitch-hikers guide to support for the welfare state', Sociology, Vol.18, No.1, pp.88-94.

Taylor-Gooby, P. (1985), Public Opinion, Ideology And State Welfare, Routledge, London.

Taylor-Gooby, P. (1986), 'Privatization, power, and the welfare state', Sociology, Vol.20, No.2, pp.228-46.

Taylor-Gooby, P. and Dale. J. (1981), Social Theory And Social Welfare, Edward Arnold, London.

Terrien, F. and Mills, D. (1955), 'The effects of changing size on the internal structure of an organization', American Sociological Review, Vol.20, No.1, pp.11-13.

Therborn, G. (1984), 'The prospects of labour and the transformation of advanced capitalism', New Left Review, No.145, May/June 1984, pp.29-33.

Thomas, D.N. and Shaftoe, H. (1983), 'Does casework need a neighbourhood orientation?', in Sinclair, I. and Thomas, D.N. (eds), Perspectives On Patch, NISW Paper 14, National Institute For Social Work, London, pp.31-37.

Thompson, J. (1987), 'Language and Ideology', The Sociological Review, Vol.35, No.3, pp.516-36.

Tilbury, D. (1971), 'The selection of method in social work', Social Work Today, 22 April 1971, pp.9-12.

Timms, N. (1968), Language Of Social Casework, Routledge, London.

Timms, N. (1983), Social Work Values: An Enquiry, Routledge. London.

Timms, N. and Timms, R. (1977), Perspectives On Social Work. Routledge, London.

Timms, N. and Watson, D. (eds) (1975), Talking About Welfare: Readings In Philosophy And Social Policy, Routledge, London.

Townsend, M. (1911), The Case Against The Charity Organization Society, Fabian Tract No.158, London.

Townsend, P. (1970), The Fifth Social Service, Fabian Society, London.

Traux, C. and Carkuff, R. (1967), Towards Effective Counselling And Psychotherapy, Aldine Publishing Company, Chicago.

Trevillion, S. (1982), 'Welfare, society and the social worker', British Journal Of Social Work, Vol.12, No.1, pp.23-33.

Turner, B.S. (1990), 'Outline of a theory of citizenship', Sociology, Vol.24, No.2, pp.189-217.

Turner, C. and Hodge, M.S. (1970), 'Occupations and professions', in Jackson, J.A. (ed.), <u>Professions And Professionalization</u>, Cambridge University Press, Cambridge.

Twelve Students (1989), Applied Social Work Course, School of Social Work, Manchester University, letter 'Breath of fresh air over social work training', <u>Social Work Today</u>, 6 April 1989, p.10.

Ungerson, C. (1983), 'Why do women care?', in Finch, J. and Groves, D. (eds), <u>A Labour of Love: Women, Work, And Caring</u>, Routledge, London.

Ungerson, C. (1987), <u>Policy Is Personal: Sex, Gender, And Informal Care</u>, Tavistock, London.

Urwick, E.J. (1904), 'A school of sociology', in Loch, C.S. <u>Methods Of Social Advance</u>, Macmillan, London, cited in Jones, C. (1983), <u>State Social Work And The Working Class</u>, Macmillan. London and Basingstoke. p.83.

Valk, M. (1983), 'Imaginative literature and social work education: an extended comment on Barker', <u>Issues In Social Work Education</u>, Vol.3, No.1, pp.17-26.

Vance, F.L. (1968), 'The psychological interview as a discovery machine', in Parker, C.A. (ed.), <u>Counselling Theories And Counsellor Education</u>, Houghton Mifflin, Boston.

Varley, B. (1966), 'Are social workers dedicated to service?', <u>Social Work</u>, Vol.11, No.2, pp.84-91.

Vollmer, H. and Mills, D. (1966), <u>Professionalization</u>, Prentice-Hall, New York.

Waldow, B. (1954), 'Role conflcit of the military chaplain', <u>American Sociological Review</u>. Vol.19, No.4, pp.428-35.

Walby, S. (1988), 'Gender politics and social theory', <u>Sociology</u>, Vol.22, No.2, pp.215-32.

Walby, S. (1989), 'Theorizing patriarchy', <u>Sociology</u>, Vol.23, No.2, pp.213-34.

Wallis, R. and Bruce, S. (1983), 'Accounting for action: defending the commonsense heresy', <u>Sociology</u>, Vol.17, No.1, pp.97-111.

Warner, N. (1986), 'Social work: a cautionary tale', <u>Social Services Insight</u>, 1 March - 8 March 1986, pp.13-15.

Warner, N. (1989), Warner, Director of Social Services, Kent Social Services Department, reported in 'News Item', <u>Community Care</u>, 22 June 1989, p.3.

Waterhouse, L. (1987), 'The relationship between theory and practice in social work education', <u>Issues In Social Work Education</u>, Vol.7, No.1, pp.3-19.

Watson, M. and Lee, P. (1982), 'Baptisms of fire: some dilemmas in becoming a social worker', in Bailey, R. and Lee, P. (eds), <u>Theory And Practice In Social Work</u>, Blackwell, Oxford, pp.136-53.

Watson, S. and Austerberg, H. (1986), <u>Housing And Homelessness</u>, Routledge, London.

Webb, A. (1980), 'The personal social services', in Bosanquet, N. and Townsend, P. (eds). <u>Labour And Equality</u>, Heinemann, London.

Webb, D. (1981a), 'Sociology', in Hardiker, P. and Barker, M. (eds) <u>Theories Of Practice In Social Work</u>, Academic Press, London, pp.117-38.

Webb, D. (1981b), 'Themes and continuities in radical and traditional social work', <u>British Journal Of Social Work</u>, Vol.11, No.2, pp.143-58.

Webb, D. (1985), 'Social work and critical consciousness: rebuilding orthodoxy', <u>Issues In Social Work Education</u>, Vol.5, No.2, pp.85-102.

Webb, D. (1987), (Review), <u>Issues In Social Work Education</u>, Vol.7, No.2, pp.157-60.

Webb, D. and Evans, R. (1976), Sociology And Social Work Practice: Explanation Or Method?, Paper National Deviancy Conference, London.

Weinstein, J. (1986), 'Angry arguments across the picket line: left labour councils and white collar trade unionism', Critical Social Policy, Issue 17, pp.41-60.

Westland, P. (1974), (Review), British Journal Of Social Work, Vol.4, No.2, pp.469-71.

White, M. (1972), 'Room for adventurous experiment', Social Work Today, 6 April 1972, pp. 9-11.

Whiteley, R. (1977), 'Organization control and the problem of order', Social Science Information, Vol.16, No.2, pp.169-89.

Whittington, C. (1977), 'Social workers' orientations: an active perspective', British Journal Of Social Work, Vol.7, No.1, pp.73-97.

Whittington, C. and Bellaby, P. (1979), 'The reason for hierarchy in social services departments: a critique of Elliott Jaques and his associates', The Sociological Review, Vol.27, No.3, pp.513-39.

Whittington, C. and Holland, R. (1985), 'A framework for theory in social work', Issues In Social Work Education, Vol.5, No.1, pp.25-50.

Whorf, B. (1956), Language, Thought And Reality, MIT Press and John Wiley, New York.

Wilensky, H. (1964), 'The professionalization of everyone?', American Journal Of Sociology, Vol.70, No.2, pp.137-58.

Wilkinson, P. (1971), Social Movement, Pall Mall, London.

Williamson, B. (1989), 'Sentiment and social change', The Sociological Review, Vol.37, No.1, pp.128-41.

Williamson, D.A. (1978), 'Perceptions of staff supervision in the probation office', British Journal Of Social Work, Vol.10, No.1, pp.27-43.

Wilson, D. (1974), 'Uneasy bedfellows', Social Work Today, Vol.5, No.1, pp.9-12.

Wilson, P. and Pahl, R. (1988), 'The changing sociological construct of the family', The Sociological Review, Vol.36, No.2, pp.233-66.

Wirt, F. (1981), 'Professionalism and political conflict: a development model', Journal Of Public Policy, Vol.1, Part 1, pp.61-93.

Wood, E.M. (1986), The Retreat From Class, Verso, London.

Woodroofe, K. (1962), From Charity To Social Work, Routledge, London.

Wright, P. and Treacher, A. (eds) (1982), The Problem Of Medical Knowledge, Edinburgh University Press, Edinburgh.

Wright, R. (1977), Consultative Document No.3: Expectations Of The Teaching Of Social Work On Courses Leading To The Certificate Of Qualification In Social Work, Central Council for Education and Training in Social Work, London.

Wrong, D. (1979), Power: Its Forms, Bases, And Uses, Blackwell, Oxford.

Yelloly, M. (1972), 'The Concept of Insight', in Jehu, D., Hardiker, P., Yelloly, M. and Shaw, M., Behaviour Modification In Social Work, John Wiley, London, chapter five.

Yelloly, M. (1987), 'Why the theory couldn't become practice', Community Care, 29 January 1987, pp.18-19.

Young, A. and Ashton, E. (1956), British Social Work In The Nineteenth Century, Routledge, London.

Young, P. (1979), 'Foreward', in Curnock, K. and Hardiker, P., Towards Practice Theory: Skills And Methods In Social Assessments, Routledge, London.

Younghusband Report (1947), Younghusband, E., Report On The Employment And Training Of Social Workers, (Carnegie UK Trust), Constable, London.

Index